Ten Moments That Shook the Sports World

One Sportswriter's Eyewitness Accounts of the Most Incredible Sporting Events of the Past Fifty Years

Stan Isaacs

Skyhorse Publishing

To Bobbie (one more time)
The partner of my soul

"Newspaper readers, like bettors and lovers, are hard to discourge."
—A.J. Liebling

Skyhorse Publishing books may be purchased in bulk at special discounts for sales promotion, corporate gifts, fund raising, or educational purposes. Special editions can also be created to specifications. For details, contact Special Sales Department, Skyhorse Publishing, 555 Eighth Avenue, Suite 903, New York, NY 10018 or info@skyhorsepublishing.com.

www.skyhorsepublishing.com

10 9 8 7 6 5 4 3 2 1

Library of Congress Cataloging-in-Publication Data
Isaacs, Stan.
Ten moments that shook the sports world : one sportswriter's eyewitness accounts of the most incredible sporting events of the past fifty years / Stan Isaacs.
p. cm.
Includes bibliographical references and index.
ISBN 978-1-60239-628-9 (alk. paper)
1. Sports—History. I. Title.

GV576.I83 2008
796—dc22
2008013920

Printed in Canada

Contents

Foreword: Not So Left Field, After All

Stan Isaacs has gone mainstream on us, highlighting the first-rate, front-line, main-event, big-picture journalist he always was, yet guilefully kept hidden behind the guise of the iconoclast.

I should hasten to add that Stan is my mentor, my friend, my role model, along with his wife, Bobbie. For nearly half a century I have been taking discreet peeks at how they conduct themselves as a thoroughly hip and loving couple. So the point is, expect no neutrality here.

We thought we were hot stuff at *Newsday* in the early Sixties. I say "we" in the way ballplayers speak fondly of their first team. As well as he did further on down the line, Don Baylor will always refer to the Baltimore Orioles as "we," where he learned to play the game right. That is how I felt about *Newsday* on Long Island, watching Stan Isaacs and Jack Mann and the rest. We thought we were the best sports section in New York, and Stan was our cleanup hitter, the sports columnist who was at these momentous events he describes in these pages.

He worked at the same time as Jimmy Cannon, Dick Young, Arthur Daley, Red Smith, Bob Lipsyte and Leonard Koppett, and he was as good, as important, as any of them. He cultivated the role of the character, which only added to his role as observer of big events. As this memoir proves, Stan was present at the major sports events from midcentury onward, and now he goes over them again, as a journalist-historian who has been around.

How jealous I was, covering high-school sports on Long Island, editing copy late at night, reading Stan's dispatches from all over the country—and Wimbledon, exotic England. He did it with a deceptive, playful approach, having fun with instant history. He was there, taking it seriously, when Jim Brown and Bill Russell and Mickey Mantle and Muhammad Ali became themselves, but he also kept sports in perspective by finding its goofy corners. He knew what he was doing when he called his column "Out of Left Field."

I can still recall the evening in the old *Newsday* office in Garden City when we learned that Stan was covering the Yankee game in Kansas City—from the sheep pasture in ramshackle Municipal Stadium. This is true. Charles O. Finley, the obstreperous owner of the A's, while somewhat misanthropic toward his employees, had a fondness for four-legged creatures. Finley had a live mule and an artificial pop-up rabbit that delivered fresh baseballs at home plate, and he also kept a flock of sheep on the steep hill behind the outfield fence.

It was easier to let sheep roam rather than try to mow the hillside. Probably cheaper, too. So Stan arranged to watch the game from the pasture. He arranged for a mystified Associated Press photographer to transmit a picture of him sitting amidst the sheep. In my memory bank, I seem to recall our caption saying: "Stanley, Is That Ewe?" I have forgotten what his take was from the pasture, but I am sure it illustrated the strangeness of the Finley menagerie, the exotica of funky old ballparks before they became the cash-cow amusement parks of today. Back in suburban Long Island, reading Stan jealously as his copy clattered home in the midnight hours, I couldn't wait to get out to America and see some of this strangeness for myself. And I think our readers felt the same way.

Stan was one of the Founding Fathers of the Chipmunks, a breed of youngish (some would say immature) scribblers, who chattered away on irrelevant matters during Big Games. (It is our eternal honor that the nickname was bestowed on us by none other than Jimmy Cannon, another of my heroes, who, I like to think, understood our enlightened irreverence.) Stan and Jack, Larry Merchant and Stan Hochman of the *Philadelphia Daily News*, Bud Collins of the *Boston Globe* and Leonard Shecter of the New York Post were sort of charter Chipmunks, and the rest of us scampered along, gibbering in their wake.

Our coat of arms, if we had had one, would have contained the Latin version of Stan's most iconic question. One day Ralph Terry, a prince of a right-hander with the Yankees, was congratulated on the birth of his first child. He had just been chatting on the phone with his wife, who was feeding the infant.

"Breast or bottle?" Isaacs asked. Gentleman that he was, Terry may even have answered the question. But the response has been overshadowed by the question, the quintessential Stan Isaacs.

Oddness like that allowed Stan to operate in a deceptive manner that James Joyce described in Ulysses as "jocoserious." But he was right there. He knew a story. When a baseball manager rambled that his black and Latin players were not mentally alert, Isaacs knew that needed to be reported. When Cassius Clay took on the Muslim name Muhammad Ali, Isaacs knew this was an important moment in America, and treated Ali's point of view with dignity.

Stan was also a pioneer of independence in the baseball press box, declining to be the paid official scorer because he thought it violated his neutrality. Today very few daily reporters are allowed to score. Under Jack Mann, our sports editor, we were not allowed to write for team programs or take gifts from teams or travel for free on team airplanes.

Behind the jokes, we were blazing some trails. Stan was out there, earlier and more often than the rest of us. Now he has gone back over the great events and trends he covered. Expect no neutrality from me. It is an education, and a treat, to read him again.

—George Vecsey
January 2008

Introduction

It was the last day of the sophomore honors English class at Eastern District High School in Brooklyn in 1944. Abe Risikoff, the teacher, said to me, "You did well in this class this term. Would you like to join the school newspaper?"

I said, "I don't like to write compositions."

He said, "You don't have to write compositions on the *Gold and White* [the school paper]. What are you interested in?

"I like sports," I said. Sports were just about all I was interested in. I was a sports fanatic who probably knew more about sports statistics at 11 than I knew when I was a professional sports reporter.

"Well, you can write sports for the paper," Risikoff said. Immediately there danced in my mind the thought that probably motivated just about every person who ever became a sports writer. I thought, "I can get into games free."

That was the beginning of a half-century of writing sports. It would take me to the four corners of the nation and beyond. Often in moments of introspection I have thought back wistfully to the debt I owe Mr. Risikoff. I was never able to thank him in person, because he went into the service after steering me onto the paper. During an English class the next term, the teacher made an announcement. He said, "Our Mr. Risikoff had died in action fighting in Europe."

When the idea for this book was broached, my first reaction was to wonder if I had been involved with enough earth-shaking events to handle the assignment. But once I started to list events that qualified, I found I had more than ten blockbuster occasions to consider.

In winnowing my list, I thought first of some less-than-earthshaking moments which made a large impression on me at the time. The first was a football game between the two New York City municipal colleges, CCNY and my school, Brooklyn College in 1946. These were hardly football titans, but that didn't matter because this was a hot rivalry. The games were played on Saturday night at Ebbets Field, which made it a perfect date night. I took my nose out of football statistics long enough to line up a young woman to be my date.

City College led, 8-6, in the waning seconds. They had the ball on their one-yard line and tried to kill the clock in the final two seconds with a quarterback sneak. The CCNY quarterback fumbled the ball, however, and Brooklyn guard Bernie Friedlund pounced on it in City's end zone for a Brooklyn College touchdown and a 12-8 victory. In the midst of the wild celebrating by the Brooklyn students, I believe I was emboldened enough to kiss my date. I couldn't imagine that 22 years later I would cover an event that had such heroics and more in a more significant game.

My professional newspaper career started while I was still in college. It was a copy boy's job at the *New York Star*, which succeeded the noble but failed the journalistic experiment known as *PM.* I then continued as a cub sports writer with the *Daily Compass*, which followed the fallen *Star* at a downtown area in Manhattan now known as Tribeca.

I covered the great City College sweep of the National Invitation Tournament and NCAA tournament in 1950. Because teams no longer can enter both tournaments, City stands as the only team ever to win both in the same year.

The *Daily Compass* was a marginal paper and it had a skeletal sports staff of three or four at best. To give the impression of heft, sports editor Stanley Woodward created two fictional names as bylines. So I wrote as Gary Fiske while covering the tournaments, both of which took place at Madison Square Garden.

CCNY won both tourneys by beating Bradley in the final each time. Because CCNY was a municipal school as was Brooklyn, I identified with and rooted with a passion for the City guys because they were a New York City team to the core, made up mostly of black players and Jews. I was professional enough in my coverage, yet I basked in the post-tournament celebrations as if it was my school that had won.

The footnote to this was a little gift that the Madison Square Garden people gave to the reporters covering the event. I still have the cigarette lighter inscribed to "Gary Fiske."

Much to our dismay the college basketball scandal erupted the next spring. Shockingly, City College was involved; the core of its team had succumbed to the lure of gamblers offering them money to shave points. Manhattan, LIU and NYU were also caught in the scandal, as were out-of-town schools, Kentucky, Toledo and Bradley. These revelations and the scuttling of New York City by the Brooklyn Dodgers and New York Giants in 1957 turned off a generation of sports fans in New York.

Texas Western's 72-65 victory over Kentucky in the 1966 NCAA final is regarded as a watershed game in college sports history because it was the first time an all-black team played in—and won—an NCAA final. It has taken on a deeper significance down through the years, though not much was made of it at the time.

I think I was reluctant to emphasize the race angle in those days and probably did not address it after the final game because I had stressed it in my column on Texas Western (now UTEP) beating Utah in the semi-final game.

I wrote:

All of the first seven on Texas Western are Negroes [the term in usage at the time] *That shouldn't be significant one way or another except that many people make it noteworthy with snickers about the racial makeup of the team.*

In the press row for example a reporter from Virginia noted at one point that Texas Western had five Negroes on the team and Utah three. "I'll say one thing," this sharp observer noted, "whoever wins this game will be the dark-horse team tomorrow night [in the final]."

His neighbor, also a Virginian, said, "What do you mean?"

"It's eight to two on the court," the first noted.

"Eight to two?" the second repeated with puzzlement. Then he grasped the meaning. "Eight to two. Oh."

The point here is that the second fellow was seeing the game for what it was: a battle of two teams. His neighbor was blinded by the color of skin. Perhaps there is a bigger point there. Who would have thought, say 10 years ago, that two schools—not CCNY or UCLA—but such outlanders as Texas Western and Utah would be involved in a game with such representation. Democracy, it's wonderful.

The most tumultuous scene I have ever experienced occurred around the first Floyd Patterson-Sonny Liston heavyweight championship fight. Boxing came together with literature, politics and farce in late September, 1962 for the bout at Chicago's Comiskey Park. Fight headquarters at the Sheraton Hotel throbbed all week with gabbing, boozing, clowning and lying. There were boxing beat writers, columnists from all over the country, from Europe. There were boxing luminaries: former champions Rocky Marciano, Barney Ross and Archie Moore, Joe Louis, even Jim Braddock. A presence in the background though he was hardly seen by anybody—and wasn't, as far as I can recall, at the fight—was Playboy publisher Hugh Hefner, who put up some celebrities at his notorious hedonistic mansion on the north side.

There were the writers: James Baldwin, Budd Schulberg, Norman Mailer and William Buckley. A dynamic aspect of the week was a debate scheduled between Mailer, the left-winger and Buckley, the eminent right-winger on the subject, "The American Right Wing." Amidst much fight talk there was merriment about the debate. Somebody put up a comic betting line, "Battling Bill Buckley (Brown Shirt) 2½-1 favorite over Norman (Ex-Boy Wonder).

Much to the surprise of many, Mailer won the debate. Buckley was used to dismissing liberals. Mailer took a radical stance, equally hard on liberals, and bobbed and weaved his way to victory.

The *New York Times* had it as a draw. This infuriated Mailer so much he went on a drunken toot and stayed on it right through the fight and most embarrassingly, the morning after.

The fight, of course, had the shocking ending of Liston knocking out Patterson in 2:06 of the first round. It was so embarrassing to Patterson, he donned a disguise to get out of town undetected. Mailer, in what he later would call "a mind half-gorged with juice," crashed Liston's post-fight press conference and made a fool of himself by injecting himself in Liston's moment. To cries of "throw the bum out" he finally was ushered away. Amazingly, instead of shrinking out of the public eye in shame, he soon wrote a piece for *Esquire* magazine in which he described the scene, not sparing himself one bit.

Many years later, doing a question and answer piece for *Newsday* magazine, I told him I was amazed at his accuracy in portraying himself as a fool. Mailer's response: "Well, I didn't do it on purpose. You know how that happened. I was half out of my head."

The Islanders hockey team shook the world of Long Island if not the nation when it won four straight Stanley Cups from 1980-1983. The Islanders were the only "pure" major league franchise on Long Island in that they were based in Nassau County, outside New York City, the area in which *Newsday* dominated.

I had moved on from sports columnist to sports editor to TV sports critic by that time. I had a different take on the Islanders fourth Cup victory in 1983 because I worked as a post-game interviewer on a *Newsday* TV channel. I ducked the champagne deluge in the winning locker room to interview the conquering heroes. I even had a chance to hold the Stanley Cup, and was surprised by how light it was, no heavier than a flower vase.

I covered the football Giants in the 1958 season and did double duty with some stories on Jim Brown of the Cleveland Browns. He was a Long Island product from Manhasset High School who would go down in the minds of many as the greatest running back in history.

The season came down to a showdown between the Giants and Browns. The Giants had to beat the Browns in the last game of the season and then beat them again in a playoff to get into a championship game against the Baltimore Colts. I recall clearly Cleveland's first play from scrimmage in the season finale. Big and fast Jim Brown broke over right tackle and ran 65 yards for a touchdown. The game eventually came down to a 10-10 tie and had Pat Summerall, who had missed two field goals, lining up in the snow for a 49-yard field goal attempt. It seemed to go wide right, then hooked left and sailed over the crossbar. The Giants won, 13-10 and beat the Browns again the next week at Yankee Stadium, 10-0.

The championship game against the Colts was played before a crowd of 64,000 in relatively mild 45-degree weather at Yankee Stadium. It was the first ever pro football game to go to a sudden death overtime.

The game featured a parade of stars: Johnny Unitas, Raymond Berry and Lenny Moore on offense for the Colts, and defensive behemoths Gino Marchetti, Art Donovan and six-foot seven-inch Gene (Big Daddy) Lipscomb who once described his tackling technique as, "I reach out and grab an armful of players from the other team and peel them off until I find the one with the ball." The Giants had Charley Conerly, Frank Gifford, Alex Webster and Kyle Rote, and tackle Roosevelt Brown on offense and a defensive line of Andy Robustelli, Jim Katcavage, Dick Modzelewski and Roosevelt Grier. And they had assistant coaches Vince Lombardi on offense and Tom Landry on defense. "With Vince and Tom," head coach Jim Lee Howell said, "all I have to do is blow up the footballs."

The Giants scored a field goal in the first quarter and the Colts scored two touchdowns in the second to lead 14-3 at the half. A comic moment was provide by Colts coach Weeb Ewbank. When Giants linebacker Sam Huff piled on Berry after a catch near the sideline, Ewbank was so enraged that all 5-foot-5 inches of him ran over and took a swing at Huff.

An 86-yard pass play led to a touchdown in the third period that narrowed the Colts' lead to 14-10. The Giants then scored on a 15-yard Conerly-to-Gifford touchdown pass and led, 17-14. After the Giants missed by inches on a third down and four situation and chose to punt, the Colts moved toward a field goal. Three straight Unitas-to-Berry passes gained 62 yards and put the ball on the Giants 13. With 19 seconds left, Steve Myhra kicked a 20-yard field goal for a 17-17 tie to force overtime.

The Giants won the toss but couldn't move the ball. The Colts took over on their own 20, and with the cool Johnny Unitas in complete command, they launched one of the most celebrated scoring drives in NFL history. As they moved down the field toward the left field bleachers in Yankee Stadium, I was looking up the field from outside the Yankee dugout at first base, pausing before going to the post-game dressing room interviews.

A 21-yard pass to Ray Berry and a 20-yard run by Alan Ameche put the ball just inside the Giants 10-yard line. This was the time to play it safe and kick a field goal. Unitas, however, was so cocky he took a colossal chance that has been questioned ever since.

After Ameche made only a yard on first down, Unitas threw a pass in the right flat to Jim Mutscheller. It was a risky call, because it could have been intercepted to nullify a sure winning field goal. But Unitas was supreme. He hit Mutscheller, who fell out of bounds inside the one-yard line. On third down, Ameche bucked through a huge hole for a touchdown that ended what would be called—at least in the years before Super Bowls took over the NFL landscape—"The Greatest Game Ever Played."

One of my favorite athletes of all time was Al Oerter, the champion discus thrower. His feat of winning gold medals in an unprecedented four straight Olympics would rank among my 10 moments that shook the sports world if more people paid attention to the discus event. "The only way the discus would ever attract any attention," Oerter often joked, "would be if we started throwing them at each other."

Oerter won the discus at the 1956 Olympics in Melbourne, in 1960 at Rome and in 1964 at Tokyo before he would try at Mexico City in 1968. He did not do well in many meets leading up to the Olympics. He suffered from several injuries and needed a neck collar to protect a pinched nerve in his cervical disc, the area at the top of his spine. By any rights he was an underdog, but there was a mystique about him that loomed large for the other competitors.

Oerter grew up in New Hyde Park on Long Island. He began his career at Sewanhaka High School when a discus landed at his feet and he threw it back past the group of throwers. He went on to Kansas U. He was 6'4", 280 pounds, sandy-haired with blue e[illegible] a broth of a man whom people would look at twice.

I once accompanied him to a local gym on Lon[illegible] lifted weights as preparation for the 1968 Games [illegible] on with awe as Oerter went through his lifts and politely stepped aside as he eventually used every piece of equipment in the room.

It was raining in Mexico City on the day of the discus competition, October 15th. The big men came out at 3:00 p.m., then left the field as thunder and lightning crackled in the air. They returned half an hour later to begin throwing. Throughout it all, Oerter paced back and forth between his throws, not looking at his competitors. I recalled a comment he had made at the Olympic trials. He said, "I wouldn't want to peak too early or I would be a raging maniac by the time of the Games."

On his first throw, Oerter hit 61.78 meters (202.6 feet). This put him third in the competition. He fouled in the second round, but held his position. The first three throws were important because only the top eight would advance to take three final throws. From where I sat in the press section across the field I focused on Oerter as he stopped his pacing and readied for his third effort.

With brisk strides, he settled into the circle, rubbing and cradling the disc, six pounds and 10 ounces of iron. He rubbed spit on it. Then he walked to the front of the circle, made a half-arc transferring the discus from his right to left hand and back. He moved to the back of the circle, set himself and quickly went into his spins, coming out of a final half-turn with his throw. It was an action combining speed with strength that didn't look quite as pretty as the famous Greek statue of *Discobolus*. Oerter had been doing this for some 16 years; he once estimated he had thrown the discus 500,000 times.

On this day Oerter did not wear the special collar to protect his neck. He said later, "If there was any separation in the neck, I ould have felt it, and I would have quit."

He ignored the pain, came out of his last half-turn and let go a heave for the ages. The discus almost seemed to be saying, "Whee, look at me." The crowd in the discus area roared when they could see Oerter's discus spinning beyond the marks of the leaders. The announcement of 64.78 meters—212 feet, 6½ inches—brought gasps and an ovation. This was the winner, the fourth time Oerter beat the existing record while winning an Olympics. For good measure, he added two more heaves that also were good enough to beat the competition.

Rain delayed the victory ceremonies for a long time. When Oerter approached the victory stand on the field, there was a crack of thunder that added a surreal quality to the moment. On the top stand he waved with one hand and bent to allow the gold medal to be placed around his collar-less neck.

The headline on the "Out of Left Field" column the next day read: "Raging Maniac Prevails Again."

The 1968 Olympics also included Bob Beamon's record long jump, six medals by Czech gymnast Vera Caslavska and, notably, the black power civil rights protest by Tommie Smith and John Carlos. But for me the world-shaking moment was Al Oerter heaving that discus into Olympic history.

Those were some of the happenings that made an impact on me. They serve as an appetizer for the events highlighted in this book. The ten events which produced moments that shook the sports world include three football games, two baseball segments, a tragic Olympics, an epic boxing match, a basketball heroic, a tennis upset and a magnificent horse race. They are described in reverse order of their impact on the world of sports.

#10

The First Super Bowl

During one of the large press conferences held a few days before the first Super Bowl, Green Bay coach Vince Lombardi told the assemblage, "Winning won't mean the end of the world as far as the Packers are concerned—or Kansas City." Listening to Lombardi poor-mouth this game, I couldn't help but suppress a giggle.

Nobody had to be on the inside at Lombardi's practices to guffaw at that whopper. Lombardi, no less than the God of football in those days, had been ranting and raving at his players for fear of losing the first match-up between the champions of the long-established National Football League and the upstart American Football League.

What Lombardi said and felt was revealed in detail in David Maraniss' excellent biography of Lombardi, *When Pride Still Mattered*, published in 1999, 32 years after this first Super Bowl. Red Cochran, one of Lombardi's assistant coaches, said, "Vince made it very clear from our first day of practice out there that we had to win that game and that he didn't want to make a squeaker out of it." Lombardi told his players, "You damn well better not let that Mickey Mouse league beat you. It'd be a disgrace, a complete, utter disgrace."

Left tackle Bob Skoronski said, "He was miserable that week." He raised the fines for curfew violations to record amounts: $2,500 for being out after curfew, $5,000 for an indiscretion. There was no relaxation for his men because he wanted no distractions. He distracted himself by watching Tom & Jerry cartoons during the week. Frank Gifford, one of the CBS announcers, interviewed Lombardi before the game. He said Lombardi was so nervous, "he held onto my arm and he was shaking like a leaf."

Lombardi knew he carried the whole National Football League on his shoulders. All the Packers' success of the previous half decade made them the kingpins of football, and he feared the disgrace it would be if the AFL champion beat his vaunted legions. Wellington Mara, the owner of the Giants, sent Lombardi a letter whose sentiments reflected those of all the NFL owners. He underscored how important it was for the league that Green Bay won and he said he was particularly happy that it was the Packers of all NFL teams who would be carrying the NFL banner. Willie Davis, the Packers' all star defensive end, recalled, "He told us 'This was for a way of life, a game of survival, a test of manhood.'"

Vincent Thomas Lombardi was born June 11, 1913 in Brooklyn, New York. An undersized 5-foot-8, 185-pound guard, he was one of Fordham's celebrated "Seven Blocks of Granite." He taught and coached at St. Cecilia, a New Jersey high school, then left for assistant coaching positions at Fordham and later West Point. He became the offensive coordinator with the Giants and took over as coach and general manager at Green Bay in 1959. His success and dominant personality made him an American icon, admired by movers and shakers as well as the man on the street. One story attached to Lombardi: he and his wife Marie are in bed on a cold, wintry night in Green Bay. Marie says, "God, it's cold." And Lombardi says, "In bed, Marie, you don't have to call me God."

I was not a fan of Lombardi. I found him overbearing, condescending, hypocritical. He demanded and got a sycophantic press. Bobby Kurland of the Bergen Record told me, "Lombardi courted the press when he was at St. Cecilia, but once he became a big name, it was as if we didn't exist." I was surprised to read Lombardi's reaction to a critical piece written about him by Leonard Shecter, a colleague with whom I had covered the Yankees and Mets. The article entitled, "The Toughest Man," which appeared in the January, 1968 issue of *Esquire* magazine, described Lombardi swearing at his players, casually dismissing their pain and injury and generally acting bellicose if not abusive. The story had a profound effect on Lombardi, David Maraniss wrote. "He was a New Yorker and Shecter was a New Yorker, and he had assumed that Shecter would intuitively understand him. During the week that Shecter was in training camp, in fact, Lombardi had noted with hometown pride that the writer was a 'real New Yorker' because he read the newspaper by folding it in eighths, the style perfected by subway riders."

Lombardi felt the story diminished him, reducing him to nothing more than another brutal football coach when he preferred to be known as a teacher, a leader, a man who preached the nobility of sport. For all his toughness, he talked about how the story had hurt his mother.

If dominated by Lombardi, the first Super Bowl traced as much as anything else to the efforts of one man, Lamar Hunt, owner of the Kansas City Chiefs. He was the ultimate prototype of the little kid who went out and bought himself a football because it was the only way he could get a game, only on a much larger scale: Hunt went and bought himself a league. The famous sudden death Baltimore Colts victory over the New York Giants in the NFL championship game in1958 symbolized the popularity of pro football in the country, and Hunt felt there was room for more teams in more cities. The established NFL had no room for new blood, so Hunt, scion of the oil wealthy Hunt family in Dallas, called for the formation of a new league on Aug. 14, 1959. The American Football League, which added Oakland, Buffalo, Cincinnati, Denver, Houston, San Diego, Dallas, Miami, Boston and New York to the football landscape, began play in 1960. Scoffers thought the idea of a new league was so crazy, the owners of the teams that formed this new conference were called the "Foolish Club."

I had a particular liking for Hunt because he was a fellow devotee of ice cream. Knowing about my annual ratings columns in which I rated, among others, the best chocolate ice creams, he tipped me off to a superior ice cream emporium in Canton, Ohio.

The NFL was in existence for 39 years when the AFL was formed. The established league regarded the AFL as, in Lombardi's words, a Mickey Mouse League. But it prospered little by little and the NFL could no longer ignore it when Al Davis, its hard-driving commissioner, threatened the old league by signing quarterback talents out from under the NFL. On June 8, 1966 a merger agreement was signed, though it wasn't finalized until 1970. What was first officially called the AFL-NFL World Championship game was also established.

Hunt, though, had other ideas. His three children played with highly concentrated rubber balls called Super Balls that would bounce high in the air. Hunt said, "The kids were always talking about these Super Balls. In the fall of 1966 at one of our joint meetings when we were discussing the game, I called it the Super Bowl. Thereafter the committee began to refer to the game as the Super Bowl." It was three years before the somewhat stodgy NFL people would accept the name, Super Bowl, but it was long part of the public discourse by then.

Pete Rozelle, who retained his title as league commissioner with the merger, predicted that the championship game in Los Angeles would be a sellout. He miscalculated by 35,054 seats. The crowd measured 61,946. Much has been made of that, with claims that the game did not have the significance of the later sold-out Super Bowls. Not so. The fact that the game was set for Los Angeles only six weeks earlier prevented the kind of build-up needed to fill such a stadium. Consider this. The Rose Bowl, which doesn't always pit the best college teams, is always a sell-out. That is because the Rose Bowl is one of the New Year's tourist attractions in the Los Angeles area. Visitors buy tour packages that include Disneyland and the Hollywood studios, among others, along with the Rose Bowl long before the teams have been set. And once the Super Bowl was established and the NFL's high powered marketing machine had time to get rolling, the Super Bowl became the country's monster one-day sports extravaganza, an unofficial national holiday.

Tickets for the first game sold for $6, $10 and $12. For the 2007 game between Indianapolis and Chicago in Miami, the top price for tickets was $700, which hawked for as much as $2,900. The real growth of the Super Bowl can be measured in the rates charged for television ads. For Super Bowl I a 30-second ad sold for $42,000. For Super bowl XLI (No. 41) a 30-second ad cost $1.3 million.

Because the first game was not a sellout, the telecast was blacked out in the Los Angeles area. Almost as significant as the battle between the league champions was the square-off between the television networks: the long-established NFL network, CBS vs. the AFL network, NBC. Each paid $1 million for the rights to broadcast the game. Each went all out to win the ratings battle and also to win honors for the best television presentation of the spectacle. CBS had its four horsemen ready to roll: Ray Scott and Jack Whitaker for play-by-play and Frank Gifford for analysis along with Pat Summerall. NBC had its Forrest Evashevski-Tom Harmon pair of broadcasters, with steady Curt Gowdy setting up star analyst Paul Christman for analysis. The post-game trophy presentation was handled for CBS by Summerall, for NBC by George Ratterman. who had to share a single microphone. Because the CBS production staff controlled the telecast, NBC's crew had little control over how the game was shot. The worst botch: NBC did not return to the air in time from a halftime commercial break for the start of the second half, and the kickoff had to be redone. Both networks taped over their copies of the telecasts so there is no known complete videotape of the game. There is only the action of Max McGee catching a pass for the opening touchdown. The telecasts were watched by 60 million people; it drew a combined rating of 40.8; the highest ever would be the 49.1 rating for the 1982 San Francisco 26-21 victory over Cincinnati .

A crowd at the airport sent the Packers off to Los Angeles to the strains of the Packer fight song. The Packers showed singing talent of their own a few weeks earlier when their flight out of Dallas was delayed. Led by Fuzzy Thurston, the redoubtable guard, they broke into song. To the refrain of "He's Got the Whole World in His Hands," they sang, "We've Got the Best Darn Coach—in This World." They went on to "Best Right End. . . " "Best Left Guard" and so on down through the lineup.

The Packers trained in Santa Barbara, 90 miles north of Los Angeles. Kansas City trained in Long Beach, some 30 miles south of the Coliseum. The Packers came in with a record of 12 victories and two defeats. They had defeated the Dallas Cowboys 34-27, at Dallas to win the NFL championship. Lombardi had inherited a team that had won only one of 12 games in 1958, and went on to win four NFL titles in six seasons. Kansas City—the franchise was moved there when Lamar Hunt's team didn't draw in Dallas—came into the big game with an 11-2-1 regular season record and a crushing 31-7 defeat of the Buffalo Bills in the AFL championship game. Green Bay chose the film of that game as one of the three KC efforts it would look at. They were not impressed. They also watched a film of a Jets game showing the full-bellied Jets offensive tackle, Sherman Plunkett. He symbolized the AFL to them, and they laughed as the film was rewound a few times to show Plunkett in action. Kansas City chose to study film of Green Bay's victories over Cleveland and Dallas in the NFL championship as well as its loss to Minnesota.

If Lombardi played down the game publicly, Lamar Hunt did not. "There will never be another game to match this one," he said. Kansas City guard Ed Budde said, "This is our chance to show what our league is all about." Linebacker Sherrill Headrick said, "Football is my whole life. After my career is over, I'd like to be remembered. This is my chance." In a sense, Kansas City quarterback Len Dawson symbolized the AFL. He had been drafted in the first round in 1957 when the Pittsburgh Steelers won a coin toss with Cleveland for the fifth pick (Cleveland then took Jim Brown with the 6th pick). He sat on the bench for five years in the NFL before making it big in Kansas City. "To me it will mean a great deal of money and prestige," he said. The Chiefs were admittedly nervous. Linebacker E.J. Holub said, "We were scared to death. Guys in the tunnel were throwing up and wetting their pants."

When the Packers boarded the bus to the stadium, Lombardi was the first man on. He took his seat, front right. As the driver started to pull out, Lombardi stopped him. He rose to his feet, stepped into the aisle and danced a soft shoe. The players loved it, shouting "Go, Coach, go." Lombardi, beaming, explained to an assistant, "They were too tight."

The pre-game ceremonies featured trumpeter Al Hirt and the marching bands from Grambling and the University of Arizona. I described the pre-game show as a production featuring "bands . . . girls . . . flags . . . flying men . . . balloons . . . and pigeons: 4,000 pigeons, the most gosh-awful number of pigeons ever released anywhere. It was an extravaganza by Mike Todd out of Cecil B. DeMille, and it couldn't have cost more than World War II." (Little did I know what would come later.) Some said the pre-game show was better than the game.

Referee Norm Schachter handled the coin toss. The officials wore neutral uniforms, different from those used in each league. When the Chiefs were on offense, the AFL ball was used; the Packers used the NFL football on offense. The Packer players felt the NFL ball was easier to catch and went farther.

The Packers were 13-point favorites. Not only did Green Bay command respect from one and all, there was an undercurrent of feeling in the land—and not only from NFL loyalists—that the game might wind up being a rout. Clif Keane, a Boston writer always fast with a quip, said the odds were even that the Packers would score a touchdown during the playing of the Star Spangled Banner. I heard somebody repeat an old line: that the Chiefs were working on survival. Because the game was new and people did not have a line on teams that played in opposite leagues, and had no common opponents, gambling on the game was light.

As a confirmed underdog rooter who resented the superior attitude of many NFL-ers I wanted the Chiefs to win—or at least do well. I picked Green Bay to win, 17-0. The writers who covered the NFL were openly scornful of the Chiefs. The AFL scribes resented this, but tended to be somewhat muted in defense of the league such was the awe for the Packers. This would change in Super Bowl III when Joe Namath's antics underscored bitter feelings between writers of the respective leagues.

In the face of the ridiule of Kansas City, cornerback Fred (The Hammer) Williamson, the Chiefs 6-foot-3 cornerback from Northwestern, emerged as a central, self-aggrandizing character in the pre-game palaver. He drew attention to himself by wearing white shoes, belittling the Packers, boasting he would use his "hammer"—a forearm karate chop to the head which bordered on the illegal—to destroy Packers' receivers Boyd Dowler and Carroll Dale.

The 1:00 p.m. start came up sunny and 72 degrees. There were few remarks about the Los Angeles smog. The Packers won the toss and Fletcher Smith kicked off. Herb Adderley, the Packers' 6-foot-2 star defensive back who once guarded the 7-foot Wilt Chamberlain as a high school basketball player, caught the ball on the Green Bay 5-yard line and returned it to the 25 before being tackled by linebacker Bobby Bell. After all the preliminaries—the pregame fustian and whim-wham, the balloons and pigeons released over the stadium, the concern about the absence of a sell-out, the fear of a rout by AFL stalwarts, the fear of a loss by NFL loyalists—the battle was joined.

Fullback Jim Taylor ran off right tackle for four yards, Elijah Pitts gained five on a sweep to the left and Taylor gained three yards to pick up the game's initial first down at the Packer 37. In that first series Packer flanker Boyd Dowler was injured and Lombardi startled veteran end Max McGee by calling his name and inserting him into the lineup. McGee, the 34-year-old who had caught only four passes all season and would retire after the following season, was a roustabout who had been up to his usual shenanigans the night before. He had arranged dates with stewardesses for himself and his soon-to-be-married roommate, Paul Hornung, who declined. McGee was up most of the night, returning to the hotel the next morning just as Bart Starr was walking through the lobby to buy a newspaper. Starr noticed that McGee was wearing the same sport coat he had on the night before. Because Dowler had been injured in the NFL championship game with Dallas, McGee had paid more attention than usual to the game films. He suggested to Ray Scott, the regular Green Bay broadcaster, that he might get into the game. He hinted there was a cornerback who would be easy pickings.

Starr's immediate pass to him was broken up. On the next play Kansas City's 6-foot-7, 285-pound defensive tackle, Buck Buchanan, sacked Starr for a 10-yard loss back to the Packer 27. I was impressed upon reading that Buchanan had bought a copy of Lombardi's book, *Run to Daylight* before the game to find out more about the Packers. Starr was sacked again on third down by defensive end Jerry Mays and linebacker Bobby Bell, resulting in a five-yard loss. Mays was playing opposite Forrest Gregg, who had preceded him at SMU and whom he admitted was "his idol." This opening defensive action was a sign to AFL fans that perhaps the Chiefs belonged on the same field with the Packers. With Green Bay back on their 22, Don Chandler punted 50 yards and Mike Garrett returned nine yards to the Chiefs 37.

Dawson, 31, trotted out onto the field to lead the red-and-white clad Chiefs. He immediately opted for a pass intended for Chris Burford. It fell incomplete. Garrett then gained four yards on a draw play up the middle, where he was stopped by left tackle Ron Kostelnik. On third down Dawson completed his first pass, an 11-yard strike to Burford for a first down into Green Bay territory, the 48-yard line. That was it for the first drive. Garrett gained only a yard on the next play, the Chiefs were penalized 5 yards for delay of game, and two incomplete passes by Dawson forced Jerrell Wilson to punt. Donny Anderson returned the punt 15 yards to the Green Bay 20.

Starr and the Packers then asserted themselves. Elijah Pitts gained three, and Starr completed three passes: 11 yards to Marv Fleming, 22 yards to Pitts, and, after a 5-yard loss, 12 yards to Carroll Dale. From the Kansas City 37, Starr passed to McGee over the middle. The 6-foot-4 McGee beat the 6-foot-1 cornerback, Willie Mitchell, with a remarkable one-handed catch, then sprinted to the goal line. McGee had found his patsy. When McGee died in October 2007, Paul Hornung said, "Now he'll be the answer to one of the great trivia questions: who scored the first touchdown in Super Bowl history?" The Packers gained eighty yards in six plays and led, 7-0, after Chandler kicked the extra point.

Chandler kicked off to Garrett, who returned the kick 23 yards. A holding penalty on the Chiefs put the ball back to the 13. After nine plays that included two pass completions (18 yards to Fred Arbanas and 7 yards to Reg Carolan) Kansas City set up for a 40-yard field goal. But Chiefs kicker Mike Mercer missed, the ball soaring wide to the right.

Green Bay failed to gain a first down on its next possession. After the quarter ended with the Packers leading, 7-0, Chandler punted to Gene Thomas, and the Chiefs next drive started at their own 34-yard line. Coach Hank Stram's innovative strategy of the moving pocket paid off here because it allowed quarterback Len Dawson to move around and find the time to spot receivers. Three completions and three short runs produced two first downs and a touchdown. He delivered a short pass to Mike Garrett who squirmed out of the arms of Green Bay's three vaunted linebackers, Willie Davis, Ray Nitschke and Lee Roy Caffey for a 17-yard gain into Packer territory. After three short runs gained eleven yards, Dawson hit the fine end, Otis Taylor, who made a sensational catch for a gain of 31 yards to the Packer 7. On the next play, a play action pass, he found Curtis McClinton in the end zone for a touchdown. Mercer's extra point tied the game at 7-7 with ten minutes and forty seconds to play in the half.

Kansas City coach Hank Stram, 44, short and stocky, dressed, as always, in a blazer, roamed the sidelines. He could feel the satisfaction of a man who had come a long way. A graduate of Purdue, he had been an assistant coach at Miami when Lamar Hunt plucked him off the campus to be his first coach. He won the AFL championship his third year (at Dallas before the franchise relocated to Kansas City) and would go on to become the only coach in AFL history to take his team to two Super Bowls when the Chiefs returned to the Super Bowl in 1970 and beat the Minnesota Vikings. Stram would be the first coach to wear a microphone for NFL Films in that Super Bowl (IV); one of the classic sound bites picks him up saying, "Let's just keep matriculating the ball down the field, boys!"

In addition to the moving pocket, Stram had devised the "stack defense"—linebackers stacked behind the linemen—and a two tight-end offense. More relaxed and amiable than most football coaches, Stram said before the game, "People think we change our offense every week, but we couldn't be a solid team if we did that. We might change our look a bit as we shift into a strange formation, but the plays are the same. It's just the same face with a different make-up. The key," he said, "is not to deviate from what we've been doing for six months. That means not adding a lot of things."

Donny Anderson returned the ensuing kickoff twenty-five yards to the Green Bay 27 before being collared by Walt Corey. After runs by Elijah Pitts and Jim Taylor gained nine yards, Starr and Carroll Dale teamed up on the longest pass play of the game, a sixty-four yard completion to the Chiefs 20-yard line. But the play was called back on an illegal procedure penalty.

Starr, 32, wearing No. 15 on his green and yellow jersey, proceeded to enjoy some of the finest moments of his 16-year Hall of Fame career. He moved the Packers seventy-three yards in thirteen plays for a touchdown. He did it by completing passes four times when the Packers faced third-down situations. He dropped back coolly and even though tacklers seemed about to hit him, let loose with passes that one writer said "were pretty enough to belong in museum." He completed these third-down strikes: from the Packer 32, a 10-yard pass to Max McGee; from the Packer 42, a 15-yard pass to Carroll Dale; from the KC 38, an 11-yard pass to Marv Fleming; and from the KC 24, a 10-yard pass to Pitts.

This set up a touchdown on the famous Green Bay sweep devised by Lombardi when he was the offensive coach with the Giants. Guards Jerry Kramer and Fred "Fuzzy" Thurston pulled out and fullback Jim Taylor swept fourteen yards around left end behind blocks by Kramer and Thurston. Don Chandler kicked the extra point. With 4:37 remaining in the second period, Green Bay had regained the lead, 14-7.

Mike Garrett returned the ensuing kickoff twenty yards to the Chiefs 26-yard line. Now it was Dawson's turn. After being sacked for an 8-yard loss by Lionel Aldridge and Henry Jordan, Dawson hit three straight passes: twelve yards to Fred Arbanas, eleven yards to Otis Taylor and twenty-seven yards to Chris Burford to the Green Bay 32. Garrett gained two up the middle before being stopped by the great middle linebacker, Ray Nitschke. Curtis McClinton lost two yards on a fumble, but recovered the ball. With a third-and-10, and needing a little bit of Starr heroics, Dawson completed a pass to Garrett up the middle for eight yards, two yards short of a first down. Stram again called on Mike Mercer for a field goal. This time he kicked a 31-yarder. Kansas City had gained fifty yards in seven plays and cut the Green Bay lead to 14-10 less than a minute before the clock ran out for the half.

What would turn out to be a wide margin of victory for the Packers would years later be regarded as a rout by a superior league champion against an inferior bunch of upstarts. But that was not the feeling at halftime when Green Bay led by only 14-10. The Chiefs had out-gained the Packers 184 yards to 164 in the first half. Dawson completed eleven of fifteen passes for 152 yards, Starr eight of fifteen for 128 yards. The Chiefs' first-half effort raised enough ominous indications of a possible upset to impress all but the morning-after know-it-alls who insisted that they knew all along that the Packers would win easily. Consider Buddy Young, one of the all-time great elusive backs who was now an NFL employee, a scout for the old league. I had a good relationship with Young because we often reminisced about the time he ran a kickoff back almost 100 yards for the New York Yankees against the New York Giants. Before the game Young, a gregarious, likeable guy, told me, "Green Bay is much too strong. No contest." When it appeared that the Chiefs could play the Packers even, I overheard Young, who was standing behind me in the huge Colsieum press box, tell a friend, "You may be seeing the makings of a great upset here." After the game Young admitted, "I was scared to death."

During the intermission Lombardi did not rant and rave. Not quite. "He had a few nice words," tackle Henry Jordan said. He told his players they were too tight. Ray Nitschke snorted at that, saying to a teammate, "Who the hell does he think got us nervous in the first place?" A major change in strategy was installed and that helped turn the game around. They had not blitzed their linebackers during the first half so the four rushing linemen were unable to get to Len Dawson. Defensive coach Phil Bengston said, "Kansas City's play-action passes were working because our linebackers were following the fakes of their ball carriers. When we put in the blitz in the second half, the linebackers disregarded their backs and went right for the quarterback."

After the second-half kickoff was replayed because NBC was in commercial, it didn't take long for the Packers to take charge. The sign of things to come was a pass rush that threatened Dawson, but he escaped and slithered for a 15-yard gain. Two short runs followed and the Chiefs had a third-down and five on their 49-yard line. Then came the turning point in the game. Dawson retreated to pass and the Packers blitzed. The line rushed and the outside linebackers, Dave Robinson from the left and Lee Roy Caffey from the right, also charged in. As Dawson threw the ball up, Caffey's hand nicked it. The wobbly ball floated into the hands of Packers safety Willie Wood. He grabbed the pass in front of end Fred Arbanas at the Packer 45 and raced fifty yards to the Chiefs 5 before being tackled by Mike Garrett, a fellow University of Southern California man. Wood was 5-foot-10, 190, and one of the fastest men in the league; he had not been drafted, and had to ask the Packers for a tryout. I unabashedly called him "Wonderful Willie Wood."

Afterward the Chiefs agreed that Wood's interception and 50-yard run was the key play in the game. "That play certainly changed the personality of the game," Hank Stram said. "We played well in the first half. We were doing things we should have been doing. Then came that one play. After that we just broke down and they got to Lenny." Dawson said, "The interception did it. It gave them the momentum. Their offense took the ball and drove it down our throats." Jerry Mays, the honest defensive end, said, "We lost our poise after the interception. That's no excuse. Great teams don't lose poise."

The Packers wasted no time after the interception. Elijah Pitts, No. 22, immediately rambled for five yards over left tackle for the touchdown. Green Bay, 21, Kansas City 10. Pitts, a graduate of Philander Smith College in Arkansas, fascinated me for the euphonious nature of his name. The name also registered for *Newsday* reader Paul Greenberg, who penned this quatrain:

There's one thing that gives me fits
Did Elijah Pitts go to Philander Smith
Or did Philander Smith
Go to Elijah Pitts?

Pitts, a six-year veteran, had taken over in October for glamour boy Paul Hornung, who was suffering with a pinched nerve in his neck. Pitts, 6-foot-1, 205 pounds, delivered workmanlike performances. Frequently running out of the Packer sweep that made Hornung famous, Pitts gained 393 yards rushing, caught twenty-six passes and scored ten touchdowns coming into the Super Bowl.

The Packers fielded eight players who would eventually be named to the Hall of Fame: defensive stalwarts Wood, cornerback Herb Adderley, end Willie Davis, linebacker Ray Nitschke, the tackles, Forrest Gregg and Henry Jordan; quarterback Starr and halfback Hornung. KC defensive standouts Bobby Bell and Buck Buchanan would be named to the Hall of Fame as well as Dawson.

Green Bay put together another scoring drive just before the end of the third quarter. Starr, who was voted the Most Valuable Player in the league during the season, went on to earn the MVP award for this game as well. It became the Starr-McGee show, the roguish end victimizing right cornerback Willie Mitchell all day. A

56-yard drive included third down completions of eleven and sixteen yards to McGee. Max then gathered in a 13-yard pass in the end zone making a spectacular juggling catch as Mitchell fell on his face at the goal line. He wound up with seven catches for 138 yards and two touchdowns, beating Mitchell most of he time by running short patterns. .

The Chiefs were awed by Starr. Defensive right end Chuck Hurston said afterward, "Once I was this close (he placed his fingers an inch apart) and he still threw a touchdown pass. He didn't even notice me." Mays called him "the most accurate passer I've ever seen." How did the Packers do it? Bill Austin, a Packer assistant, said, "They kept completing the same simple patterns they always had. It was a case of execution."

Starr had one mishap and poor Willie Mitchell had a momentary reprieve. On Green Bay's first possession of the fourth quarter, he threw deep from midfield intending to hit McGee, but the pass was picked off by Mitchell on the Kansas City 11-yard line. It was the first interception of Starr since October and ended a streak of 173 straight pass completions.

Ray Nitschke, the great Packer linebacker who called the team's defensive signals, said, "We blitzed at least six times in the second half." With Dawson contained, the Chiefs advanced into Packer territory just twice in the second half, and never made it past the Packer 44 yard line. Stram conceded the game by the middle of the fourth quarter, inserting Pete Beathard at quarterback to replace the confused Dawson.

The Packers clinched the game with their fifth touchdown. After a 61-yard punt into the end zone by Jerrell Wilson, the Packers started from their own 20. Starr completed three passes, a 25-

yarder to Carroll Dale, a 37-yard pass down the middle to McGee and another 7-yarder to Dale. Two plunges by Taylor then set up Elijah Pitts for a 1-yard push into the end zone. Starr left after that with the Packers leading, 35-10.

For the remaining eight minutes of the game, the Packers attended to stopping the demoralized Chiefs and running out the clock on offense. Zeke Bratkowski, the veteran replacing Starr, threw only one pass. He was content to hand the ball off to Donny Anderson and Jim Grabowski for time-consuming runs. The second time Anderson carried the ball resulted in an action that, in a sense, underscored the ecstasy of triumph for the NFL legions wanting to humiliate the upstart league. Anderson ran around right end for three yards where he was met by Fred Willlamson. In the collision, Anderson's leg banged into Williamson's head, knocking him unconscious. Williamson was taken off the field on a stretcher, much to the delight of Packer partisans. On the Packer bench there were cries of "Who was it, who got hit?" and the answer from Willie Wood, "The Hammer. They nailed the Hammer."

Williamson recovered enough to talk, however woozy, in the dressing room. "I don't remember a thing," he said. "Did I make the tackle?" Stram, ever supportive, said, "Fred got his share of tackles." Unabashed, Williamson went on to a short career in movies and for a short time joined the list of inept analysts trotted out by ABC on its "Monday Night Football" telecasts.

Super Bowl I soon was all over but the counting. The finances: 40 percent of the receipts went to the players pension fund, 15 percent to each team, the rest to team managements and the league office. This netted the Green Bay players $15,000 each and the Chiefs $7,500, which at the time amounted to the largest single game share ever in sports. Packer tackle Henry Jordan said, "I am going to take all that money in one-dollar bills, fill up a bathtub with it—and jump in."

Afterward the steamy Packers locker room was relatively quiet. Lombardi met the press shifting a football from hand to hand. "The boys gave me the game ball," he said, and added with a twinkle, "an NFL ball." He was gracious, yet honest. Well, almost, because he really didn't have a high opinion of the Chiefs. He said, "Kansas City is a good football team. But their team doesn't compare with the top National Football League teams. The Chiefs have great speed, but I'd have to say NFL football is tougher." He declined to say how much tougher or how many teams he rated higher than the Chiefs, or which teams.

Losing locker rooms usually make the best story, but I wasn't able to get to the Kansas City players because of a tight deadline. Frank Litsky wrote in the *New York Times*, "After the loss it was difficult to tell in the Kansas City locker room whether they had won, lost, tied or even played. There was no crying, no outbursts of temper. There was disappointment with their performance and, to a lesser degree, there was praise for the Packers as a good—but not perfect—team."

I had made my way down to the locker room area from the huge press box atop the vast Los Angeles Coliseum in an elevator. It reminded me of a time several years earlier when I was out in Los Angeles for post-season baseball. I decided at the last moment to cover a UCLA-Southern California night football game at the Coliseum so I didn't get the proper credentials to send my story via Western Union. After doing locker room interviews I did not trek all the way back up to the press box. I scribbled my story in a notebook and, in the semi-light at a street telephone, called my story in to the *Newsday* sports desk. My colleague, Steve Jacobson, who accompanied me to the football game, warmed the cockles of my heart whenever he told people about it.

Despite the lack of a full stadium, despite the reluctance of some to use the word, "Super" as in "Super Bowl—"it sounds like a comic strip," Lombardi said—and despite the concern about how big the production was (little did we all know what was to come) "an undercurrent of merriment pervaded the scene," I wrote. "Those of us here cannot be sure of what came across on the television screens to the record sports audience of 45 million viewers, but everything here was first-class, positively . . . er . . . super."

The Packers had held up the honor of the National Football League, solidified their dynasty. I summed up the game by writing, "The Packers illustrated what most people have thought: The National Football League—the oldest, reliable, permanent pro football league in existence—is putting out a better product right now than the American Football League" The New York Jets victory over the Baltimore Colts was still two years away.

Lombardi retired after the 1968 Super Bowl. The man who had refused to talk to players who asked for raises broke his own contract with the Packers by moving on to take over the Washington Redskins in 1969. He started to turn the Redskins around in his two seasons, but developed intestinal cancer in the summer of 1970 and died on Sept. 3, 1970 at the age of 57.

It was the passing of a giant. He was celebrated as a national hero, a man looked on by many as a spokesman for traditional values at a time when many objected to what they saw as the permissive attitude in society. Thousands of people attended funerals for him in Washington and New York. Hard-nosed football players cried openly. President Nixon sent a telegram of condolence to Maria Lombardi. He was inducted into the professional football Hall of Fame in 1971, the year that the $20,000 Super Bowl Tiffany trophy was renamed in his honor.

#9

John McEnroe's Wimbledons

The tumultuous events at Wimbledon in 1980 and 1981 produced the drama that earns the John McEnroe-Bjorn Borg rivalry a place among the ten moments that shook the world of sports. On July 5, 1980, McEnroe and Borg played a 34-point fourth set tiebreaker in the final. A year later, on July 4, 1981 outrageous behavior in the early rounds by McEnroe led up to a tense, suspenseful second successive final between the pair on the sacred greensward of Wimbledon.

Borg, a Swede and McEnroe, an American, were players with far different temperaments. Borg the cool. McEnroe the hot. In 1980 McEnroe won the legendary fourth set tiebreaker, 18-16, but did not ultimately win Wimbledon. In 1981 he made a fool of himself in the early rounds, but went on to win the tournament.

Bjorn Borg was born June 6, 1956. He grew up in Sodertalje, a town near Stockholm. When he was a youth he became fascinated by a golden tennis racquet his father had won as a prize at a table tennis tournament. His father gave him the racquet, and that was the start. He progressed to train with Percy Rosberg, the leading coach of the day, at the Salk Club in Stockholm. For five years he stuck with a rigorous after-school schedule, commuting to Stockholm. His parents supported him even though his devotion to tennis took a toll on his schoolwork. In his first two years of playing Borg held the racquet with both hands—even when he hit forehand shots—because the racquet was too heavy. As he continued playing he grew stronger, and he discovered that it was easier to hit the ball with topspin if he adopted a one-handed forehand. He kept the two-handed backhand for his entire career, though.

With his long blond hair and stolid demeanor he preferred to battle from the baseline, trading groundstrokes tirelessly in long rallies. He waited patiently to outlast his opponents. He gained a reputation for remaining cool under pressure, so cool and reserved that he would earn the nickname, "Ice Man." While other players argued with referees over questionable calls, Borg let the calls pass. The Swedish press said he had "ice in the stomach." His sportsmanship commanded respect and he would receive it from the media, the fans and the other players, notably McEnroe.

Borg won his first tournament at age eleven. Over the next four years he swept every junior championship in his age division. In 1972, at the age of fifteen, he became one of the youngest players ever to represent his country in the Davis Cup, and won his debut singles match in five sets against New Zealander Onny Parun. Later that year he won the Wimbledon junior singles title. In 1973, the sixteen year old Borg reached the Wimbledon quarterfinals in his first appearance at the British classic.

In 1974 he won his first Grand Slam title at the French Open, coming back from two sets down in the final to defeat Manuel

Orantes of Spain. He retained his French Open title in 1975, beating Guillermo Vilas of Brazil in straight sets in the final. He then reached the quarter-finals of Wimbledon again before losing in four sets to the eventual winner, Arthur Ashe.

In 1976, Borg began his reign as the dominant player in tennis, winning the first of five straight Wimbledon titles. In the finals he defeated Ilie Nastase (1976); Jimmy Connors (1977 and 1978); Roscoe Tanner (1979); and, in 1980, McEnroe in the five-set classic marked by the 16-18 fourth set tiebreaker that he lost.

McEnroe was born February 16, 1959 in Wiesbaden, Germany while his father served as an officer in the U.S. Air Force. When his father got out of the service, eventually to become a lawyer, the family moved to an apartment in Flushing, Queens, then to Douglaston, Queens near the borderline between New York City and Nassau County, Long Island. It tickled me to know that, among other things, McEnroe delivered *Newsday*, meaning he was distributing my column, "Out of Left Field," to the good burghers of Douglaston. In the summer of 1967, the McEnroe family moved north to the lovely enclave of Douglas Manor. McEnroe often talked of himself as a tough product of Queens, but Douglas Manor was a suburban jewel far from any mean streets. It was at the neat Douglaston Club that McEnroe first started playing tennis at the age of five. When he was twelve, he started working as a ballboy at the U.S. Open Tournament, held in those days at Forest Hills.

McEnroe came under the tutelage of Tony Palafox and the legendary Australian teacher, Harry Hopman at the Port Washington Tennis Academy. By the time he was eleven he was number eighteen in the country in the twelve-and under category. At twelve he was number seven. He won his first national title when he was sixteen. He showed his temper early and at one point was suspended for six months by the Port Washington Academy. His outrageous behavior led to heavy fines and suspensions throughout his career. At the 1990 Australian Open he would suffer an extraordinary suspension for showering abusive language on court officials.

His game took off after he was graduated from Manhattan's prestigious Trinity School. He made his first splash at Roland Garros in Paris in 1977, teaming with Douglas Manor friend Mary Carillo—later to become a broadcasting partner—to win the mixed doubles championship. He then went on to a sensational debut at Wimbledon, becoming the first qualifier and youngest player, eighteen, to reach the semi-finals before being eliminated in four sets by Jimmy Connors. That fall he entered Stanford University, won the NCAA singles championships and led the team to the NCAA title. He left Stanford after only a year to turn pro. In 1979 he won his first U.S. Open championship, beating his friend Vitas Gerulatis in straight sets. But he was eliminated in the fourth round at Wimbledon that year by Tim Gullikson.

At 5-foot-11 (he said six feet because he insisted he was five-foot-11-and-a-half) and 170 pounds, McEnroe was described by tennis sage Bud Collins as "a magnificent volleyer with a feathery touch, perhaps the most skilled of all players." He combined shot-making artistry with a fast, attacking style of play. His game had variety, delicacy and quickness.

He also had extreme competitive fire and a volatile temper. Some people claimed his temper tantrums were a means of motivating his play. McEnroe said that may or may not have been true, but it did not bother him if those outbursts threw off his opponents. He said, "I know people have seen me as a caricature, a spoiled, loudmouthed, ill-tempered crybaby. I don't deny I've acted that way a lot, though I have always instantly regretted it." Yet he reacted with amusement to the report that when the actor Thomas Hulce was studying for his role as a mercurial young Mozart in the movie, "Amadeus," he looked at videotapes of McEnroe acting up on the court.

McEnroe would apologize time and time again after explosions. "When you rise quickly to the top ranks of tennis at an early age," he said, "the oxygen doesn't always flow to your brain." But the bad behavior would continue and he, Connors and Ilie Nastase became a terrible threesome, rotters who inspired disgust in the public.

Curiously McEnroe was a different hombre against Borg. "I never acted like a jerk when I played Borg," he said. "I respected him too much; I respected the occasion. Whether I won or lost was always less important than that I got to be a part of history." In his autobiography, *You Cannot Be Serious*, McEnroe wrote, "The first time I saw Borg—I was twelve or thirteen—I thought he was incredible looking—the long hair, the headband, that little bit of scruff on his face, the tight shirts and tight shorts. I loved that stuff. I thought he was magical—like some kind of Viking god who'd landed on the tennis court. He didn't have much to say, on or off the court—but then he didn't have to say much. The way he looked—long, tan legs, wide shoulders—and the way he played, the vibe he gave off, all that was more than enough."

On his run to his fifth straight Wimbledon championship in 1980, Borg lost only two sets in six matches before the final against McEnroe. He had lost to McEnroe in May on a fast indoor carpet, but this was the first time they would meet on grass. To reach the final, McEnroe had to survive a four-set semi-final conflagration with his tempestuous countryman, Jimmy Connors. The bad blood between the two produced constant bickering over officials' calls and they mouthed obscenities when they passed each other on court changes.

McEnroe won the first set of the final, 6-1. He had noted that Borg had a habit of standing far back to receive serve, so he got to the net quickly after his serve and took command of the angles. "Early on," he said later, "I was amazed at how easily I was winning."

McEnroe then took a 5-4 lead in the second set. But with visions of a huge upset in the air, he tightened up. Borg got his serve going. He came back to win three straight games and take the second set, 7-5. Borg then took the third set, 6-3, and seemed ready to put McEnroe away when he scored the only break of serve in the fourth set. At this point, down 3-5 on his serve, McEnroe rallied to hold serve. Borg then had two match points, serving at 5-4, 40-15, but McEnroe climbed back from that hurdle with two crucial winners, the last one on a backhand cross-court service return. The crowd, which had been rooting for Borg, responded with cheers for McEnroe's pluck.

The tiebreaker took 22 minutes, only five less than the entire first set. It was excruciating for the players, as well as for the spectators. Both lunged, stretched, sprawled onto Wimbledon's heavily-played scarred Centre Court turf. As McEnroe recalled in his autobiography, "The crowd was very excited, vociferous, and then dramatically hushed at other moments. Somehow—maybe because I'd saved those match points earlier—I could sense that even the people who didn't want me to win the match wanted me to win the tiebreaker."

I always had mixed feelings about McEnroe. Because he was a local guy, who had, as I said, delivered my newspaper, *Newsday*, to Queens neighbors, I was inclined to root for him. Yet his behavior always got in the way. As much as I was torn, I invariably admired his ability to make spectacular shots, to hit his spectacular wide serve from thie advantage court—his "can-opener" serve.

It wasn't only the spectators who felt the tension in such matches I always have felt that tennis players, more than any other athletes, face more pressure situations, one after another than those in any sport As much as I try to approach an event with professional aplomb, I find it excruciating sometimes when a match see-saws between scores of deuce, advantage-in, deuce, advantage-out, deuce. A tennis player can face such nerve-racking moments more times in a match than a quarterback has to deal with crucial situations or a baseball pitcher deals with such make-or-break moments.

The tiebreaker went back and forth, back and forth, with both players hitting tremendous winners but neither able to put the other away. McEnroe, serving second, survived five match points. Australian Fred Stolle, the ex-player-TV commentator said, "How the guy got up to serve those match points, I don't know." On the third match point McEnroe saved himself with a forehand volley that died on the grass after Borg had made a tremendous forehand return of a second serve. McEnroe got his first set point at 8-7. This time, Borg drove a forehand return of service down the line. McEnroe dived in vain at it, tumbling to the ground.

It seemed as if match points and set points were played on almost every succeeding point. *New York Times* reporter Neil Amdur called the action, "a blur of brilliance." They hammered first serves, attacked, scrambled, sometimes missing the lines by inches, other times splattering chalk. McEnroe recalled one special moment:

"I hit one winning forehand—a winner down the line as it turned out—and ended up practically in the crowd when I stopped. I could feel the excitement coming off those people in waves."

After more than 20 minutes, McEnroe took a 17-16 lead when Borg drove a forehand service return wide by inches. On the seventh set point for McEnroe the tiebreaker finally ended. Borg, attacking off serve, netted a forehand volley. McEnroe 18, Borg 16. On to a fifth set.

Borg served the first game and when McEnroe won the first two points, he began to think Borg would be utterly deflated by having lost that heartbreaking tiebreaker. So did many of the fans and experts in attendance. But Borg was indomitable. He rallied to win that game and didn't lose another point on serve until the 10th game. Afterward he said that he told himself, "Don't give up, don't get tight."

Borg got stronger, McEnroe weaker. John was hard-pressed to even score points on Borg's serve. One break of McEnroe's serve won it for Borg. At 15-all he ran around McEnroe's second serve and drove a forehand down the line, inches inside the chalk. McEnroe, behind, 15-30, hurriedly netted a forehand volley. That made it, 15-40.

The final point: McEnroe, attacking off a second serve, punched a forehand volley into the right corner. Borg countered with a backhand cross-court winner. After three hours and 53 minutes, Borg won, 1-6, 7-5, 6-3, 6-7 (16-18), 8-6.

"Electrifying," said Fred Stolle. Amdur wrote, "If this marathon was not the greatest major championship final ever played—and tennis historians treasure the past with reverence—it ranked as one of the most exciting." Lance Tingay of the *London Telegraph*, who was watching his 43rd final, put it at the top of his Wimbledon list.

Borg said later, "For sure it is the best match I have ever played at Wimbledon."

The crowd erupted with waves of applause. The ever-appreciative British saved their loudest applause for the loser. McEnroe The Bad had won over the crowd, and when he stepped up to the Royal Box and bowed deeply from the waist, his head lowered and one foot pawing the turf, the cheering swelled.

The fourth set tiebreaker eventually took on mythic overtones. Looking back on his career, McEnroe said, "After people talk about my temper, the main thing everybody wants to discuss is my first Wimbledon final when I won the fourth set tiebreaker, 18-16. People usually think I won that match, even though I lost it in the fifth. That's OK with me."

The following year, 1981, Borg came to Wimbledon looking for a modern-day record of six straight Wimbledon championships. Willie Renshaw had won six straight titles from 1881 to 1886, a somewhat lesser achievement because in those days the defender played only in the final.

I had been to Wimbledon before but this year I covered the tournament in a dual capacity at *Newsday*. Now the TV sports critic, I would report on the background of the NBC telecasts, and compare it to the British Broadcasting Company (BBC) efforts. I would also revert to my old role as "Out of Left Field" sports columnist and cover the tennis action.

I am an anglophile who is a sucker for the pomp and circumstance of Wimbledon—the white-clad tennis players, the velvety green lawns of the courts early in the tournament, the presence of royalty, strawberries and cream—tradition, tradition, tradition.

I love the story about the time the women tennis players asked for equal treatment by the Wimbledon authorities, the presence of a masseur in the locker room. When the authorities could not find a female masseuse, they solved the problem of propriety in dealing with women by employing a blind male masseur. And there was the time American announcer Bud Collins said over a quick TV shot of a member of royalty picking her nose: "Nice backhand."

Ah the privileges of the insider. One day, I met with NBC sports head Don Ohlmeyer head at his hotel, and we went out to Wimbledon in his chauffeur-driven Bentley. In the plush NBC-hospitality tent, I enjoyed the delectables of the moment topped off by strawberries and cream. On another day I was scheduled to meet with the super sports agent Mark McCormack at the NBC tent. He had extended his reach and was now the commercial representative for Pope John Paul II in the Pope's approaching visit to London, and I thought that would make a good column. I spotted McCormack inside the tent and was about to make a beeline for him when I noted he was chatting with a beautiful blonde woman and a dumpy-ish middle-aged man. In a flash I realized that they were Princess Grace Kelly and her husband Prince Rainier. McCormack's assistant came over and said this might not be a good time to talk to McCormack. Between tennis and TV duties, I never came up with a column about McCormack and the Pope.

In the early rounds Borg defeated Peter Rennert, Mel Purcell and Rolf Gehring. He beat one of his favorite patsies, Vitas Gerulaitis for the umpteenth time and Peter McNamara in the quarter-finals. He then lost the first two sets against the dogged Jimmy Connors, before putting together 6-3, 6-0, 6-4 sets to qualify for the final against McEnroe. "He had to play his best stuff to beat me," said the never-gracious Connors.

McEnroe had a turbulent odyssey through the tournament. The histrionics started in the first round against American Tom Gullikson. McEnroe, who said he often was especially nervous in the early rounds of tournaments, recalled that he was "tight as a piano wire" in 1981. He didn't feel any better when the umpire, Ted James, who knew whom he was dealing with, told him just before the match started, "I'm Scottish, so we're not going to have any problems, are we?" McEnroe responded curtly, nervously, "I'm Irish."

He won the first set, 7-6, and there seemed no reason for alarm, but when Gullikson went ahead 4-3 in the second set on what McEnroe labeled "a miserable line call," he smashed his racket, drawing a warning from James. Later, when a linesman called a serve deep that McEnroe thought threw up a spray of chalk, the hot-head slammed his new racket and gave a scream that has echoed through the years.

He yelled, "Man, you cannot be serious." As boorish as it was at the moment, it came to be McEnroe's trademark. Attitudes toward him mellowed with his future successes, and he chose *You Cannot Be Serious* as the title of his autobiography.

After uttering that piece of eloquence, McEnroe walked up to the umpire and demanded to know if he had seen the chalk fly.

"There was chalk," James said, "but it was chalk which had spread beyond the line." To give McEnroe his due, he had phenomenal eyesight and usually was correct in how he saw shots. But I thought it was the height of arrogance for him to be so adamant about his opinion when he was disputing a shot landing at the far baseline, the line across the court farthest from him.

At 1-1 Gullikson hit a serve that McEnroe thought was long, but wasn't called. This produced another wail that certainly had never been uttered at Wimbledon before. He cried, "You guys are the absolute pits of the world!" That was more than the umpire—old enough to be McEnroe's father, perish the thought—could stand. It cost McEnroe a second penalty point. He would claim later that he should not have been charged the penalty for uttering an obscenity because the umpire had mistakenly heard "piss" for "pits." In any case he called for the referee to come out and within a few seconds yelled an obscenity at him. For good measure he pointed at poor Edward James and yelled loudly enough for TV and most of Court One to hear, "We're not going to have a point taken away because this guy is an incompetent fool."

This was probably the worst of the worst of McEnroe's explosions. Bunny Austin, a British player beaten in Wimbledon finals by Ellsworth Vines and Don Budge, was so upset by McEnroe's boorish display that he wrote a letter to the *London Times* recounting an anecdote. In the midst of a Don Budge-Gottfried von Cramm match, Budge argued with the umpire about a call. On the change of court von Cramm admonished Budge about complaining. "But Gottfried," Budge said, "I was complaining about the call being in my favor." Von Cramm answered, "Still, you should not have done that. You embarrassed the poor fellow."

I wrote in *Newsday* after the Gullikson incidents, "By any standard of good manners, John McEnroe deserved to be thrown off the court and out of the tournament for putting on one of those asinine, spoiled, pipsqueak tantrums like the one that erupted at Wimbledon yesterday." I would later turn around and give him credit. For all his poor behavior, he showed up at the post-match press conference and faced the hostile treatment. In contrast, Jimmy Connors frequently ducked press conferences when he lost.

The London tabloids went wild after the Gullikson match. One headline read in bold caps: "THE SHAME OF JOHN MCENROE; DISGRACE OF SUPER BRAT." The *Daily Mirror* quoted a psychologist at a local hospital, who called him a classic example of a "hysterical extrovert." A woman even wrote to the *Daily Mail* complaining about his use of "you know" in a post-match interview. "I counted 49 'you knows' by him in the interview," she wrote, "and it is disheartening because I have been trying to discourage my son's frequent use of this abominable phrase."

Nor did he get much sympathy in the American press. Pete Axthelm wrote in *Newsweek*, "In private this devastating athlete can be a nice enough kid . . . but when he steps to the service line, with his perpetually put-upon expression and his insistence that every line call and crowd reaction go his way . . . Call it spoiled." Barry Lorge wrote in the *Washington Post*, "He comes across as a precocious brat . . . immensely talented, spoiled and rather obnoxious." McEnroe's father, John Sr., tried to explain. He said, "John sets high standards for himself and doesn't suffer fools gladly. What you might say about John is that he shoots from the hip through his mouth."

There were several sides to McEnroe. For all his boorishness, petulance and frequent lack of sportsmanship in his fearsome desire to win, he was a loyal tennis man. He knew and respected tennis history. Where others like Jimmy Connors and, later, Pete Sampras, ducked Davis Cup play because there was no money in it for them, McEnroe often said "what a great honor it is to play for one's country." He held the American record for most years of Davis Cup matches played; he had a singles record of 41-8, was 18-2 in doubles play and led the United States to five Davis Cup victories. In 1981 he was the first to sweep Wimbledon, the U.S. Open and the Davis Cup finals since Don Budge had in 1937.

In September of 1980 he and Borg were offered $750,000 each to play a one-day exhibition in the South African state of Bophuthatswana. McEnroe turned it down because of the apartheid policies of the South African government.

Though McEnroe eventually beat Gullikson in straight sets, 7-6, 7-5, 6-3, he just could not rest easy even when he was ahead. He said, "The devils were crawling all over my brain that afternoon." In his autobiography he offered this explanation: "My confidence in myself made me nervous deep down in places nobody knew about. One of the hardest things for me has always been to live up to my potential—to beat the guys I shouldn't lose to in the early rounds, and get to the finals where I was supposed to be. . . . I could be dominating a guy, 6-2, 6-2, 2-0 and 40-0 on his serve—but if he somehow got out of that game, the negative thoughts would start creeping in."

In that 1981 Wimbledon, McEnroe was hit with a $750 fine for obscenity, another $750 for the unsportsmanlike comment about the umpire and $750 more for accusing a lineman from India of being biased toward the two Amritraj brothers of India. He was threatened with an additional $10,000 fine and possible suspension from the tournament if he "engaged in any further aggravated behavior." The fine was never levied and he was not suspended from the tournament though he had some more rabid moments in his 7-6, 6-4, 7-5 semi-final victory over Australian Rod Frawley. He grumbled his way to victory, complaining 19 times by one account. He dressed down tournament referee Fred Hoyles after informing the umpire, R.A.F. Wing Commander George Grime that he was "a disgrace to mankind." This produced another $10,000 fine that McEnroe got off on appeal. The brouhaha continued in the press room as McEnroe took on the gossip-hungry British tabloid press. There followed a hilarious dialogue on the nature of journalism that wound up with an Englishman and an American rolling on the floor in a scuffle.

Anticipation was sky high for the July 4, 1981 final between Borg and McEnroe. Their 1980 match with the mythic 34-game fourth set tiebreaker had given them the aura of heavyweight fighters meeting for a return match. McEnroe's temper tantrums added an element of spice. Though he had never behaved badly against Borg, there was no telling what the mercurial American might do. They took the Centre Court where $22 seats were scalped for as much as $1,000. A capacity crowd of 15,000 included European royalty, celebrities and standees who had lined up outside the grounds in sleeping bags for more than a week for standing room admittance.

Neil Amdur wrote in the *New York Times*, "Even before the first serve spectators shouted the names of the players with cries of 'hooray' and 'boo' as if they were in a soccer stadium and not in a setting laden with tradition. But then the two weeks, with record crowds, large fines against players and enraged fans throwing cushions in the Centre Court to protest a doubles match curtailed by darkness had brought Wimbledon further than ever from its traditional roots."

Watching from the press rows, I frequently had been disgusted by McEnroe's actions on the court, but I couldn't help but be impressed by his brilliance, his artistry with the racquet. I normally was not given to making predictions, but wrote these lines before his confrontation with Borg:

"I think John McEnroe is going to win Wimbledon this year. I believe this because I believe in the inevitability of the epic triumph. It will happen because it would be one of the great stories of sports. It has the elements of controversy that preceded the Cassius Clay upset over Sonny Liston, the Jets upset of Baltimore in the Super Bowl. One begins to develop a feel for this kind of upheaval, and this one fairly cries out for a tumultuous climax."

McEnroe had won the doubles championship the day before with Peter Fleming. Before this match he went over notes he had written about his serve that he had stored in his racquet cover: "Keep the head up, throw the toss more to the left, try to stay ahead." He had watched Borg come back from two sets to beat Connors in the semi-final two days earlier and reasoned he would not play like Connors. His strategy was to "hit the ball softer, dink, chip and come in."

Coming off his remarkable comeback over Connors, Borg entered the final with a record 41-match winning streak at Wimbledon. He hadn't lost at the All England Lawn Tennis and Croquet Club since being beaten by eventual champion Arthur Ashe in the quarter finals in 1975. The London bookies made him a strong, but not an overwhelming favorite.

No doubt aware of the 1-6 first set he lost to McEnroe the previous year and the poor start against Connors in the semi-final, Borg struck early. At 2-all in the fifth game, he broke McEnroe at deuce and then ran out the set, rallying from 15-40 and four set points in one game. McEnroe would say later that he got off to a sluggish start.

In the second set, each held serve during some terrific action, both keeping the ball in play against what seemed like certain winners. In the tenth game of the set, Borg, serving at 4-5, struggled up to a 40-30 game point. All the wizardry that McEnroe could put on a racquet came into play here. He hit three topspin forehands, each so deep they drew gasps. Borg drove them all back. McEnroe then hit two slices just over the net to draw Borg in and make him bend. On the second one Borg somehow passed McEnroe for a winner that was so stunning, McEnroe spun his racket in the air in disbelief. The crowd roared for both men. "Better than last year's match up to this point," McEnroe said later. They went to a tiebreaker. McEnroe dominated it, getting in all four of his first serves. He won an early mini-break for a 2-0 lead, broke Borg again at 4-1 and ran out the points to win the tiebreaker, 7-1.

Borg took a 4-1 lead in the third set. The key game was the tenth with McEnroe down 4-5 and serving at 15-30. Attacking behind his serve, McEnroe punched a forehand volley that the linesman signaled good. Here, Bob Jenkins the umpire who had officiated at two previous McEnroe matches, overruled the linesman. "The ball was out," Jenkins announced.

Thinking the shot was good, McEnroe paused in the backcourt. Spectators waited, fearing or expecting a tantrum from the volatile American. McEnroe balanced the ball on his racquet, seemingly uncertain about what he wanted to do. Instead of 30-all, McEnroe was down 15-40, double set point. If ever there was a time for a Mt. McEnroe eruption, this was it. He looked up at a fan who yelled, "Play on, John." Finally, he served, attacked and won the serve with an overhead. A service winner to the forehand brought it to deuce. Before McEnroe would win the game to tie, 5-all, there were six deuces and McEnroe would survive three set points. He finally broke through to gain a tiebreaker after the sixth deuce.

His restraint about that call symbolized his behavior in the match; it showed he could control his temper. Afterward Borg said the overruled call was correct. The ball "was clearly out," he said. And "maybe it was good for him that he controlled himself." Borg, of course, was always the cool Swede. Once, when he got the benefit of a call against Vitas Gerulaitis, he made what was for him a vigorous attempt to correct the call. He arched an eyebrow at the umpire and said, "Was good?" The umpire nodded a "was good" to him.

Borg led the third-set tiebreaker, 3-2. McEnroe won his two serves, then swept Borg's two serves, the first with a looping forehand cross-court pass and then a backhand pass down the line. He went on to win the tiebreaker, 7-4. Borg said afterward, "You can't play scared on your serve in a tiebreaker." McEnroe missed only one of ten first serves in the two tiebreakers. His can-opener serve, a big hook from the advantage court to Borg's backhand, was deadly time and time again. It would push Borg wide and when he returned, he left the court open for McEnroe to whack his return for a winner.

After the first tiebreaker, it seemed as if McEnroe had begun to gain the tiniest of edges. The wide serves were coming at the right times, and he repeatedly read Borg's attempted passing shots, stabbing his racket out to intercept them and volley backhand crosscourt winners. When he had to win crucial points, he invariably got his first serve in and dominated the play. He won 82 of 104 points played on his first serve, a remarkable 79 percent. Borg was under 50 percent for his first serves until the middle of the third set. At one point, as they probed each other for weaknesses, looking for a short ball to jump on, a statistician in the press box passed along this note: Borg was ahead, 194-191—which would have made for a sizzling table tennis match.

As the fourth set started McEnroe led 4-6, 7-6, 7-6. He remembered only too well that he had lost his edge in the second set the year before and that Borg's superior condition had worn him down in the fifth set. He was determined not to let the match go to a fifth set. After each man averted crises and held first serves in the fifth, McEnroe saved two points from 15-40 to hold serve for the third time in the set. Then Borg came back from 15-40 to tie the match at 4-all. Once more McEnroe held serve for a 5-4 lead, Borg serving.

Volleying was never Borg's strength. With a 30-15 lead he came in behind his serve only to stroke a backhand volley long. The score: 30-30. And then it was match point, 40-30, for McEnroe when he attacked a second serve and Borg missed a two-handed backhand. But Borg, always a fighter, rallied, winning the point with a serve and volley. "If I held to 5-all," he said, "I felt I could break him."

At this crucial point he couldn't get his first serves in. McEnroe moved in on a second serve, pressured Borg's backhand and won the point with an overhead. Match point. Another second serve allowed McEnroe to take the offensive. He moved in and clinched the match with a touch volley up the line. The lights on the scoreboards behind the players lit up with these numbers for McEnroe: 4-6, 7-6, 7-6, 6-4. He won the tiebreakers by 7-1 and 7-4 scores. He sank to his knees in victory à la Borg, saying later, "I was thinking that I will go to my knees like Bjorn, but I better get up."

My lead in *Newsday* read: "Wimbledon—All the fuss and furor of the past two weeks here culminated for John McEnroe yesterday in an upset victory that put him in the ranks of brash-young-upstarts-turned-conquerors, like Cassius Clay and Joe Namath. He put all the winds of controversy out of his mind and brought down Bjorn Borg, the King of Wimbledon no more."

When it was over, McEnroe raised both arms in victory, punched the air with his fist, and paraded around the court with the shiny Wimbledon trophy. "There was applause," *New York Times* columnist Dave Anderson wrote, "for his championship, applause for his behavior and applause for his talent as a tennis player."

McEnroe gestured with the trophy to standees on both sides, none of whom applauded louder than the two rogues who had waited on line for the men's finals for a week, one dressed in a jester's outfit, the other as a clown. Above them waved an American flag for the Yankee Doodle Dandy who had shocked the world of sport at Wimbledon 1981. When McEnroe moved on to the BBC-TV interview room, he shyly waved an American flag. "Now that I've gone through these two weeks and I'm over it, I think it will make me a better person" He said.

"We're sorry we made it so difficult for you," said a BBC radio man.

McEnroe flashed two fingers at him and said, "Peace be with you."

As Humphrey Bogart said about Paris to Ingrid Bergman in the movie, *Casablanca*, McEnroe would "always have" the fourth set tiebreaker of Wimbledon, 1980, and the championship in 1981.

POSTSCRIPT ONE:

Shortly after the match, a Wimbledon official asked McEnroe if he planned to attend that night's victory dinner. McEnroe said he was exhausted, but would be willing to stop by for coffee and dessert and "say a few words." The invitation was withdrawn and shortly afterward it was announced that for the first time in a hundred years, Wimbledon decided not to give the men's champion an automatic membership in the All England Lawn Tennis and Racquet Club (He was awarded the membership when he won two years later).

POSTSCRIPT TWO:

My wife and I took off for Ireland shortly afterward. While dining at Doyle's restaurant on the Dingle Peninsula, I was talking about the McEnroe phenomenon when a woman at the next table, grasping that we were Americans, complimented us for McEnroe's victory. She loved McEnroe because she felt he had stuck it to the British establishment. I told her that I admired McEnroe's tennis artistry but didn't share her appreciation for his behavior because I regarded his displays as childish temper tantrums, rather than measured assaults on British snobbery. It turned out that Gemma Murphy was a member of the Irish legislature and we had a stimulating three-hour discussion about McEnroe, tennis, Irish political and literary history. We closed the joint.

#8

Secretariat's Belmont

The first time I ever went to a racetrack was on June 3, 1944, the day of the 76th Belmont Stakes. This was at a time when minors were not allowed into New York racetracks. I was 15 years old, taken there by my cousin Moey, a degenerate horseplayer and a rollicking, full-of-jokes guy. He put a large fedora on me to make me look older, to get me past the ticket taker. The turnstile guy wasn't fooled. He said light-heartedly, "I see him under that hat"—and let me pass through the turnstile anyway.

I saw Bounding Home win that Belmont, ridden by G. L. Smith. He beat the favorite, Pensive, and paid the tidy sum of $34.70. I became an instant fan of horseracing, of Belmont Park, and of the Belmont Stakes. Over the years, I covered many Triple Crown races. And I bet on them. Horse racing is, afer all, a betting sport, and it is a rare scribe who doesn't get involved. At least some of the richness of the sport revolves around betting. I cashed win bets on Northern Dancer, Lucky Debonair and Kauai King in the Kentucky Derby, on Northern Dancer in the Preakness. But up until 1973, I had never won a bet on my favorite race, the Belmont Stakes.

So, when the 1973 Belmont loomed and an infatuation with Secretariat and his bid to win the Triple Crown had taken over the racing world, I decided I would confront my jinx. I would bet two dollars on the nose of Secretariat. If he won the race and completed a long-awaited Triple Crown victory, I would finally cash a winning bet on the Belmont. If he lost, I would think even he couldn't overcome my Belmont Stakes jinx.

By 1973 I had left the column-writing ranks to oversee what turned out to be a Marx Brothers regime as sports editor of *Newsday*. On the first day of my stewardship, the only member of the sports department who had a key to the office did not show up. So we had to wait an hour for security before we could begin work on the section. I came to see this as symbolic of my trials in running a sports department. We made mistakes. Before two years were out, I asked for and was relieved of the sports editor's chair.

We did some good things, though. For one, we utilized the reporting and writing of Bill Nack. The editor of the paper, a racing fan, knew of Nack's love for horse racing and moved him to the sports department just as I became sports editor. When I heard that Nack kept a photo of Swaps, the winner of the 1955 Kentucky Derby, in his wallet, I knew we had our racing reporter.

Newsday in 1973 was a burgeoning giant in the newspaper business. It was the suburban colossus, well-written, with a large circulation and much respect in the trade. But it was on Long Island, not New York City, and it was common to hear from non LIers, "I haven't read *Newsday*, but I hear it is an excellent newspaper."

Long Island for most people meant the two counties outside of New York City—Nassau and Suffolk. When I became sports editor of *Newsday* in 1972, there was only one sports event of national significance that took place on Long Island: the Belmont Stakes. The Islanders hockey team had only just joined the National Hockey League so this was before their run of Stanley Cups when they became a centerpiece of *Newsday* sports coverage. And the Mets played in Queens—like Brooklyn a part of Long Island, but not considered so by chauvinistic suburbanites.

I was determined to make the Belmont a showcase for *Newsday's* sports coverage. We had a terrific department and now, I felt, was the time to show our stuff. We would treat the Belmont the way the *Louisville Courier* treated the Kentucky Derby. Well, almost. In any case, I launched our coverage the Sunday before the 1972 Belmont. In addition to stories on the horses, we had pieces on the history of the Belmont Stakes, nostalgic remembrances about the Belmont Stakes, stories about the businesses bordering the track, even a guide to eating at Belmont Park.

At the heart of the coverage were columnist Ed Comerford, a fine writer, and Nack, reporting from Belmont almost as if he were sleeping at the Belmont barns. And in due time he *would* be sleeping at the barns, when he covered Secretariat's Belmont Stakes. The year, 1972 was Riva Ridge's year. He had won the Kentucky Derby and then lost the Preakness. He came into the Belmont the favorite over No Le Hace and Key to the Mint, horses he had beaten in the Derby but had finished behind in the Preakness, won by Bee Bee Bee, a non-entrant in the Belmont.

Nack was 31. He had been a beat reporter on town, county and state government. He went on to cover environment stories with an emphasis for a time on the impact of sewers on groundwater supplies. He liked to say, "Even today I know more about the tertiary treatment of sewage than any sports writer who ever lived." Nack seized on my suggestion that during the week of the 1972 race he walk the mile-and-a-half of the Belmont—the longest track in America—with a jockey. Nack corralled Braulio Baeza, who had ridden three Belmont winners. They walked the mile-and-a-half Belmont track, Baeza recalling his ride aboard Arts and Letters with whom he won the 1969 Belmont. It was a terrific piece. The sense of it is in these excerpts:

Baeza, the white rail running beside him, walked toward the first turn, pointing toward the dirt about eight feet off the fence. "He was lying third around here," he said, recalling the position of Arts and Letters in the first dash for the turn. "There was no speed in the race and everyone was taking their horses back." He laughed.

Baeza headed toward the far turn, past the three-quarter pole, then the five-eighths pole where he made a critical decision that day in 1969. "At this point I started moving," said Baeza. "I said, 'Oh, this [slow pace] can't go on.' They couldn't keep going the way they were. At this point I felt that way."

During that week Nack formed a relationship with Riva Ridge's connections: owner Penny Tweedy, trainer Lucien Laurin and jockey Ron Turcotte. He formed a bond with them because he was a fine writer, an outstanding, hard working reporter, loved racing, and was good with people. He commanded the respect of the Meadow Stable people and it paid off for him the following year when he became, in effect, the chronicler of the Secretariat saga, first in the pages of *Newsday* and later in a gem of a book about Secretariat, entitled, *Big Red of Meadow Stable*.

Secretariat was born just after midnight at the Meadow Stud farm in Virginia, March 30, 1970. He was sired by Bold Ruler (the preeminent sire in America) out of Somethingroyal (the dam) whose sire was Princequillo. The foal was a huge chestnut with three white feet—the right front and two behind with a blaze of white down his face. Looking at him, Howard Gentry, the farm manager, said, "There is a whopper."

The foal was named by Elizabeth Ham, the longtime secretary to Christopher Chenery, Penny Tweedy's father. The Meadow sent to the Jockey Club six names, two sets of three names each. The first set was quickly rejected: Scepter, Royal Line and Something Special. (Names are rejected if they duplicate the names of horses that had run in the past 20 years; the names of great horses of the past can never be used again.) From the second set of names Penny Tweedy's suggestions of Games of Chance and Deo Volente (Latin for "God Willing") also were rejected. Elizabeth Ham had been the personal secretary to a man who had been the chief delegate to a disarmament conference in Geneva, Switzerland, the home of the League of Nations' secretariat. From that she came up with Secretariat, a name that seemed more fitting as Secretariat progressed and became a national icon.

Secretariat made his first start, July 4, 1972, a five-and-a-half furlong sprint for maidens at Aqueduct racetrack in Queens. He had made such a strong impression in training, he went off the favorite—as he would in every race he ran—at $3.10 to one. After a slow, rough start, he came with a rush at the end and finished fourth, beaten only a length and a quarter by a horse named Herbull. Eleven days later, again ridden by apprentice Paul Feliciano, he broke his maiden, winning a six-furlong maiden race at Aqueduct by six lengths. He paid $4.60

Ron Turcotte, the Meadow Stable's main rider who had ridden Riva Ridge to glory the previous year, couldn't ride Secretariat in his debut July 4 because he was committed to ride a stakes race at Monmouth Park. Turcotte then missed Secretariat's second start because he was laid up after a serious accident at Aqueduct; he was out of action for 20 days. Though not 100 percent, Turcotte was anxious to get on the horse that was stirring the juices of the Meadow people who still were basking in the glow of the near Triple Crown success of Riva Ridge. Trainer Lucien Laurin put him on Secretariat for a six furlong $9,000 Allowance sprint on opening day at Saratoga, July 31. The colt brushed the side of the gate at the break, trailed the field in the early going and then started to pick up horses at the far turn and pulled ahead to win by a length-and-a-half.

Turcotte was born July 22, 1941 in the Canadian province of New Brunswick. He was one of fourteen children, the son of a lumberjack. It was a hardscrabble life. He left school in the eighth grade to help support the family. He worked on farms and found work as a lumberjack, too. His first meaningful experience with horses was hauling logs behind a team of horses. Somebody noted his small stature and suggested he try riding horses at Woodbine Race Course in Toronto. He found a job at the track working for E. P. Taylor's Windfield Farm stable at the lowest level of backstretch toil: as a hot walker cooling out horses. He eventually went to Taylor's farm and learned to break yearlings under tack. Within two years of showing up at the track, he made his debut as a jockey in 1961. He was extremely powerful and used his strength to push racehorses down the lane. He was not afraid to take the dangerous inside route on the rail. He rode his first winner in 1962. In 1965 he won the Preakness on Tom Rolfe.

Secretariat won the Sanford and Hopeful Stakes at Saratoga and the Belmont Futurity over Stop the Music. He beat Stop the Music again in the Champagne Stakes, but was disqualified for bumping into him on the turn. He was a 1 to 10 favorite in his last two races as a two-year-old. He won the Laurel Futurity and the $298,000 Garden State Stakes. He finished his two-year-old season with seven victories in nine races and earned $456,404. He joined Native Dancer and Moccasin as the only two-year-olds to be voted Horse of the Year.

Secretariat won almost all of his races by coming off the pace. He impressed people with his confirmation, his racing style. I didn't pretend to know anything about a horse's confirmation—I find most thoroughbreds to be handsome beasts—but I sensed something special about him. He was big with a neck like a buffalo, a back as broad as a sofa. Horses are measured from the ground to the withers, the highest part of the back, in a unit called hands, and Secretariat stood five feet, 6 inches, a massive 78 inches around the body. He weighed 1150 pounds, at least 200 pounds heavier than the average thoroughbred. People around the stable called him, "Red." Others preferred "Big Red." His stride measured 25 feet, almost as much as the legendary Man o' War, and he seemed to be attacking the dirt as he gobbled up ground. Some turf reporters, always on the lookout to spot a potential Triple Crown champion, began heralding him in stories. People talked about Secretariat having "a presence about him, a sense of greatness." An artist who wanted to sketch him talked about his "look of eagles."

These were the best of times for Laurin, however nervous he was when his prize horses took the track. He had come a long way from Joliette, Quebec in Canada where he was born March 18, 1912. At 60 he had Riva Ridge, the 1972 Kentucky Derby and Belmont Stakes winner and he had the winter book favorite for the 1973 Kentucky Derby, Secretariat, in his barn as well.

Laurin's racing career began in 1929 as a jockey at Delormier Park, a half-mile track in Montreal where he had first exercised horses. He had only moderate success as a jockey and he was ruled off the track in 1938 when a battery—which can be used to shock a horse into running faster—was found on him at Narragansett Park. He worked on horse farms for awhile and, when the ban was lifted, went back to riding before becoming a trainer. He trained cheap horses on minor league tracks, building a reputation as a hard worker and a shrewd judge of thoroughbreds. It led to a job with Reginald Webster and first success with Quill, the champion two-year-old filly in 1958. He won the 1966 Belmont Stakes with Amberoid and was near retirement when the call came from Penny Tweedy's Meadow Stable.

Roger Laurin, Lucien's son, worked as a trainer at Meadow Stable. When Roger accepted an offer to work for the powerful Ogden Phipps stable, he suggested to the Chenery family that his father might help on a temporary basis. The stable was having financial difficulties, but that changed with the emergence of Riva Ridge as champion two-year-old in 1971.

Secretariat turned three in Florida in 1973. Before he ever ran as a three-year-old, syndication had been worked out for him as a stallion. They brought him up north on March 14 and he settled into Stall 7 in Barn 5 at Belmont Park. Barn 5 lay a few hundred yards from the noisy car and truck traffic on Hempstead Turnpike adjoining the barn area. It was one of the barns closest to the main

Belmont track, the largest track in America at a mile-and-a-half, the distance of the Belmont Stakes.

He started his three-year-old campaign at Aqueduct, winning the Bay Shore at Aqueduct. He won the Gotham. But he did not win the Wood Memorial. He was beaten by his stablemate, Angle Light—and Sham, the horse that figured to be the main opposition in the race. Angle Light set a leisurely pace, didn't fold, and beat Sham by a head. Secretariat finished a disappointing four lengths behind.

When the Wood was over, a remarkable scene ensued in the Meadow Stable box. Laurin looked around and asked Tweedy, "Who won it?"

"You won it," she said with a hint of anger.

"Angle Light?" he said with incredulity. He had just won the Wood Memorial, but with the wrong horse. He did not have the look of a happy camper. Another person with mixed feelings was Edwin Whittaker, the owner of Angle Light. He liked his horse, but he didn't think he would ever be a threat to the wondrous Secretariat. Now he had beaten Secretariat and was accompanying a confused Laurin to the winner's circle. Penny Tweedy told him, "Congratulations." He said, "I'm sorry."

There was consternation all around among the Secretariat people: by Mrs. Tweedy, Laurin, Turcotte. In the morning, veterinarian Manuel Gilman had noticed an abscess about the size of a quarter inside Secretariat's upper lip—the lip with his tattoo number, Z20660. He told Laurin he didn't think it would bother him. Groom Eddie Sweat put hot towels on the wound and they hoped for the best. Sweat had noticed, though, that Secretariat shied when he tried to put the bit in his mouth before the race. And afterward Turcotte said, "He just didn't fire."

There were recriminations as well. Penny Tweedy was furious. She lambasted Lucien Laurin. She threw senseless accusations at him about Angle Light being a better horse than he had told her. She said the other jockeys in the field didn't fear Angle Light so they let him get on the lead with a slow pace that enabled him to have energy to finish well. She was so angry she even had a confrontation with Angle Light's owner, Whittaker. She accused him of coming between her and Laurin. She later apologized. She had harsh words for Ron Turcotte as well. She reminded him that he had misjudged the distance in a workout earlier in the week. She believed Turcotte had misjudged the pace in the Wood and let Angle Light steal away with it. She actually thought about taking Turcotte off Secretariat and finding another jockey. This would have been a panic move, and she eventually thought better of it.

Helen Bates (Penny) Tweedy was born in 1922, the youngest of Christopher Chenery's three children. She was graduated from Smith College as a history major in 1943, and made her debut in New York society in Westchester County. She attended Columbia's school of business, and married John Tweedy in 1949. They raised four children and when her father's health failed, she became the major force in the operation of the Meadow racing enterprise. She was a tough manager. Somebody wrote, "Behind the friendliness and the warmth, behind all the charm, gentility and good Episcopalianism—was a mind with a thermostat idling at sixty degrees."

For Turcotte this criticism was an old story. For years he had been faulted in the press. He did not react well to criticism. He held grudges against certain reporters, actually hitting one whom he thought had been particularly unfair to him. He had come under sharp attack particularly for his ride on Tom Rolfe, who finished third in the 1965 Kentucky Derby. Though he had done splendidly in guiding Riva Ridge to victories in the Derby and Belmont Stakes, there often were reminders of past failures when he lost.

Turcotte had no explanation for Secretariat's lackluster Wood. He couldn't understand it and could say only, "He just didn't fire, he just didn't fire." Lucien wondered, too, whether Secretariat could go the distance. His sire, the great Bold Ruler, was one of the great sires of all time, but he had not been able to handle the Derby distance and there was that lingering doubt about Secretariat after his failure in the mile-and-an-eighth Wood.

The day after Secretariat arrived at Churchill Downs for the Derby, another veterinarian looked at him. He spotted the abscess on the horse's upper lip, and noticed that it had grown larger. He told groom Eddie Sweat to bathe it with hot towels. For two days Sweat put scaled hot towels on the horse. Gradually, the abscess drained and there was no need to lance it.

Sweat was a short, stocky 34-year-old black man with a sense of racetrack wisdom about him. He was born in a small farmhouse in the town of Holly Hill not far from the coast of South Carolina, the sixth of nine children. They were a poor family of tenant farmers. Sweat helped support the family, working after grade school, picking cotton, digging sweet potatoes and harvesting corn. At the age of eight he was doing a man's work.

One day Sweat stopped by the thoroughbred horse farm down the road owned by Laurin. He was hired at 15 dollars a week to dig fence holes. By 1955 he was walking hots and grooming horses; he was too heavy to become a jockey. He was smart, serious, responsible about his work. He mucked out stalls, changed horses' bandages, rubbed their legs. Within three years of Laurin first taking him to the racetrack, he developed into Laurin's ablest and most trusted groom.

After the abscess was drained, Secretariat perked up. One morning Laurin, who had been in a funk about his big horse, approached Sweat and asked, "How is he?"

"He's all right," Sweat said, "All he wants to do is eat."

Laurin heaved a sigh. "Good, let him eat." Things were looking up.

Just before Turcotte left for Kentucky, he learned from a New York racing official about the abscess. This was startling and encouraging news for Tucotte; because it explained for him the listlessness of Secretariat in the Wood. Laurin and Tweedy would also come to believe that the abscess, not any poor decisions by the trainer and jockey, had led to the defeat in the Wood.

None of this was known to a public beginning to wonder about Secretariat. On the backstretch at Louisville rumors about Secretariat were rampant. There was talk that the colt was walking wide in front, a sign of bad knees. They said he had bone chips on his knees, bad ankles and bucked shins. The rumors of unsoundness exasperated Laurin. Wherever he went people asked him if it were true Secretariat was standing in ice for a bad knee. It got so ridiculous that the Associated Press actually ran a story by the great pretender of knowledge, Jimmy (The Greek) Snyder, saying the colt had no right to be the 1-5 choice in the Wood; he insisted the barn was putting icepacks on Secretariat's knees. (I had seen one aspect of The Greek at Belmont Park one Saturday. After a race, he pulled out a mutuel ticket on the winning horse. A friend of his told me with a laugh that Jimmy made sure to have a winning ticket to show by buying tickets on all the horses in a race.)

Meanwhile, Sham was training well, and trainer Pancho Martin was feeding the rivalry with big talk about his horse. He noted that the only time Secretariat ran a bad race was the one time he met Sham. He said, "In my estimation I've got the best horse. My horse is in top condition, he loves the track. And I got [the great jockey, Lafitt] Pincay."

Thirteen horses entered the 99th Kentucky Derby, May 5, the first Saturday in May. Secretariat, coupled with Angle Light, went off at 7½ to 5, the only time in his career he would not be the odds-on favorite. Sham was the second choice at 2½ to one. Also in the field was Forego, a relative unknown at the time.

These were the lines on the two favorites in a smashing winning Kentucky Derby performance by Secretariat and Turcotte.

	PP	¼	½	¾	Mile	Stretch	Finish
Secretariat	10	11	6	5	2	1	1
Sham	4	5	3	2	1	2	2

Sham, close up in the early going, momentarily led in the stretch until Secretariat took charge at the three-sixteenths pole. He swept past the leader, Shecky Greene (his jockey, Larry Adams, said Secretariat "looked like the Red Ball Express") collared Sham and won going away by two-and-a-half lengths.

The time of 1:59 2/5 set a Kentucky Derby record. Remarkably, Secretariat ran each quarter-of-a-mile faster than the previous quarter. "All I did was fasten the seat belt," Turcotte said after the race. Our Native finished third. Far back, in fourth place, was

Forego, something that would become pertinent for me the day after the Belmont Stakes.

Two Saturdays later, May 19, a field of only six horses was entered in the Preakness. Pancho Martin, Sham's trainer, still needed convincing. He said he would be disappointed, "very, very, very disappointed" if he didn't win. Emboldened by what he called "a terrific" workout at Pimlico, he said, "I think Sham is going to win easy. I don't think the Derby was a true race."

Secretariat went off at 30-cents on the dollar, Sham 3-1. The four others in the race went off at odds of 11 to 1. Ecole Etage and Torsion led in the early going, but were passed by Secretriat and Sham after a half-mile.

Secretariat awed even the most veteran racegoers by the move he made swooshing from the rear to take the lead and win. There was controversy, however. The infield flashed a time of 1:55 for the mile and three-sixteenth race. Though two *Daily Racing Form* clockers had a time of 1:53 2/5 and that was corroborated by a CBS replay of the race, the track accepted the clocking of 1:54 2/5 by its official timer. It wasn't until 1999 that the Maryland Racing Commission finally awarded Secretariat his rightful time of 1:53 2/5. This enabled him to surpass 1971 winner Canonero II as the holder of the Preakness record and gave him the best-ever times for the first two Triple Crown races.

The Triple Crown races had a magical aura about them. By 1973, only eight three-year-olds had won the Kentucky Derby, Preakness and Belmont. The first of them was Sir Barton in 1919, at a time when there was no Triple Crown concept. It was later that Charles Hatton, a columnist for the *Morning Telegraph* and *Daily Racing Form*, originated the concept of the Triple Crown when Gallant Fox won the three races in 1930. The idea solidified with subsequent Triple Crown successes: Omaha in 1935; War Admiral in 1937; Whirlaway in 1941; Count Fleet in 1943; Assault in 1946 and Citation in 1948.

By 1973, 24 years had passed without a Triple Crown winner. Since Citation's victory, seven horses had won the Derby and Preakness, then failed in the Belmont. They were: Tim Tam in 1958; Carry Back in 1961; Northern Dancer in 1964; Kauai King in 1966; Forward Pass in 1968; Majestic Prince in 1969; and Canonero II in 1971 (Later, after Affirmed completed the triple in 1978, no Triple Crown winner would come up for 27 years through 2007).

The day after the Preakness, Eddie Sweat drove the van that took Secretariat back to Belmont Park. They arrived at 3:00 p.m., and when they unloaded the big red horse at Barn 5, a small crowd watched him join Riva Ridge and Angle Light among others in Lucien Lauren's barn. There were stable workers, racing officials, photographers, newspeople from the wire services, the *New York Daily News* and Bill Nack. A horse who had left New York for Kentucky with many doubts about him had returned a national celebrity. He and his people were the subjects of newspaper stories throughout the country. The two wire services had men covering him daily. He was on the cover of *Time, Newsweek* and *Sports Illustrated.* Television and film crews came by regularly.

I had made it a point one morning to go out to the barns area with Nack. To be in that enclave off Hempstead Turnpike in Elmont was to be in a bucolic world far from the bustle of the city. Trainers and exercise riders and grooms went about their business of getting horses ready to race. Sleek thoroughbreds came off the training track glistening with sweat. As grooms doused them with water, then brushed them dry, the early morning sun reflected pools of light off them. These scenes have long appealed to painters. Horse racing is glamour and glory, the involvement of betting and the roar of the crowd—and it is also the farm life activity on the backstretch in the morning.

Some people saw the glory of Secretariat and his pursuit of the Triple Crown as a relief during a troubled time. The cataclysmic Vietnam War wracked the country. As details of the Watergate scandal filtered out to the public, they marked the beginning of the end of President Richard Nixon's presidency. On the morning of the Belmont the front page of the *New York Times* included two stories related to Watergate, with John Ehrlichman and Robert Haldeman in one headline.

Secretariat settled down to his regular routine. He thrived on work. He loved to eat; he was what racetrack people called "a good doer." He ate 16 quarts of grain a day, seven more than the average horse. He devoured his hay and oats and sweet feed and mash even after strenuous workouts. One morning after one of those workouts and while Secretariat was being walked around Barn 8, Sweat prepared Stall 7, laying down a fresh, foot-deep mattress of golden straw, hanging a bucket of water on the wall. Another four-legged animal was in that barn. He was Billy Silver, the stable pony, who would join Secretariat grazing on the grass between the barn and Laurin's offices. Billy Silver adored Secretariat. "I never saw a pony so crazy about a horse," Laurin said. "Yeah," said Sweat, "But Red don't care nothing about the pony."

Surely Secretariat had a mind of his own. When he was taken out for a workout, exercise rider Jimmy Gaffney came to know what to expect. Secretariat would stop at the gap leading to the track, and stand there for several seconds, looking to the left and right, raising his head, looking off into the distance. Gaffney would not hurry him but let him stand and watch the morning activity of horses galloping, cruising, exercise riders chirping at them as they ate up ground on the rail. Gaffney said Secretariat liked to stop and see what he was getting into before he got into it.

Secretariat had just set records for two of the biggest races in America, but the mile-and-a-half Belmont loomed as the most grueling challenge of all. Laurin worked him hard, getting to what horse people called "the bottom of the colt." Secretariat galloped two miles every morning, stretching his almost 25-foot stride, flashing by photographers anxious to capture the beauty in motion of the reddish gold, almost copper coat.

Now it was the morning of the Belmont Stakes, three weeks after the Preakness. Work continued apace. Secretariat was fed as usual at 10:30. But his meal was cut to one quart of dry oats from the regular three. Sweat, clad in a red undershirt, knocked on the door of Laurin's office a few yards from the barn and asked, "Which of those nose bands do you want him to wear—the blue or the white?" Laurin said, "The white." It was Secretariat's day, but the other horses had to be worked. Laurin sent out horses in sets. They came back, the day wore on and it was quiet again at Barn 7.

Past 11:00 a.m., fans filed into the huge complex on the county line between Queens, New York City and suburban Nassau County. The course was named Belmont Park after August Belmont, whose name, when he was born in Germany, was August Schonberg, which translates to "beautiful mountain." When he flourished in the United States in the late 1800s and became a force in politics and horse racing, he changed his name to Belmont, which, in French, also means "beautiful mountain." I wonder sometimes how it would sound if we were instead going to the Schonberg Stakes at Schonberg Park.

People filled up the clubhouse and the grandstand. Unlike Churchill Downs and Pimlico, Belmont does not allow spectators in the infield for its races. The closest thing to the colorful infield crowds in Kentucky and Baltimore was the picnic gatherings on the lawns adjoining the paddock behind the stands. A festive feeling was in the air. More than a few people talked about the feeling of being in on a coronation; not even an uncomfortably muggy day seemed to dampen enthusiasm. The races began at 1:30 p.m. and the crowd grew to 69,138, at that time the second largest ever to watch a Belmont Stakes.

Eagerly awaiting the race on television, like millions of others, was Vic Ziegel, the *New York Post* scribe. He had covered Secretariat's victories in the Derby and Preakness. Then, a week before the Belmont Stakes, the sports editor told him he was needed to cover the Yankees in Kansas City. *The Post* had no Sunday paper then, so Ziegel, a dedicated racing fan, took a bus to the Ak Sar Ben (Nebraska spelled backward) track in Omaha just to watch Secretariat again.

Owner Penny Tweedy arrived at her box seat with her husband Jack, sister Margaret and brother Hollis. She was wearing a blue and white dress, the Meadow colors, over whose sleeveless top hung a golden pendant. Standing in the mezzanine, she looked down on the crowd below, accepting good wishes. The CBS television cameras panned to her waving to the crowd. This may be as close as any American woman might get to feeling like a queen.

The tension built as the races went off. Spanish Riddle won the fifth race, Whole Truth the sixth. Angle Light, not anywhere the horse he was when he won the Wood, finished next to last in the seventh race, an allowance race at a mile and a sixteenth for three-year-olds. It was won by Forego, the even money favorite, in fast time. Little did I know at the time that this horse would come back to haunt me in the near future.

I was watching the race in the box seat area with a few friends. There was a little part of me that wanted to be working the event as a reporter, but I was *Newsday's* sports editor now, and I was comfortable with the assignments we had for blanket coverage of the day. Columnist Eddie Comerford would write the main story of the race; Sandy Padwe would record Sham's day for better or worse; George Usher would clean up with odd items and interviews of pertinent figures. I had also asked *Newsday's* talented feature columnist Mike McGrady, a horseplayer, to provide his take on the race.

And we had the indefatigable Bill Nack to zero in on Secretariat. He was alternately euphoric and nervous about Secretariat. He had decided to sleep at the *Newsday* office in Garden City, some five miles from the track. At 2:00 a.m. he woke and drove to Belmont Park to begin his long day's journey into early evening. He fell asleep against a tree, woke to the crowing of a rooster, and recorded the movements at the barn that began stirring at 5:00 a.m.

Horses in the early races were shiny sleek as they walked down the macadam paths into the tunnel leading to the paddock. They came back dripping with sweat, dirt encrusted. Their grooms were asked by stable help how they did, an occurrence that happens after every race at every track, big and small, across the racing landscape.

At 5:10, half an hour before post time, a small crowd gathered to monitor Secretariat's walk to the paddock. Dave Anderson wrote in the *New York Times*, "It was like the way people waited for a heavyweight champion to come out of his dressing room before a fight." Just as Secretariat came out of the shed, Sham and trainer Pancho Martin were moving toward the tunnel. Then, with stable pony Billy Silver leading, Eddie Sweat led him down the tunnel toward the paddock, which was 200 yards away. A racing official kept the crowd at a distance from the horse.

Soon Secretariat was moving under the tall oak trees of the Belmont paddock. He circled the walking ring, past the ancient white pine that is the symbol of Belmont Park. Owners and trainers, press and officials were packed together standing on toes to get a glimpse of Secretariat. The women were dressed in summer finery, chiffons and silks, as if it were a garden party. Sweat took the handsome chestnut to Stall No. 1 for saddling. Laurin was waiting for him. He was wearing a red plaid sports coat, white shirt and pants, white shoes and a purple and white tie. He put the blue-and-white hooded blinders on and adjusted the bridle. His nerves were on edge; he didn't appreciate CBS-TV analyst Frank Wright asking if the heat might bother the horse.

The jockeys came out. Turcotte trotted up the stairs from the jockeys' room leading to the paddock, holding a whip in one hand while adjusting the leather No. 1 strapped to his left arm. He was chewing gum. He wore the Meadow Stable silks of blue and white blocks. At the same time the other jockeys ambled toward their trainers in the grass area. Laurin met Turcotte in the ring. They had already discussed the race, and Laurin reviewed their strategy. "Don't take him back too much, Ronnie," he said. "See how they're going.

Many Belmonts have been won on the lead. If he wants to run early, let him. But don't send him. Don't choke him . . ." He lapsed into French: "*Utilise ton propre jugement*" (use your own judgment).

"Riders up," the paddock judge shouted.

Bugler Sam Koza in his colorful red coat played, "Call to the Post" on his Aida trumpet, the signal for the riders to mount. The crowd in the walking ring was so tight that Laurin was unable to get through to help Turcotte. The assistant trainer, Benny Hoeffner had to step in. Turcotte held his stick in one hand and moved to Secretariat's left side, raising his left boot behind him at the knee. Hoeffner reached down, grabbed the boot and raised Turcotte up onto the saddle. As Secretariat and the others circled the walking ring, the crowd looking on from outside an iron gate shouted cries of encouragement. One man yelled, "Triple Crown, baby, Triple Crown in New York." Others looked on respectfully. There were wisecracks from two-dollar bettors aimed at Turcotte and Laurin that they had better win. Accompanied by outriders in front and behind, the horses circled the ring, then turned right onto the path under the stands out onto the track. A few years later an imposing silver statue of Secretariat became a striking centerpiece of that paddock.

As the horses arrived on the track, Secretariat appeared cool and dry despite the heat: Sham was washy, wringing wet with white perspiration. The band played "Sidewalks of New York." This didn't have the schmaltzy appeal of "My Old Kentucky Home" which brings tears at Churchill Downs, but some people sang along.

In the post parade the horses walked past the stands in single file. At Pimlico, before the Preakness, Secretariat suddenly stopped in midstretch, raised his golden tail and defecated. The crowd loved it, cackling and applauding. He provided no such entertainment this time. Because of the heat, none of the other jockeys galloped his horse. Turcotte, after telling Charlie Davis on the pony, Billy Silver, that he thought Secretariat needed some warming up, galloped him around the turn and back into the stretch toward the gate.

The betting windows were busy. People at the rear of mutuel lines fretted that they might not get their bets in. They rushed back to the infield apron, to their seats in the grandstand, the Terrace dining room and the boxes to be there for the start. One of the best things about the Belmont as a mile-and-a-half race on a mile-and-a-half oval, is that the start is right in front of the stands. People got a close-up look at the loading of the horse into the starting gate, a jungle gym of bars and doors. Shouts of encouragement for Secretariat. But there were always rooters for the underdog in a New York crowd. "You can beat him, Sham," a man in an orange sleeveless shirt shouted from the rail only a few feet from the gate.

The horses loaded in order. This was the lineup:

Post	Horse	Jockey	Trainer	Odds to $1
1.	Secretariat	Turcotte	Lawrin	.10
2.	Pvt. Smiles	Gargan	George Poole	14.30
3.	My Gallant	Cordero	L. Goldfine	12.40
4.	Twice A Prince	Baeza	John Campo	17.30
5.	Sham	Pincay	Frank Martin	5.10

Secretariat was 1 to 10, the lowest odds permissible. Because the mutuel board cannot show double digits, he was listed on the board at 1 to 9.

Longtime New York racetrack starter George Cassidy stood on a green platform by the inside rail twenty feet in front of the gate, watching the horses move into the metal enclosure. These were poised horses, and there were no delays. An assistant starter took hold of Secretariat's rein on the left side, and led him into the first stall closest to the inside rail. As the door slammed shut behind him, Turcotte pulled a pair of plastic goggles over his eyes. The big red horse stood quietly as the others were loaded next to him.

It was 5:38 p.m.

The bell clanged, the doors in front of each stall sprang open and the five colts rushed from the gate. The crowd roared. The roar seemed to continue from start to finish, reaching a crescendo at the end. Secretariat broke well. He did not drop back as he usually did, and was close to the lead immediately. My Gallant was expected to take the early lead, but Angel Cordero, seeing Secretariat challenging him early, settled his horse behind Secretariat into the turn. Sham's jockey, Laffit Pincay, had been told to try for the lead at the start so he rushed from the outside to challenge Secretariat. He joined Secretariat in the turn. The others had already fallen back so it began to look like another race between just these two, a match race. Fleeting visions of Seabiscuit vs. War Admiral, Swaps vs. Nashua danced in the heads of racetrack cognoscenti.

Secretariat, with Turcotte in the blue and white silks, was on the inside; Sham, with Pincay in yellow and green, on the outside. Secretariat put a head in front after 220 yards, an eighth of a mile, out of the gate. Turcotte knew the pace was fast, but Secretariat was running so smoothly he was not concerned. As they raced side by side, lapped on each other, they almost seemed like only one animal to the crowd and to the viewers watching on television. They were putting together 12-second eighths of a mile. It was faster than Pincay wanted to go, but he didn't want to let Secretariat get away. Before they had run a quarter-of-a-mile, Sham inched ahead, by a head, then a neck, by almost a half-length. It was a match race for sure.

They were sizzling along at a killing pace down the backside of the track. Turcotte could feel the surge of power in his horse and let him roll. Secretariat came back at Sham, within a neck, then closed to a head-bobbing nose. By the time they had run a quarter of a mile, he had taken the lead. The timer on the board flashed 0: 23 3/5 for the quarter mile, sprinter's speed. My Gallant was third, six lengths back, Twice A Prince fourth and Pvt. Smiles fifth. The jockeys on these horses wondered if the two big horses in front of them might have nothing left at the finish.

Secretariat and Sham continued to race together from the quarter to the half-mile marks of the race. Turcotte was confident. "When I want him to go faster," he said later, "I would simply pick up his head and say 'okay, big boy.' Big Red was really a push button horse, just like driving a car." Now, Turcotte chirped at Secretariat. The colt was moving effortlessly, doing it all on his own. He was about to switch leads.

Horses stretch out with one front leg. They lead with their left foreleg going around a turn while turning left, and switch to the right leg for the straightaway. Secretariat had been on the left lead around the turn, and as he banked and straightened into the backstretch, Turcotte felt the hitch in his rhythmic stride; nine jumps into the backside straight. The colt then switched to the right lead and leveled out into long, smooth and powerful strides.

After they went a half mile in 0:46 1/5, Secretariat was in the lead by a head. The better-than-12 seconds per eighth-of-a-mile was getting to Sham. He was beginning to wilt. Pincay could feel it, Turcotte could see the wet, lathering neck of Sham. Some ten lengths behind them My Gallant and Twice A Prince were running head to head. Baeza, on Twice A Prince, saw Sham falling back, and began to think he could finish second. Right next to him was My Gallant. Baeza shouted to Cordero, "I'm going to be second, man." Cordero shouted back, "Screw you, man. You gotta beat me."

Secretariat raced the fifth furlong in 0:12, giving him five-eighths of a mile in a sensational 0:58 1/5. They were still running faster than Spanish Riddle had zipped five furlongs in a shorter earlier race, faster than Man o' War, Count Fleet and Citation had run the first five furlongs of the Belmont Stakes. He had taken charge of the race. They were no longer racing as one. The crowd saw this and the roar from the stands grew louder. It would accompany him around the turn and into the stretch as he lengthened his lead, while Sham fell further and further back. Sham finished last, as if this had been a boxing match and he had been knocked out.

The crowd was not concerned with times. It saw only a horse taking charge of a race and pulling away. There was concern, though, among the Secretariat people. Lucien Laurin saw the clocking of 1:09 4/5 for the six furlongs and worried. He could see his great horse moving along smoothly with no sign of discomfort but this was a suicidal pace. His face was rigid, his lips pursed. His hands were gripping the box-seat railing in front of him. He waited and watched.

Down on the track racing official Pat O'Brien stood by the finish line looking at the teletimer and his mind jumped back to the afternoon of June 15, 1957 when Secretariat's sire, Bold Ruler, raced through the first half-mile of the Belmont in 0:46 4/5, the three-quarters in a suicidal 1:10 2/5 and almost slowed to a walk in the stretch, finally finishing third. Remembering that, O'Brien said afterward, he wondered if the sins of the father were visited on the son.

Secretariat was stretching his lead with every stride, putting more daylight between him and Twice A Prince and My Gallant. Racetrack regulars were used to seeing a horse pulling away down the stretch, but Secretariat was doing this on the turn. I was standing in the back of the mezzanine looking on with awe at the power of this horse. Anytime anybody talks about Secretariat's Belmont, I can picture that turn as he put more and more daylight between himself and the others.

Turcotte looked back to his left in the stretch to see the other horses. He also noted the time on the teletimer and realized his horse could set a record. He let him run all out down the stretch. In the announcer's booth announcer Chick Anderson's voice rose to the occasion. In what has become one of the best-known American sports calls, Anderson captured the moment. He shouted:

Secretariat is blazing along. The first three-quarters of a mile in 1:09 and four-fifths. Secretariat is widening now! He is moving like a tremendous machine! Secretariat by twelve, Secretariat by fourteen lengths on the turn. Sham is dropping back. It looks like they'll catch him today, as My Gallant and Twice A Prince are both coming up to him now. But Secretariat is all alone! He's out there almost a sixteenth of a mile away from the rest of the horses! He's into the stretch. Secretariat leads this field by 18 lengths and now Twice A Prince has taken second and My Gallant has fallen back to third. They're in the stretch. Secretariat is opening a 22-length lead! He's going to be the Triple Crown winner! Here comes Secretariat to the wire. An unbelievable, an amazing performance!

Secretariat's winning margin was 31 lengths—a distance it took careful examination of videotape and trackside photographs to measure. His time of 2:24 was a world record that no horse would come close to challenging into the next century. During Anderson's call of the stretch run, the CBS camera had to pull back to keep the colt and his opponents in the frame. This caught the backs of thousands of Belmont Park spectators cheering and applauding as Secretariat neared the finish.

As Turcotte galloped Secretariat back to the winner's circle, the crowd applauded them in waves. The jockey doffed his helmet, and the crowd responded with another ovation. The cheering followed Turcotte, Laurin, Tweedy and Secretariat to the winner's circle. Turcotte held one white carnation. Edddie Sweat put a blanket over the sweat-glistening colt and walked him home to Barn 7, passing dignitaries and backstretch workers. Thousands of people lined the tunnel back to the barn to clap for them.

This is the official *Daily Racing Form* on the epic race:

Horse	Jockey	PP	¼	½	1Mi	1¼	Str.	Finish
Secretariat	Turcotte	1	1	1	1	1	1	1^{31}
Twice A Prince	Baeza	5	4	4	3	2	3	$2^{1/2}$
My Gallant	Cordero	3	3	3	4	3	2	3^{13}
Pvt. Smiles	Gargan	2	5	5	5	5	5	$4^{3/4}$
Sham	Pincay	6	2	2	2	4	4	5

With the quaint understated commentary:

Secretariat sent up along the inside to vie for the early lead with Sham to the backstretch, disposing of that one after going three-quarters, drew off at will rounding the far turn and was under a hand ride from Turcotte to establish a record in a tremendous performance. Twice A Prince, unable to stay with the leader early, moved through along the rail approaching the stretch and outfinished My Gallant for the place. The latter, void of early foot, moved with Twice A Prince rounding the far turn and fought it out gamely with that one through the drive. Pvt. Smiles showed nothing. Sham alternated for the lead with Secretariat to the backstretch, wasn't able to match stride with that rival after going three-quarters, and stopped badly.

The experts now agree there has never been another race like this. "Spectacular, just sensational" respected trainer Elliott Burch called out as Secretariat walked by him back to the barn. Many other horsemen were dazzled. People saw this as a performance that went beyond the sport of horse racing. *Sports Illustrated* rated it the second greatest sports performance by an individual athlete, ranking second only behind Wilt Chamberlain's 100-point game. Two weeks after the race, Secretariat graced the covers of *Sports Illustrated, Time* and *Newsweek*.

Eddie Comerford wrote in *Newsday* that "in the Triple Crown races Secretariat looked like Pegasus flying past Clydesdales." Columnist Mike McGrady wrote, "Secretariat is too good to be believed . . . he has been whatever we wanted him to be—and maybe, just maybe too good for us. It is easier somehow to relate to the horse that stumbles, the favorite who finishes fifth. What's a beautiful animal like this doing in a world like ours? Who can believe in something like that?"

Bill Nack chronicled Secretariat's day from the time he awakened from sleeping under a tree at the barn in the dawn hours. He would write that this was "the greatest single performance ever by a running horse, an unprecedented feat of power, grace and speed." He quoted Charles Hatton, the man who coined the term, Triple Crown, calling Secretariat the greatest single horse he had ever seen "in 60 years of covering and observing the American turf, even greater than Man o' War."

Later, Nack would be riled by a *Blood Horse* magazine poll of the Top 20 Horses of All Time. Man o' War finished first ahead of Secretariat, but only because one expert skewered the vote by placing Secretariat 14th on the list. Everyone else had him first or second. Nack said "I told the *Blood Horse* editor that, had I known one judge was going to do that, I'd have done the same thing to Man o' War just to nullify the idiot's vote."

Secretariat was retired to stud after his three-year-old season. He ran six more times after the Belmont Stakes, winning four of six races. In his last race he won the Canadian International at Woodbine Park by six-and-a-half lengths. He ran 21 times, won 16 and was out of the money in only his first race. On Oct. 4, 1989, when he was suffering from laminitis—a painful hoof disease—he was put down. He was 19.

The chorus in praise of Secretariat echoed throughout the Belmont weekend. There was one cynic. Me. Acting as a wizened sports editor meant to suggest some sober analysis of the race, I wrote a short editorial note hoping to put some of it in perspective. I wrote that Secretariat had really dominated only one horse, Sham, in the Triple Crown races. And I pooh-poohed Secretariat's world-record winning time by saying that the track must have been particularly fast because a "serviceable allowance horse" ran only a fifth of a second off the track record in the race before the Belmont. Well, that "serviceable allowance horse" was none other than Forego, who would go on to become one of the greatest horses in American history, voted eighth in the *Blood Horse* poll. Nack, who has gone on to be one of the premier sports reporters of our time, has never let me hear the end of that. "Serviceable allowance horse" he says with a grin; I don't blame him.

And, oh yes, I cashed a ticket worth $2.20 on Secretariat. I broke my Belmont Stakes betting jinx. I was a loser again, probably, because in this age of sports collectibles the ticket might well be worth more than that now and in succeeding years.

#7 The Miracle Mets

Casey Stengel called them "The Amazins." He was only seven years early.

And it didn't matter in the midst of the Mets' mystique of 1969 that Stengel was being sarcastic in those early days when the classically inept Mets hardly resembled a major league baseball team. In order to appreciate the achievement of the 1969 Mets, we have to go back to their beginnings and their years of ineptitude—comic ineptitude for sure. All that led up to the glory of a pennant, a playoff and the World Series—when for legions of their fans they truly were amazin'.

The Mets got going as an expansion team in 1962. There was much excitement the previous winter about the new team. Stengel, a national icon who had been fired by the Yankees, was named manager. George Weiss, who had helped build the Yankee dynasty and was fired as well, came out of retirement to be the Mets general manager. This occasioned the celebrated comment from his wife about having an inactive husband around the house. She said, "I married George for better or worse, not for lunch." In the enthusiastic glow of anticipation, optimistic souls like me actually thought Stengel's wizardry with the Yankees might translate into a golden touch with the Mets. There was derision of Leo Durocher when the Lip ridiculed the idea that the group of retreads and unproved humpties the Mets inherited in the draft of other teams' leftovers would be winners.

I had been covering the Yankees after the New York Giants and Brooklyn Dodgers deserted New York following the 1957 season. As a National League fan in a National League town I was excited about covering the Mets, the new team in town. Not everybody understood that. I recall a conversation with Les Biederman, a veteran Pittsburgh baseball reporter. When I told him I was looking forward to covering the Mets, he gave me the look of a man who felt he was talking to a fool. He said, "I don't think that is such a good idea. When you cover a successful team like the Yankees, people associate you with them and their success. That wouldn't be so with a new team that won't be a winner."

The much-awaited opening day of the Mets first spring training at Miller Huggins Field in St. Petersburg arrived in February, 1962. The players heard a speech from Stengel and trotted out of the clubhouse for calisthenics and a rag-tag sprint around the baseball field. The desultory ambling style of the not-at-all svelte athletes galumphing along wasn't something that inspired visions of grandeur.

Reporters met with them en-masse when they returned to the clubhouse for their lunch-break. With pen and trusty reporter's pad in hand, I approached Sherman (Roadblock) Jones, a 6-foot-4, light-skinned, freckled black man from Winston-Salem, North Carolina who certainly *looked* like a real ball player. He had had brief, inconsequential stays with the San Francisco Giants and Cincinnati Reds before the Mets plucked him from the Reds in the draft that stocked the Mets and Houston Colts.

I said, "Hi, I'm Stan Isaacs from *Newsday*."

He said, "*Newsday*? That's a newspaper, ain't it?"

I said, "Yes, it is."

He said, "I believe only 12 percent of what I read in newspapers."

I was taken aback. "12 percent? Why 12 percent?"

He gave me an inscrutable look, shook his head and repeated, "12 percent."

Roadblock Jones played one season with the Mets. His most significant achievement was his appearance as the starting pitcher in the Mets home opener at the Polo Grounds, a game which the Mets lost. He earned no victories against four defeats before fading back into the minor leagues and out of baseball. I came across his name several years later when I read—with some excitement I must say—that he was running for a minor office in Kansas. A few days later I read that he won. Subsequently, I read that he had been unopposed.

The Mets went on to make a prophet of Leo Durocher, the onetime manager of the Dodgers and Giants. They evolved into the worst team in history, setting a record of 120 losses (with only 40 victories) that has been the low-water mark into the 21st century. I may be one of the few people who recall that the highlight of that first season may have been a victory, not during the season, but during spring training. It was the first spring game against the

Yankees and it loomed as an important game because of what the Yankees represented. They were the powerhouse of baseball, the ever high and mighty team who had long dominated baseball. They were the natural target for New York National League fans who had seen them dominate the Brooklyn Dodgers and New York Giants for so many years. And they had, of course, fired Stengel.

Stengel was all fired up for the game. He talked it up in his inimitable style. He managed it to the hilt. And the Mets won the game by coming from behind. I knew of the dangers of becoming too excited about any spring training game, but by this time I sensed that the Mets would flounder during the regular season and that a victory over the lordly Yankees—even under these circumstances—would be major. I wrote a much longer story than usual about the game. The wizened editors back in the office scoffed at my enthusiasm for a spring training game. They attributed my excitement to being too close to the scene, and the story was cut. I was, in truth, correct. The Yankee victory provided more one-day glory for the Mets than any of their paltry 40 victories during the season.

These are some excerpts from my piece:

St. Petersburg, Fla.—This was the slightly manic Casey Stengel after the Mets beat the Yankees yesterday:

"You can't beat gettin' to home plate."

"They [the Mets] were amazin'. If ever it was good to be good, this was the time. If you can beat the Yankees, you should know you can beat many clubs in the National League."

"We looked good in our uniforms. They're [the uniforms] just as good as the other sides."

"There is some ability in these players if we can get it out of them."

On Joe Christopher, the man who led off the ninth inning with a triple that led to the winning run: "I love him. I love him. Tonight I love him. Last night I didn't."

Then he did a little jig and away he went.

If you were at Al Lang Field yesterday, you might believe the Mets' 4-3 victory over the Yankees was one of the greatest baseball games ever played. It wasn't of course, but you might have believe it if you were there.

After describing the game details in which the Yankees led, 2-0, the Mets rallied for a 3-2 lead, then the Yankees tied, 3-3 on some shoddy fielding by the Mets, the story ended with this paragraph:

The finish: Joe Christopher lined a drive to left which was too much for Hector Lopez. Christopher made third. Gary Blaylock, the third Yankee pitcher, retired Don Zimmer on a foul. Now Stengel was thinking again. Up came Richie Ashburn, pinch-hitting for Howie Nunn. Ashburn lined a single to right and Christopher sprinted home. A few of the Mets rushed to shake his hand. The old people in the stands cheered, not the polite claps with which they greet most plays, but with lusty cheers.

"You're the best, Casey," a white-haired man behind the dugout yelled. "You're the best."

A *New York Daily News* headline got that game just right. It read: "Break Up the Mets."

The Mets then went into the season, winning friends and fans as they lost games. Symbolic of something or other was the incident of passion during the opening game at the Polo Grounds (the one started by Roadblock Jones). A couple was pulled into the police station for indecency, namely an act of fellatio in the stands behind home plate. It was learned later that they were married.

Obviously, the Mets inspired them to such heights of passion, they couldn't wait to get home to the privacy of their abode.

The Mets were so inept, there was a celebrated incident attending one of their few victories, a slugfest win over the Chicago Cubs. A fan reportedly called a radio station to get the score. When he was told the Mets had scored 19 runs, he responded, "But did they win?"

The saga of Harry Chiti is noteworthy. During the season the Mets acquired catcher Harry Chiti from the Cleveland Indians for a player to be named later. After being exposed to the talents of Chiti for a few games, the Mets sent him back to Cleveland as "the player to be named later." Some wondered if the Mets got the better of either deal.

The best Mets player, probably the only one who performed with any kind of distinction that first year, was Ashburn, who eventually was voted into the Hall of Fame for his long, distinguished career with the Philadelphia Phillies. A scrapper, a basestealer, the personification of a lead-off man, he was a significant Met, not only because of his play, but because he was second only to Casey Stengel in conveying an aura of charm about the Mets.

He was an engaging guy. I, a liberal Democrat, enjoyed good-natured jousting with him, a solid Republican from Tilden, Nebraska. He had a dry wit that served him well later on as a beloved broadcaster of Phillies games. It was Ashburn who helped nurture the phenomenon that was Marvelous Marv Throneberry.

Throneberry came over to the Mets from the Baltimore Orioles early in their first season after he flopped with the Yankees and Kansas City Athletics. He idolized Mickey Mantle to the extent he copied Mantle's mannerisms at bat, but without the same results. He was an uninspired ball player, and he started out badly with the Mets as well. He became a target of boos, but somewhere along the line there developed a fondness for him in the sense that he was so bad he became good. I was the first to comprehend this. I wrote a column in the midst of the booing pointing out that love was the other side of hate, and that a lovefest would emerge from the dislike of him.

That is exactly what happened. Throneberry's screw-ups became the stuff of lovable legend. The most celebrated incident was the time he hit what should have been a triple, but was called out by an umpire for failing to touch second base. When Stengel went out to argue, first base coach Cookie Lavagetto told him not to bother. "He missed first base, too," Lavagetto said.

Throneberry, a laid-back Tennessean, did not scintillate as a personality; he tended to bitch and moan. He lockered next to Ashburn at the Polo Grounds, and Ashburn kidded him out of his morose moods. And it was Ashburn who good-naturedly passed on to reporters Throneberryisms—goofs in language or daily living—that served to endear Throneberry as something of a folk hero. Years later the Miller Lite beer people selected Throneberry to appear in one of their commercials. When a limousine picked him up at the airport upon his arrival from Tennessee, he chose to sit in the front with the driver.

He hit only .244 in his one full season with the Mets, but he slugged 16 home runs, a few big ones, notably one where he came off the coaching line to contribute a big pinch-hit. Ashburn batted .306, was the only Met selected to the All Star team and never stopped battling umpires to get on base no matter how helpless the Mets' cause.

Banners caught on early with the Mets at the Polo Grounds, though it took management some time to appreciate or at least tolerate them. A noteworthy occurrence was the ridiculous act of censorship that boomeranged on the Mets. After they had moved to Shea Stadium and had solidified themselves as big-time losers, two fans showed up with a sign in right field that read, "Welcome to Grant's Tomb" a bow to Mets executive Donald Grant, the former hotel clerk who held owner Charles Payson's hand and had all too much say as a spokesman for the Mets. A security patrol headed by Matt Burns tore down the sign. The sign man, Karl Ehrhardt, and a friend, wended their way to the press box to complain. Their cause was taken up by colleague Steve Jacobson and me in *Newsday*. The Mets' Gestapo backed off. They suffered the next sign by Ehrhardt & Co. It read, "We Scribble while Matt Burns."

Ehrhardt, an advertising graphic artist, went on to gain fame as "The Sign Man" of the Mets. He captured the mocking spirit of Mets fandom by coming up with clever, pithy messages, expertly designed—some 1200 of them— that highlighted Mets foibles. He agreed later that he went too far when he flashed, "The Big Stiff" as an exclamation point underlining the inept play of Eddie Kranepool. Eddie was not a big fan of Ehrhardt. Nor were the Mets, but they grudgingly accepted him for the presence he became at Shea. He died in 2008 at 83.

The Mets finished tenth (last) their first four years, moved up to the stratosphere of ninth place in 1966, fell back to tenth in 1967 and were back to ninth, 24 games out of first place in 1968 before they launched their dizzying heroics of 1969. The frogs who would emerge as princes began forming in 1965 with the arrival, as day-to-day players, of shortstop Bud Harrelson and outfielder Ron Swoboda. Catcher Jerry Grote and left fielder Cleon Jones became regulars in 1966. Third baseman Ed (The Glider) Charles became a significant player in 1967, center fielder Tommie Agee came over from the Chicago White Sox in 1968, second baseman Ken Boswell became a regular that year and Al Weis developed into a super-sub. A key mid-season trade brought first-baseman Donn Clendenon from Montreal.

The heart of the Mets was their pitching, and the most important addition was the arrival of Tom Seaver in 1967, who won 16 games with a last place team. Jerry Koosman came of age in 1968 with 19 victories. Nolan Ryan joined the group in 1968. In 1969 Tug McGraw matured into a reliable relief pitcher along with Ryan, starting and relieving. And significantly, Gil Hodges, an original Met, became the club's fourth manager in 1968, following Stengel, Wes Westrum and interim 1967 manager Salty Parker.

They finished 24 games out of first place in 1968. They had lost their opening day games their first seven years, and didn't break the string in 1969, either, losing 11-10 to the Montreal Expos at Shea Stadium. In the first year of divisional play, the Mets took hold. They ran off a club-record winning streak of 11 games. In June they delighted their fans who morphed into Mets rooters when the Giants and Dodgers scuttled New York, by sweeping the San Francisco Giants and Los Angeles Dodgers in back-to-back series. Seaver retired 25 straight Chicago Cubs before losing a no-hitter in July. They fell 9½ games behind first place on Aug. 13, then won 38 of their next 49 games to take over first place for good on Sept. 10. They clinched the National League East championship on Sept. 24 with a 6-0 victory over the St. Louis Cardinals, and finished 8 games ahead of the second place Chicago Cubs.

The Mets then swept the Atlanta Braves in three games in the best-of-five league championship series. In game one, trailing 5-4, in the top of the eighth, the Mets rallied for five runs, gaining a 9-5 win, though Seaver struggled. He allowed five runs in seven innings. In game two, two-run home runs by Tommie Agee, Ken Boswell and Cleon Jones powered an 11-6 victory. They came back to New York for game three and won, 7-4 before a rousing crowd of 53,195. A two-run homer in the fifth by Wayne Garrett, a 21-year-old carrot-top who I wrote, "looked as if he should have been dating Rebecca of Sunnybrook Farm," put the Mets ahead for good. Nolan Ryan earned the victory.

And then came the World Series against the Baltimore Orioles. The Orioles won 109 games, finished 19 games ahead of the defending champion Detroit Tigers. They won their second pennant in four years, and swept the Minnesota Twins in three games in the American League championship series. They were 8-5 favorites over the Mets in the Series. Under a *New York Times* headline that read, "Mystical Quality Imbues the Mets," reporter Joe Durso wrote, "The Orioles add up to a juggernaut. They are methodical, the Mets are 'amazing.' The Orioles are mathematical, the Mets mystical. It is precisely that element—the intangible, perhaps the emotional—that gives the Mets the aura of the 'team of destiny.'"

I agreed with Durso. In a column on the eve of the Series, I conjured up images of another glorious time in New York and adapted the immortal home run call by Russ Hodges about Bobby Thomson's "Shot Heard 'Round the World" home run in the 1951 playoffs. I envisioned an announcer screaming, "The Mets win the pennant . . . the Mets win the pennant . . . I don't believe it, I don't believe it . . . They are going crazy here . . . Woweee . . ."

Baltimore was the city of Francis Scott Key, H.L. Mencken, Babe Ruth and stripper Blaze Starr. The Democratic mayor of Baltimore, Thomas D'Allesandro, whose daughter Nancy Pelosi would become the majority leader of the House of Representatives in 2007, ruefully noted that the Colts of Baltimore had been beaten by the Jets of New York in a huge upset in the Super Bowl earlier in January. I made it a point to call him. He said that "while he was aware of the so-called Mets syndrome," he felt that the Series represented a "splendid opportunity to rectify the situation." Baltimore fans' dread of New York extended as well to the fact that the Knicks had whipped their Bullets in a National Basketball Association playoff earlier in the year.

The Orioles took part in a downtown parade after working out the day before the opening game. The Mets followed on the Municipal Stadium turf and seemed loose. In a larkish attempt to fool onlookers, Seaver swapped his uniform 41 for the 39 of Gary Gentry.

An almost sellout of 50,429 for the opener included Pat Nixon with her daughters Tricia and Julie along with Julie's husband, David Eisenhower, who was the baseball expert in the family. Earlier that year before the All Star Game was played in Washington, President Nixon invited former ball players, officials and reporters to the White House for an afternoon get-together before the night game. Nixon reminisced about his time as a young man when he was listening on the radio to the 1929 World Series between the Chicago Cubs and Philadelphia Athletics. He recalled the epic seventh inning rally by the Athletics when they came back from an 8-

0 deficit to score 10 runs and win the game. He proceeded to recite a play-by-play of every player's at bat. I was both amazed and skeptical about such recall, though I noted that Lefty Grove, the great Hall of Fame lefty standing next to me, seemed enthralled by Nixon's recollection. I found out later that Nixon had called David Eisenhower earlier and asked him to get the exact sequence of the inning from a sports columnist acquaintance. Nixon was an avid baseball fan. He had no need to impress. But he was, after all, "Tricky Dick."

New York Mayor John Lindsay, whose identification with the Mets did not hurt him in his winning re-election bid, sat with Mets officials next to the dugout at Municipal Stadium. Right off, it appeared that any Mets aura disappeared in the first inning of the first game. After 23-game winner Mike Cuellar set the Mets down, Oriole leadoff man Don Buford smacked Seaver's second pitch over the right field fence. For a moment I thought Ron Swoboda could catch the ball, but his jump was awkward and the ball eluded him.

The Orioles touched Seaver for three more runs in the fourth inning after two were out. Elrod Hendricks singled to right, Davey Johnson walked, and Mark Belanger singled to right to score Hendricks and move Johnson to third base. Cuellar blooped a single that scored Johnson, then Don Buford doubled off the right field wall to give the Orioles a 4-0 lead. Seaver left after five innings. "I think I ran out of gas," he said.

The Mets had only one good chance to break through against Cuellar. Clendenon opened the seventh inning with a single, Swoboda walked. After Ed Charles flied out, a Jerry Grote single loaded the bases. Al Weis hit a sacrifice fly, scoring Clendenon with the first World Series run ever in Mets annals. Pinch-hitter

Rod Gaspar then topped a roller to the left of the mound. It appeared to be the kind of lucky hit the Mets were getting in the latter part of the season. But the cognoscenti didn't call Oriole third baseman Brooks Robinson "Hoover" for nothing. He scooped up everything. He charged in, swept the ball one-handed and threw to first base in time to retire the not-too-slow Gaspar. An observer said, "Not one third baseman in a million could make that play, but Brooks *is* one third baseman in a million."

Cuellar pitched a complete game, limiting the Mets to six hits, two by Clendenon. Only Buford had two hits for the Orioles. Don Cardwell and Ron Taylor mopped up after Seaver. Nobody had any complaints with the work of home plate umpire Hank Soar, a former defensive back with the New York Giants. He revealed that he was being paid $6,500 for his World Series stint. When the Giants won the National Football League championship in 1938 he got $200 a game, $2,200 in all.

The Orioles were 3-2 favorites for the second game on Sunday. The oddsmakers couldn't have anticipated the influence of a bevy of fair women—Mets women—on the game. The Mets took the lead on a bases-empty home run by Clendenon off Dave McNally in the fourth inning. Jerry Koosman had a no-hitter going for six innings. Paul Blair got the first hit off him to lead off the seventh. After Frank Robinson and Boog Powell were both retired, Blair stole second and scored on a single by Brooks Robinson, his only hit of the Series. The game was tied, 1-1.

Enter the Mets wives in the top of the eighth inning. The park started buzzing when a large white banner started moving up the aisle from the right-field sector. I borrowed the field glasses that Dick Young of the *Daily News* always toted with him, and made out the banner's message. It read, "Let's Go Mets." It was carried by four delicious things in miniskirts and pants suits. They were four Mets wives: Ruth Ryan (miniskirt, brunette); Nancy Seaver (miniskirt, blonde); Lynn Dyer (pants suit, blonde); and Melanie Pfeil (pants suit, brunette).

The Mets wives dared go out into treacherous territory to inspire their men. They went out there with no less derring-do than their husbands battling Frank Robinson & Co. They were greeted by a smattering of cheers and boos, and some lowlifes threw peanuts at them. Not many people threw anything, though, because a pretty face generally triumphs *uber alles.*

After completing their mischievous tour, they went back to their seats in the rear rows of section 34—in the boondocks of the right field corner. In the aisle an exuberant young man reached up and kissed each of them. It was all right, they said afterward. He was a Met fan.

Only a misogynist would claim *Les Femmes des Mets* didn't help inspire their menfolk to victory. Shortly after they had settled down, the Mets staged their winning rally in the ninth inning. With two out, Ed Charles singled off McNally. Gil Hodges called for a hit and run and Jerry Grote singled through the left side, enabling Charles to go all the way to third. The heretofore overlooked Al Weis then stroked a single to left field that brought Charles home for a 2-1 Mets lead.

Now it was up to Koosman, the personable 26-year-old lefty from Appleton, Minnesota. Buford flied to Swoboda in right field, Blair fouled off a pitch and then grounded out to shortstop. With the dangerous Frank Robinson up, Hodges put on a shift designed to prevent an extra-base hit. Second baseman Al Weis was moved to the left field corner to give the Mets four outfielders, the other infielders staying at their regular spots. It turned out to be more intriguing than significant. Koosman went to a 2-2 count, Robinson fouled off a pitch, then took two balls for a walk that put the tying run on base. Merv Rettenmund came in to run for foot-sore Robinson, who had hit a ball off his instep in batting practice. The dangerous Boog Powell went to a 3-1 count, took a mighty swing and missed. He walked.

As Koosman struggled to get the final out, the Mets women in right field came up with a clap cheer to the words, "Here we go, Kooz, here we go . . ." It was right out of the high school gyms of Alvin, Texas; Fresno, California; Half Hollow Hills, Long Island and all the places that button-eyed dancing girls do their all for athletic hunks.

The walk to Powell put both the tying and winning runs on base. Out of the dugout, in a leisurely, stride came Hodges again. He pulled Koosman for Ron Taylor, the 31-year-old Canadian who had struck out three of six batters in the first game (Taylor would go on to become a doctor who would treat ball players on occasion.) Now he faced Brooks Robinson, who he had struck out in a non-crucial situation the day before. The count went to 3-1. Robinson fouled off a pitch, then hit a slow grounder to third base. Ed Charles started to move toward third base for a force out, but Rettenmund was ahead of him. He turned and threw to first base instead. It was a low throw. Donn Clendenon dug it out of the dirt in plenty of time to retire the not-swift Robinson. The Mets won, 2-1, to tie the World Series and move on to New York.

The four Mets banner women had been welcomed vociferously by the other wives. I was among a few reporters who went out to join them for the rest of the game. We enjoyed what was the best show in the ball park. More noise came from that section than any part of Municipal Stadium. They brought a little slice of Shea Stadium to Baltimore. They made up in noise for the distance of their seats from the field. Their husbands had been angered about their poor location and used the rallying cry, "Win it for the wives."

The banner was the idea of Lynn Dyer, wife of the Mets' third-string catcher, Duffy. Lynn told me, "I stole a bed sheet from the hotel and I got some black shoe polish and made up the sign. We didn't go out with it earlier because Jerry [Koosman] had a no-hitter and we wouldn't want to jinx him." Ruth Ryan, a champion tennis player at a Texas high school, and the choice of many keen observers as the prettiest of all the Mets wives, said, "When I saw the banner, I volunteered to help Lynn carry it. So did Nancy. We needed one more and Melanie raised her hand." Melanie Pfeil was a bigger contributor than her husband, Bobby, a substitute infielder who sat on the bench, ineligible for the Series.

Ball games are won on the field with base hits and runs, but a team captures the fancy of the public with intangible qualities. The Mets women added to the mystique about the team. Even third-base coach Eddie Yost got into the act and added a touch of charm to the Mets saga. Yost, who was called "The Walking Man" in his playing days because he was so proficient at drawing bases on balls, played the gallant gentleman in the sixth inning when the stadium dust girl came around to dust the bases with her broom. As was her custom she finished up by dusting the shoes of the Oriole infielders and the visiting third-base coach. When she got to Yost, she handed him the broom, saying, "Now, it's your turn," meaning that she had dusted him the day before. Yost dusted the shoes of the 13-year-old girl, made a big bow and doffed his cap. She rewarded him with a lovely kiss. A wonderful scene.

After the game the Mets' husbands praised their wives. Nolan Ryan showed mock anger and threatened to speak to his wife harshly. He was warned by those of us who had sat out in the stands with the wives that if he did so he would be branded as a wife-beater in the press. Seaver echoed Ryan's comments and laughed. Duffy Dyer was delighted. He said, "She told me she might do it, but I didn't believe her. She's a great girl." Cleon Jones, whose wife, Angela, was in the thick of the cheering, said, "Wives are as good as their husbands make them."

After a day off, the Series moved to Shea Stadium for Game Three, played under a solid, overcast sky. The bookmakers were not yet impressed enough with the Mets and made the Orioles 13-10 favorites based on a match-up of Jim Palmer (16-4) against the Mets' Gary Gentry (13-12).

This was the Agee game. Tommie Agee hit a lead-off home run and then made two outstanding catches. His catches prevented five possible Oriole runs from scoring. What could have been a 5-5 game was instead a 5-0 Mets victory and a 2-1 lead in the World Series.

Agee's 400-foot home run over the center field fence in the first inning was his first Series hit in nine times at bat. The Mets scored twice more in the second. With two out, Jerry Grote walked, Bud Harrelson singled him to second and then Gentry, who had been hitless his previous 28 times at bat, popped a ball over the head of Paul Blair, often celebrated for playing more shallow than any centerfielder. The Mets led, 3-0.

In the fourth inning, when the Mets led, 3-0, Frank Robinson stroked his first hit of the Series. Boog Powell singled him to third. Brooks Robinson struck out. Then lefty-hitting catcher Elrod Hendricks lashed a drive to left-center field. Agee sprinted to his right as the ball kept fading away from him. Close to the fence, he reached with a backhand stab, gloved the ball and then cushioned the impact of bouncing off the fence at the 396-foot sign with his right hand. He held the ball up to show the precious piece of white stuck in the webbing.

The Orioles threatened again in the sixth, putting two men on base with two out. Gentry bore down and got Brooks Robinson to fly out to right field. The Mets then added a run in their half of the inning on an infield single by Ken Boswell and a double by Jerry Grote. They led, 4-0, and Ed Kranepool homered in the eighth inning off Dave Leonhard for a 5-0 lead.

With two out in the seventh, Gentry lost his control and walked Mark Belanger, pinch hitter Dave May and Don Buford in succession to load the bases. Out came manager Gil Hodges with his long, calming stride again. He removed the 23-year-old Gentry for the 22-year-old Nolan Ryan (a future Hall of Famer, but an often-erratic hard-thrower as a youth with the Mets). Blair hit one of Ryan's blazing fast balls to right-center field. Agee streaked to his left toward the Long Island Railroad depot, patted his glove instinctively, then dove and caught the ball with the glove on the dirt cradling the ball. It saved three more runs, possibly four, because Blair said he had reached second when Agee caught the ball, and might have had an inside-the-park home run if Agee had missed the catch and the ball spurted away from him.

After the game there was some spirited, light-hearted discussion about which of Agee's catches was better. Hodges, usually not one given to hyperbole, called the second catch the greatest World Series catch he had seen. Agee said he thought the first one was tougher. "I saw the ball well because the sky was cloudy, but I knew it would be tough because it was away from my glove side. I had to backhand it," he said. I had fun putting a rating on the catches. I gave the first catch "Four Gloves" and the second "3½ Gloves," subtracting half-a-glove because of the little pat; it told us he knew he had the ball even before he reached it.

Agee was a soft-spoken 27-year-old bachelor from Mobile, Alabama. One of 11 children, he had been Rookie of the Year with the Chicago White Sox before he was traded to the Mets in 1968. He was hitless in 34 consecutive times at bat early in his first season with the Mets. He hit only .217 that year, before gaining his stride in 1969 with 26 homers and a .271 batting average and four lead-off homers that helped the Mets win the pennant. He had been rejected from the army because of a heart murmur. "It flutters when I get charged up," he said. "I get bothered by it sometimes, but not today."

In Chicago, manager Eddie Stanky had disliked that Agee invariably caught a ball, hard or easy, while on the move. This offended Stanky because it was a baseball tenet that a man can do better if he can come to a stop before settling under a fly, rather than timing it so that he catches it on the run. Stanky's formative years in baseball, like mine, came when Joe DiMaggio was in his prime and nobody looked more graceful than DiMaggio getting to the spot, stopping and letting the ball drop into his glove. Agee never seemed to get the hang of that. Stanky promised to buy him a suit if he caught 10 straight balls while standing still. Agee never won the suit. "If I caught 10, he'd ask me to catch 10 more," Agee said.

The Mets had two black players from Mobile—Agee and Cleon Jones—but enlightenment had not yet reached the sports pages of the Mobile area papers. Agee's heroics didn't make any headlines there. A reporter surveyed Mobile before the Series and found people generally unaware of Agee and Jones. "The people back home," Jones said, "haven't been reading much about us. My relatives and friends get clips from out-of-town papers, but that's about it. As far as I know no reporter from Mobile has come up to me during the playoffs or World Series."

The Shea crowd of 56,335 for the third game included Jackie Kennedy Onassis and her two children, John and Caroline, who stayed until the end; her husband, Aristotle, left early. Also on hand were New York Gov. Nelson Rockefeller; and Mayor John Lindsay. When Lindsay was asked if he was associating with the Mets to help him get re-elected, he answered with a smile, "Not at all. That's ridiculous. I'm here because I love 'em. Don't we all?" As the game wound down, fans in the stands and watching on TV noted the huge sign raised in the third-base boxes by The Sign Man, Karl Ehrhardt. It read, "The Orioles Are For The Birds."

The largest crowd of the Series to date, 57,367, showed up on Wednesday, a day of national protests against the Vietnam War, which had started in 1959 and would not end until 1975. The *New York Times'* lead story the next day read, "Vietnam Moratorium Observed Nationwide By Foes of War; Rallies Here Crowded, Orderly."

The Mets now ranked as 3-2 favorites to win the Series, though the Orioles were 11-10 favorites to win the fourth game.

After the first ball was thrown out by Casey Stengel, a crisp well-played pitchers' duel between Tom Seaver and Mike Cuellar came down to a wacky 10th inning that added to the mystical feeling about the Mets. I joked to Steve Jacobson that "maybe they were, after all, Destiny's Tots."

The game was spiced up in the third inning by the ejection of the Orioles' feisty manager Earl Weaver. He argued a strike call to Mark Belanger and was thrown out of the game by home plate umpire Shag Crawford. "I don't have to take that stuff," Crawford said. Weaver had once said, "The job of arguing with an umpire belongs to the manager because it won't hurt the team if he gets thrown out of the game." Belanger then singled and went to third base on a single by Cuellar. Buford hit into a force play. Paul Blair tried to bunt for a hit, but was thrown out by Seaver, Belanger holding third, while Buford moved to second. The threat ended with a dramatic confrontation between Seaver and the dangerous Frank Robinson. Seaver won the battle when Robinson fouled out to first base.

In the Mets half of the second inning Clendenon drove a Cuellar pitch into the visitor's bullpen in left field for his second homer of the Series, to give the Mets a 1-0 lead. Seaver, displaying the form that enabled him to win 25 games that season, retired 19 of 20 hitters from the third inning on until Frank Robinson singled with one out in the ninth inning. Boog Powell then singled Robinson to third. That brought up Brooks Robinson. He laced a drive to right field that looked as if it would drop in for a hit. Ron Swoboda, known more for his genial personality than for his fielding prowess, made a desperate dive for the ball. He somehow snared the ball back-handed as he slid on the grass. It would represent his single finest moment in a seven-year career with the Mets.

It was a wild play by Swoboda because if he missed the ball, it would have gone through to the outfield and given the Orioles a 2-1 lead. Swoboda didn't see it that way. "There was no way of my playing it safe," he said. "That's a do-or-die play. I had to cut across to try and catch it or get my glove on it." Ken Boswell, the Mets sly young second baseman, said with a smile, "Why, I thought Swoboda should have got Robinson, too. I thought he was slow getting up after catching the ball." Frank Robinson, of course, had trotted home from third base after Swoboda's heroics. Now it was a 1-1 game.

Eddie Watt, who had replaced Cuellar in the eighth, set the Mets down in both the eighth and ninth, and Seaver survived one more challenge in the tenth. An error by Wayne Garrett and a single by pinch hitter Clay Dalrymple put two men on with one out. Buford then flied deep to Swoboda and Seaver struck out Blair to end the inning.

The Mets tenth started with Jerry Grote popping a fly ball to left field that went all of 195 feet. The sun and the shadows fooled left fielder Don Buford. He broke back, then came sprinting in too late. Shortstop Mark Belanger ran into short left and just missed making an outstanding catch over his shoulder. Grote reached second base and was replaced by pinch-runner Rod Gaspar. He was the obscure Met whose playoff celebration boasts had inspired the Orioles to go into the Series with the mock cry of "Bring on Ron (sic) Gaspar. Who the hell is Ron Gaspar?"

With Marx Brothers madness waiting in the wings, here the strategy wheels turned. The Orioles ordered an intentional walk to supersub Al Weis who had reached base seven times in three games and had won the second game with a ninth-inning hit. Gil

Hodges sent lefty J.C. Martin up to bat for Seaver and acting Oriole manager Billy Hunter countered with lefty Pete Richert, who had played for Hodges for two years when Hodges managed the Washington Senators. J.C. Martin laid down a good bunt on the grass ten feet toward first base. Hendricks had the better position to field it because he was facing first base. He yelled, "I got it, I got it." But Richert didn't hear him because of the crowd noise. He grabbed it, whirled and threw to first base toward second baseman Davey Johnson covering the bag. The throw struck Martin on the left wrist and bounced toward second base.

Gaspar ran from second to third.

"I saw the catcher throw the ball," he said.

"But it wasn't the catcher, Rod."

"It wasn't? I guess my eyes must be bad."

Now the ball was skittering around behind first base. J.C. Martin was taking off for second with a whoop and a holler, but Gaspar wasn't making any big move toward home plate. He said afterward, "I didn't see anything. It was all shadows. I'm only 23 years old."

In those split seconds that seemed an eternity to the Mets, third base coach Eddie Yost, tried to get Gaspar running home. He started to run himself, acting the rabbit to Gaspar. Rod, (he was only 23 years old) finally got the idea. Yost raced three-quarters of the way home ahead of Gaspar and the young man continued the rest of the way unaided. Swoboda said, "They were running around like a Chinese fire drill."

There was some post-game conjecture that Martin had run inside the baseline, which was illegal, allowing him to get in the way of Richert's throw. The Orioles would have had to contest the play at the time, but it probably would not have been accepted by the umpires, no matter what the photos in the next day's newspaper showed.

In the clubhouse, Pete Richert shook his head. He said, "Maybe Seaver was right." He was referring to a conversation between Seaver and Sandy Koufax while the Mets were beating the Atlanta Braves in the League Championship Series. Koufax asked, "Is God a Met?" and Seaver answered, "I don't know, but I understand he has an apartment in New York."

During the game, while Seaver was mowing down hitters, a group of young people wearing armbands were distributing a leaflet outside Shea that said, "Mets Fans for Peace." The cover of the leaflet quoted Seaver saying, "If the Mets can win the World Series, then we can get out of Vietnam." Seaver later said his picture appeared without his permission. It was of course, unusual for any athlete to express a political opinion at that time. He quickly backed off any public comment, saying that after the Series was over, he would do something about the Vietnam issue, but on his own, not with any group. A front-page report in the *New York Times* the next day that ran next to the Series story reported that two Blackwood, New Jersey high school students, the president of the debating society and a cheerleader, had died in an anti-war suicide pact.

The fifth game featured zany events that solidified the mystic feeling about the Mets that had taken hold even among press box cynics. The Orioles, who had not led since the first game, got off well with two home runs off Jerry Koosman in the third inning. After Mark Belanger singled, pitcher Dave McNally homered into the visitors' left field bullpen. This was no fluke. McNally had hit three homers, including a grand-slam the year before, and a homer earlier in the season. Two outs later, Frank Robinson hit his only home run of the Series, a shot over the left-centerfield fence. The Orioles led, 3-0, but would be shut down the rest of the way by Koosman. He allowed only one single in the final six innings, retiring 19 of the last 21 hitters. He pitched a complete game, something that would become something of a rarity in the 21st century.

The Orioles began to be afflicted by extraterrestrial forces in the sixth inning. With one out, an inside fastball plunked Frank Robinson on his left thigh. Robinson started making his way to first base, but the home plate umpire, Lou DiMuro, ruled that the pitch had first glanced off Robinson's bat. Earl Weaver, the feisty manager, who had been ejected from the previous game, came out and argued vociferously. He wanted DiMuro to check with the other umpires, but DiMuro thought he had seen the play clearly. Weaver lost the argument.

The game was delayed for five minutes while Robinson descended to the runway behind the Baltimore dugout where trainer Ralph Salvon treated his thigh with a freezing medication. Robinson wanted the umpire to come down and take a look at this, but the umpire desisted. When Robinson returned, he was greeted by a sea of waving handkerchiefs. He struck out.

Now the Mets sixth. Leadoff hitter Cleon Jones was struck on the right instep by a curve ball. DiMuro called it a ball. Jones insisted he had been hit. Mets manager Gil Hodges retrieved the ball from the dugout where it had rolled after the play. He persuaded the umpire to look at the ball. DiMuro duly looked and decided that the swatch of black on the ball was from the shoe polish on Jones's shoe. He reversed himself and awarded Jones first base.

Out came Weaver to argue again. Not as vociferously because, as he said later, the umpire had made the right call this time. The buzzing about the situation—the umpire rules against an Oriole getting hit and reverses himself to say a Met had been hit—had hardly died down when Donn Clendenon belted a 2-2 pitch off the left field auxiliary scoreboard. It was his third home run of the Series and solidified his election as the Most Valuable Player of the Series.

Al Weis could be called the Almost Most Valuable Player because he tied the game with a 371-foot home run off McNally in the seventh inning. Weis had never hit a home run at Shea Stadium in his two seasons with the Mets.

The Mets eighth: with Eddie Watt pitching for the Orioles. Cleon Jones led off with a double off the center field fence. Clendenon grounded out. Then Swoboda lined a ball down the left field line. Don Buford made a valiant try, almost back-handing the ball on the grass. Jones scored to put the Mets ahead, 4-3, and Swoboda slid into second base for his sixth hit of the Series. Charles flied to Don Buford in left, then came another play in which the Orioles defeated themselves. Grote hit a ground ball which Oriole first-baseman Boog Powell bobbled. He chased the ball, then threw to Watt too late to retire Grote. And when Watt juggled the ball, it allowed Swoboda to score an insurance run. The Mets led, 5-3.

The Shea Stadium crowd of 57,397 roared on every pitch by Koosman as he tried to put the Orioles away in the ninth. He wavered at first, walking Frank Robinson to lead off the inning. Then Powell forced him at second, and Brooks Robinson flied to Swoboda. Righty batter Davey Johnson was the Orioles' last hope. Fifteen years later Johnson would become the Mets manager and would graciously accept the kidding he took for what happened at Shea Stadium in his at bat against Koosman. He lifted a soft fly to Cleon Jones in left-center field. Jones squeezed the ball and raced with center fielder Tommie Agee to the Mets bullpen to run under the stands to the clubhouse. The series was over, and the Mets were World Champions.

Such words as "fantastic," "preposterous," "stupendous," "colossal," "inconceivable" and "wonderful" were used to describe the Mets. The Orioles and baseball people scoffed at this. They insisted the Mets were a good ball club with excellent pitching who had played good baseball. All of this was true for sure, but the events in the final game only underscored that there was some magic at work above and beyond sound baseball that made the Mets, in that Stengelian word, "amazin'."

I wrote that I couldn't buy "good baseball" as the full explanation for the Mets wizardry. Seeing them benefit from good breaks after bad breaks for the Orioles and seeing Gil Hodges manage like a master—the man didn't do one thing wrong—I started thinking about all the things that went wrong for the Mets in their bumbling past. When the Mets were the worst team in baseball, it seemed that not only were they inept, but they seemed to get much more than their share of bad breaks. I believed that all those years of the breaks going against the Mets somehow served to set up a huge bank of good breaks in their favor.

It is one thing to say a good team makes its own breaks—and the Mets did that—but the events in the sixth inning of the final game, Thursday, were beyond "good baseball." Frank Robinson of the Orioles gets hit with a pitch, the umpire doesn't see it and he refuses to check with the other umpires; Cleon Jones of the Mets gets hit on the shoe, the umpire doesn't see it, but he heeds Hodges's suggestion that he look at the shoe polish on the ball, and he reverses himself. It is no wonder that the Orioles' thoughtful Davey Johnson, the future Mets manager, said, "Right now, if they played an All Star team, I think they would win."

Game Five ended at 3:17 in the afternoon of Oct. 16 when Cleon Jones squeezed that fly ball by Davey Johnson. The Mets won the eastern division, they swept the playoffs and were now World Series champions. They had shook the sports world because they were 100-1 shots who had come home winners.

At that moment the fans took over. George Vecsey wrote in the *Times* that young fans "came over the barricades like extras in a pirate movie. For almost a half-hour they sacked Shea Stadium. They ripped gaping holes in the turf, tore up home plate, captured the bases, set off flares and firecrackers, and wrote messages on the outfield fences."

The city reacted with spontaneous celebrations. Wall Street was inundated in a tickertape blizzard that some people compared to the 5,438 tons of paper that fell when Charles Lindbergh came back from his New York to Paris trip. Midtown traffic was clogged with horn-sounding cars and trucks. A Madison Avenue bus driver stopped collecting fares. "Everyone on free," he said. It seemed that everybody was a Mets fan. Isaac Stern, the famous violinist, echoed Seaver's statement, saying, "If the Mets can win the Series, anything can happen—even peace."

There is an old canard in the sports writing dodge that says, "no cheering in the press box." Having covered the Mets from their inception, I naturally was caught up in their dizzy success story. If

I didn't cheer for them in the press box, I at least did a lot of chuckling along with Leonard Koppett of the *Times*, my pal Len Shecter of the *Post* and Dick Young, the *Daily News*; we all had written about the Mets from the beginning.

An extra bonus for me came in the form of an invitation from Karl Ehrhardt, who I had dubbed "The Little Old Signmaker of Shea Stadium," to ride with him in the Mets parade down Broadway after the Series. Mayor Lindsay's office had the inspiration to include Ehrhardt in the festivities. As we rode down the avenue the crowd spotted the familiar figure in his black cardboard derby hat with the orange band. "The Sign Man!" they shouted. "Atta way to go, Sign Man!" I sat in the open car with him and basked in the cheers for The Sign Man as the confetti fluttered down from the tall buildings and he flashed the custom-made epistles he worked up for the occasion: "Beoootiful" . . . "Wunnerful, Wunnerful" . . . "Outta Sight" . . . "First."

Some time after the tumult and the shouting I recalled something Baltimore mayor Thomas D'Allesandro told me before the Series: "I'll tell you this," he said, "If we lose this thing, I may pass an ordinance forbidding us to play New York teams anymore."

#6

Harvard Beats Yale, 29-29

In 1959 Red Smith, the esteemed columnist, called Charlie Loftus, the longtime Yale athletics official, to tell him he wouldn't be able to make that year's Yale-Harvard game at the Yale Bowl. "What!?" Loftus responded with surprise and disappointment. "You're going to miss THE Game?" Smith liked the sound of that and used it in his column.

The name took hold the next year when Harvard's hip sports information director Baaron Pittenger adopted the title for the program of the Yale game. It stuck. Other home games at Harvard might be titled, "The Columbia Game," "The Brown Game" or "The Penn Game," but every other year the last game of the season came to be revered as THE Game.

I was surprised when I learned this because I had assumed the Yale-Harvard match-up had always been known as The Game. The rivalry had started on Nov. 13, 1875 with a game played on the infield of Hamilton Park, a private racetrack on the outskirts of New

Haven. Harvard won, 4-0, on kicks. Seven Harvard students were arrested at post-game parties for "hooting and singing in the public streets" and fined $5.29 each.

What a rich rivalry it is. Harvard and Yale have played a football game almost every year except for 1885, when football was banned at Harvard, and the war years of 1917-18 and 1943-44. They played to a 0-0 tie in 1881, Yale awarded the game on safeties. The Yale Bowl was dedicated in 1914 with a 36-0 Harvard victory before 70,000 fans. One report said, "Yale had the Bowl, but Harvard had the punch."

When the official Ivy League was formed in 1954 with the adoption of a sanity code, it underscored the amateurism of its athletics. The de-emphasis continued with the Ivies' classification as Division 1-AA in 1982. Ever since, the Yale Bowl usually has been only half-filled except for Harvard games. I recall once being in the ABC-TV production truck for a Yale-Brown game before a small crowd of no more than 10,000 spectators. Television doesn't like empty seats so the game director had a little trick to mask the sparse crowd. When a back punted, the camera stayed on the punter for a sustained period. The cameras did not show the ball in the air lest it reveal the sea of empty seats in the background. As the receiver was about to catch the ball, the camera zoomed in on him. Hence viewers did not see the near-empty stadium.

There is some question about who coined the term "Ivy League." I had always assumed that sometime in the 1930s Caswell Adams, a columnist for the *Daily Mirror*, used a phrase about the Ivy-covered walls at the venerable New England schools. Others claimed Stanley Woodward, the revered *New York Herald Tribune* sports editor and college football purist, used "Ivy colleges" first in 1933 to describe the eight Ivy schools plus Army. And Associated Press sports editor Alan Gould allegedly used the exact term, "Ivy League" first in 1935 (I worked under Woodward in my first newspaper job at the *New York Daily Compass*, where he helped launch the paper as sports editor some years after he left the *Tribune*).

In 1935 future President Gerald Ford was an assistant coach at Yale. The Elis boasted the second Heisman Trophy winner, end Larry Kelley, in 1936 and repeated with halfback Clint Frank in 1937. Kelley, who taught history at the Peddie School in New Jersey after graduation, later sold his Heisman Trophy for $328,000 to benefit his nephews and nieces. (OJ Simpson sold his trophy for $230,000.) Kelley died in 2000 at the age of 85 from a self-inflicted gun shot wound.

In 1952 Yale inserted team manager Charlie Yeager to catch a two-point conversion in a game that culminated in a 41-14 rout. This was dubbed the "ultimate insult" to Harvard. I remembered this a few years later when I was captivated by the name of another Yale manager, Charles Cotesworth Pinckney III. I struck a historical lode in writing about him because he was descended from a long line of Charles Cotesworth Pinckneys at Yale, going back to an ancestor who represented South Carolina at the Constitutional Convention of 1787.

Bobby Kennedy was on the Harvard squad in 1946 and '47. Ted Kennedy caught a pass for Harvard's only touchdown in a 21-7 loss in 1955. Kennedy doesn't need much prompting to talk about it. "The memory comes flooding back," he says, "and I glance at an old photograph on the wall of my office that shows a young Harvard football player holding up the ball he has just caught in the

Yale end zone. I hardly recognize myself now, but I still remember the thrill of that magical moment in my life. The memory would be even sweeter if we'd won the game."

Harvard and Yale dominated the early All American teams chosen by Walter Camp into the 1930s. So much so that in a 1932 book, entitled *King Football*, a young man named Reed Harris, a former editor of Columbia University's newspaper, *The Spectator* condemned the football landscape dominated by the Ivy League: "The football of the colleges today is a royal mess," he wrote. "It is the sore thumb of our educational system . . . College football as conducted these days is only a symbol for the super-materialistic, utterly hypocritical attitude which pervades administrations of the great universities and the tiny colleges. To put forth winning football teams, alumni, faculty and trustees of the college will lie, cheat and steal unofficially."

The heated language may have overstated the case at least a little, yet the Ivy League has come a long way since then in stressing academics over athletics. By the time of World War II Ivy League football was overshadowed by the behemoths around the country—the Alabamas, Notre Dames and Southern Californias. Still the prospect of a battle of the undefeated on this late fall day in 1968 whetted the appetites of the old grads—and the young ones. Some of them may have even agreed at one time with the immortal comment of Yale coach T.A.D. Jones who told his squad before the 1923 game, "Gentlemen, you are about to play football for Yale against Harvard. Never again in your lives will you do anything so important" (Yale won, 13-0).

The 1968 game would be played against a backdrop of unrest in America. Martin Luther King Jr. and Bobby Kennedy had been assassinated in the spring. The Vietnam War raged on. The Tet offensive helped persuade a dispirited President Johnson not to run for another term. Students facing the draft were protesting the war at campuses all over the country; this would lead to the killing of four Kent State students two years later. Protests spilled onto the streets of Chicago during the Democratic National Convention. Police beat up protestors in what was later judged to be a police riot. The Game was played only a few weeks after Richard Nixon defeated Hubert Humphrey for President as the Vietnam War raged on. I did not, however, see or read of any protests before the game.

More than an appetite for football was evident among the cognoscenti in sports cars and station wagons that filled the parking fields on the banks of the Charles River outside Harvard Stadium. Hours before the 1:30 start, I strolled amid the smoke from barbeques and pungent odors to feast, at least with my eyes, on the array of foodstuffs. Beyond hamburgers and hot dogs were sumptuous feasts on folding tables draped with good linen, a veritable treasure trove of Hammacher-Schlemmer picnic supplies. A candelabra? I spotted more than one of those. Food spilled out of wicker baskets: quiches, pates, lobster newburg, cheeses, salads, even caviar. And, at a Yale station wagon, a cake decorated with a miniature bulldog. Thermos bottles of tea, coffee, hot chocolate. Red and white wines, beer, soda. A few tweedy men and women offered me a taste or two, but I desisted. One wore a button that read, "Go to hell Yale." A red banner tacked to a fence read: "When Better Women Are Made, Harvard Men Will Make Them."

Being in the midst of it I could understand the comment of A. Bartlett Giamatti, the Yale president who went on to become commissioner of baseball. He said The Game was "probably the last great 19th century pageant left in the country. It has all the tradition and texture and color of a coming together of rival families. In many ways The Game is a celebration of the comradeship of competition."

The day before featured the traditional games between Yale and Harvard houses. Harvard swept the six games. A 7-7 tie between the junior varsity elevens foreshadowed the varsity game.

In the 84 games leading up to 1968 Yale led the series, 46 victories to 31 with seven ties. No game was greeted with more anticipation and fervor than the 1968 game because for the first time since 1909 both teams came into the game unbeaten. The game would be played exactly five years to the day of the assassination of President John Kennedy. Both had nine victories, seven in the Ivy League:

Their records:

Yale	**Harvard**
Connecticut, 31-14	Holy Cross, 27-20
Colgate, 49-14	Bucknell, 59-0
Brown, 35-13	at Columbia, 21-14
Columbia, 29-7	Cornell, 10-0
at Cornell, 25-13	Dartmouth, 22-7
Dartmouth, 47-27	Penn, 28-6
at Penn, 30-13	at Princeton, 9-7
Princeton, 42-17	Brown, 31-7

Eight Yale players, including the two stars, quarterback Brian Dowling and halfback Calvin Hill, were selected to the All Ivy team. Five Harvard players made it. Yale had the league's most potent offense, averaging 479.2 yards and 36 points per game. Dowling hadn't lost a game he finished since 6th grade. The previous week against Princeton he ran a punt back for the first time ever in college and gained 32 yards. He had 13 Ivy touchdown passes going into the Harvard game. In 1967 he threw a 66-yard touchdown pass to Del Marting in the last two minutes to beat Harvard, 24-20 after Harvard came back from 17-0 and led, 20-17 in the fourth quarter. The running attack was a balance of speed and power, led by the 6-foot-4 Hill, a future National Football League All-Pro. Harvard, whose defense was called "The Boston Stranglers," held opponents to an average of 7.6 points and limited the opposition to 230.2 yards per game

In their book, *The Only Game That Matters* celebrating the Yale-Harvard rivalry, Bernard Corbett and Paul Simpson wrote:

At Yale in 1968 football was religion, Brian Dowling was God. His followers believed the charismatic quarterback and captain of the Bulldogs enjoyed an iconic status at the New Haven campus and beyond. Students held candlelight vigils beneath Dowling' dorm room window . . . When rain poured down on the fans at one game, they chanted for Dowling to make it stop. He hardly knew what to make of a six-page philosophical letter he received from a high school girl in Hartford. For fervent Yale rooters it was this: Frank Merriwell, Yale 1897, Brian Dowling, Yale 1968.

After the season's first game, a football player, wearing No. 10 on his jersey and named B.D., appeared in a cartoon in the *Yale Daily News* called *bull tales*. In one of the episodes B.D. is in the huddle admonishing his teammates for mistakes.

He says, "Well, I let you guys take the last play and what happened? You butchered it. Your big chance for you to make it without me and you blew it." In the second box, B. D. continues: "You all repeatedly refuse to run these plays right. You force me to do all the scoring. None of you have one ounce of speed, endurance or brains. In fact what does one of you have that I don't? Huh? What?" A black player wearing No. 30 says with a smile, "Soul, baby."

The whimsical exchange between Dowling and Hill was the work of Dowling's classmate, cartoonist Garry Trudeau. *The New York Times*, the only major paper in the country that doesn't run comic strips, ran one of the cartoons a few days before the 1968 game. *Bull tales* of course morphed into Trudeau's nationally popular, satirical strip *Doonesbury* in which B.D. continues to be a character.

Dowling did not have Calvin Hill's success in pro football. Drafted by the Minnesota Vikings, he was cut in training camp and then played briefly with the New England Patriots and Green Bay Packers. He had two touchdown passes over his three-year NFL career.

Yale came into The Game with a 16-game winning streak. It had lost its opener the previous year and won the next eight. It entered the game ranked in the nation's Top 20, unheard of for an Ivy League team. Yale was last unbeaten in 1960. Harvard hadn't been undefeated and untied since 1913. It went into the 1931 season undefeated, but lost, 3-0, on a field goal by the Yale immortal Albie Booth. The oddsmakers made Yale a seven-point favorite.

The big day came up bright and sunny, a crisp 45-degree New England fall day. A capacity crowd of 40,280 filled Harvard Stadium, the oldest in the country, built for $310,000 in 1903. The game had been sold out for weeks; $6 tickets now cost $100 and more. Gordon Page, the longtime Harvard ticket manager, estimated that the Harvard community alone requested more than 70,000 seats. He felt that they could have sold 100,000 seats—Big Ten numbers—for the game. A record of 400 sports reporters covered the game, not all from the northeast. *Newsday* usually didn't pay attention to Ivy League games, but I had no trouble getting the okay to do a column on this game. The Yale Club of New Haven sponsored a closed-circuit television broadcast at the New Haven Arena.

Yale dominated the game almost from the beginning. An early Yale drive ended when Harvard linebacker John Ignacio picked off a 15-yard pass into the flat by Dowling. Later in the quarter, Yale linebacker Mark Buscaren recovered a fumble on the Yale 20-yard line. Dowling promptly engineered an 80-yard drive for a touchdown. He mixed runs by Hill, fullback Bob Levin and halfback Nick Davidson with passes to Hill and left end Del Marting. The big gainer: a 37-yard inside reverse by Davidson to the Harvard 36. Hill and Levin hammered the ball to the three-yard line and Dowling scored the touchdown on an option run around right end. Rolls of toilet paper, "the ticker tape of the Ivies," Bob Lipsyte wrote in the *New York Times*, tumbled out of the Yale side. Bob Bayless added the extra point for a 7-0 Yale lead at the end of the first quarter.

Harvard quarterback George Lalich couldn't get the Crimsons moving, stymied by the strong defensive play of Yale middle guard Dick Williams and end Scott Robertson. Yale moved again shortly afterward, but they were momentarily stopped when Harvard safety Tommy Wynne broke up two successive Dowling passes.

Yale moved down the field again to set up a first down on the Harvard 3. Dowling seemed to be trapped as he faded back to pass. But in the magical style Yalies came to expect from him, he escaped pursuers and stayed alive until he threw to Hill free in the end zone. This ended a thrilling play that went for only three yards, but it resulted in a touchdown.

The score enabled Hill, playing despite a serious tongue infection, to set an all-time Yale scoring record with 144 points, surpassing the record set by Albie Booth in 1931. Hill went on to an outstanding professional career with the Dallas Cowboys. No less impressive, he married Janet McDonald, a roommate of Hillary Clinton at Wellesley College and together they produced the illustrious Duke and pro basketball player, Grant Hill. The young man at guard for Harvard, Tom Jones, who was described in the media guide as "a talented thespian," eventually gained greater recognition in Hollywood as the actor, Tommy Lee Jones. A Texan, Jones roomed with another southerner, Al Gore, and delivered one of the seconding speeches when Gore was nominated for President at the Democratic National Convention in 2000.

Yale ran and passed off the "I" formation. They ran plays off-tackle and inside end and worked the pass option often. To mix it up, on one play Dowling went downfield on a halfback option but the pass was broken up. Harvard just didn't seem able to stop the Dowling-Hill combination.

Yale scored again with eight minutes remaining in the second quarter. A Harvard punt from its own end zone was blocked by safety Ed Franklin and Yale recovered on the Harvard 5. Dowling went back to pass and again did a hasty retreat eluding would-be Harvard tacklers. Yale rooters held their breath as he went back, back, back, looking for Hill the whole time. Finally, he spotted end Del Marting in the end zone and threw him a 30-yard strike for a touchdown. Yale added two points on another pass from Dowling to Marting, and led 22-0. A rout? It seemed that way and more than a few Harvard fans started thinking about leaving at the half.

Jerry Nason, the veteran *Boston Globe* columnist revered for his longtime championing of the Boston Marathon, wrote the next day: "Dowling's control of the game seemed complete. The Johns [Harvard, that is] were psyched by his wild scrambling and off-balance throwing and his uncanny ability to brain-pick what every Ivy expert rates as the finest defensive unit in the league."

Harvard was struggling both with its running and passing. Gary Singleterry would wind up punting eight times in the game. Captain Vic Gatto had to come out for a time with a bad knee and Ray Hornblower, the league's leading ground gainer, was hobbling on a bad leg. And senior quarterback George Lalich floundered. He completed only two of six passes for 22 yards. One Yale player said, "We saw the runners limping and believed that we need only focus on the quarterback."

Harvard coach John Yovicsin, sporting a green Tyrolean hat, paced the sideline debating a change. He could see the game getting more out of hand when Yale launched another drive. After Yale moved into Harvard territory, Harvard got a break. The usually reliable Calvin Hill broke into the open for 20 yards, but then suffered a hard hit by safety Pat Conway. He fumbled and Harvard recovered on its own 36. It was one of three fumbles on the day by Hill caused by Conway, who was named to the All Ivy League team by the league's coaches.

Conway was not your usual college student. He had entered Harvard in 1963, did not do well, and joined the Marines. He was sent to Vietnam, was injured in combat and returned to Harvard, delighted to accept coach Yovicsin's offer to go out for football again. He came back to a campus full of discontent against the Vietnam War.

Conway took a perverse pleasure in baiting war protestors. "I made it a regular habit," he said, "of wearing my olive green USMC [United States Marine Corps] utility jacket. I'd find classrooms that were being picketed and walk right through the picket lines." Harvard had other players who were Vietnam veterans, some of whom belonged to the anti-war Students for a Democratic Society. He was greeted warmly. "I never felt any resentment," Conway said.

Because there was a draft, college students felt more keenly about what they considered an unjust war than they would three decades later when the United States waged war in Iraq with a volunteer army. The anti-war protests faded into the background the week of The Game in anticipation of the battle of the unbeatens. Yale's Charlie Loftus cracked, "Our kids are so busy rooting for their ball club that they don't even think about burning their draft cards."

Down 22-0, Yovicsin decided, however reluctantly, to change quarterbacks. Starter Lalich had been the junior varsity quarterback and the number three quarterback as a junior. He was erratic as a senior for a team that relied mostly on its ground game. He had passed for only three touchdowns that season and had completed only two of six passes for 22 yards when Yovicsin summoned unheralded backup quarterback Frank Champi, a junior from Everett, Mass. who had thrown only 12 passes in his entire collegiate career.

Champi was an odd duck. Here Yovicsin was giving him a chance to play in The Game and how was he feeling? Angry. He told author Al Silverman, "When coach put me in, he said he had confidence in me and that's all fine and dandy. But the way I took it is, hell, I'll be damned if I'm going to be made a fool of out here." He somehow feared he would be made a scapegoat. He said, "So my attitude was I don't give a damn what happens . . . Actually it worked in my favor to be angry at the beginning. I didn't go in there with nervous butterflies. Then, as I got focused . . . I just wanted to win the game."

Taking over on his own 36-yard line, Champi drove the Crimson in 11 plays to the Yale 15. He faked a handoff to John Ballantyne, looked downfield, and spotted sophomore end Bruce Freeman on the eight-yard line. He hit him with a bullet pass and Freeman bulled his way into the end zone. The extra point was missed. Harvard, which had gained only 18 yards on the ground in the first half, was on the board. It trailed, 22-6, at the half.

If nothing else this continued the Harvard tradition of the Little Red Flag. Whenever Harvard scored a touchdown, a designated "most loyal Crimson fan" would wave a crimson pennant with a black H attached to a walking stick. This started with freshman Frederick Plummer in 1884, another unique feature enriching The Game.

Despite Harvard's touchdown, Carmen Cozza, the ever calm Yale coach, had no reason to be overly concerned at halftime. "I told them to keep playing our game, not to let up, " he said afterwards. Cozza was a solid citizen at Yale now after a none-too auspicious start. When he took over for John Pont in 1965, Yale lost to its unheralded neighbor, the University of Connecticut, for the first time in history. A telegram sent to Cozza from an irate alumnus read: "There's a train for New London at 5:40 p.m.; be under it." Cozza's team then lost to Harvard his first two years by embarrassing 13-0 and 17-0 scores. Yale then started its 16-game winning streak after losing its first game in 1967.

In the Harvard locker during the intermission there was frustration. Pete Varney, the senior end, later said, "We knew that we played poorly, but we also knew that we didn't get any breaks. We knew the next score would be important."

Inexplicably, Yovicsin put Lalich back in at quarterback to start the second half. Three plays did not produce a first down and Gary Singleterry punted. Mike Bouscaren caught the ball on the Yale 16 where he was hit hard by guard Bob Jannino. He fumbled and Bruce Freeman pounced on the ball on the Yale 25. Back came Frank Champi, No. 27, at quarterback, destiny's tot in the making.

His first play lost a yard. He then teamed with end Pete Varney for a 24-yard gain to the one-yard line. The revived Harvard offensive line opened up a huge hole for fullback Gus Crim to score. Rich Szaro, the left-footed soccer style kicker who had made his varsity debut the week before, added the extra point. Yale's lead was cut to 22-13 two-and-a-half minutes into the third quarter.

Yale dominated the rest of the quarter but couldn't score, the first time in 26 quarters that the Bulldogs were blanked. Fullback Bob Levin fumbled on the Yale 46, then Hill fumbled again, after gaining 25 yards to the Harvard 10 before Conway jarred the ball from him again.

The sun started to dip behind the stands with the beginning of the fourth quarter and the retro-stylish ones in the crowd snuggled in their raccoon coats. Harvard threatened twice. Champi failed twice on sneaks as he tried to gain the one yard needed for a first down. John Ballantyne gained 15 yards on a nifty run, but that went for naught when two Champi passes failed.

Momentum had shifted to Harvard enough for Yale partisans to be a little uneasy. Harvard's "Boston Strangler" defense led by All-Ivy end John Cramer, cornerback Rick Frisbee and linebackers John Emery and the banged-up Gary Fanetti forced four Yale fumbles. Early in the fourth quarter, Brian Dowling took over from the Harvard 40. Two rushes netted a first down, then Dowling hit Bruce Weinstein with a pass to the Harvard 22. Two more runs sandwiching a penalty put the ball on the five. Here Dowling faked a run and skedaddled around end for a touchdown. Bob Bayless kicked another extra point and Yale led, 29-13. Dowling had been involved in 26 of those 29 points

It was estimated that some 5,000 spectators, most of them Harvard fans, left the stadium at this point. I recall that Red Smith picked up his typewriter and started to leave the press section, anxious, I assumed, to beat the traffic on the Merritt Parkway. Yale fans waved white handkerchiefs and taunted the Harvard people. They chanted, "We're number one." The sophisticates shouted, "You're number two."

Some of the more loyal Harvard fans who were prepared to stick to the bitter end might have been heartened with a bit of Harvard lore. Back in 1908 the legendary coach Percy Haughton called his minions together and strangled a live bulldog to inspire them to go out and whip the Elis. They did, 4-0, to complete a 9-0-1 season. So what if the story wasn't completely true; it was revealed that he had throttled a fake bulldog.

Harvard tackle Bob Dowd was infuriated by the white handkerchiefs. He told John Powers of the Boston Globe, "And every time we came up to the line we were taking it pretty good from the Yale players—a lot of crap about how big a game it was and how badly we were losing."

Yale then appeared to be on its way to a crushing score. Moving from the Harvard 32, Dowling dumped a screen pass to fullback Levin. He streaked down the sideline to the 20, where he was hit by guard Michael Georges. He foolishly tried to lateral to Calvin Hill, but the ball bounced free and was pounced on by end Steve Ranere at the Harvard 14. This would be the last time that Yale's offense would touch the ball.

Frank Champi went back on the field and the sight of No. 27 renewed the confidence of the Crimsons. Several of them said later that they felt at that point they could turn the game around. Ranere said, "I still quiver when I think about that game."

Champi went to work with only three-and-a-half minutes left on the clock, Harvard on its own 14.

Here is the sequence:

- A loss of two yards.
- John Ballantyne gains 17 yards to the 29.
- Incomplete pass to Ballantyne.
- Champi dropped for 12-yard loss, but a Yale penalty for holding gives Harvard a first down on the Yale 47.
- Incomplete Champi to Bruce Freeman pass attempt.
- Completed pass, Champi to Freeman gains 17 to Yale 30.
- Incomplete flat pass attempt, Champi to Gus Crim.
- Champi thrown for eight-yard loss to Yale 38.

- (Harvard third and 18 with less than a minute remaining)
- Champi trapped, tries to lateral to Crim, tackle Fritz Reed picks up the ball and runs 25 yards to the Yale 13, the longest play of the day.
- TOUCHDOWN: Champi, trapped again, scrambles and gets off a pass to Freeman on the 5, and he runs into end zone.

In two minutes, 49 seconds Harvard moved 86 yards in 9 plays for the score. Harvard went for a two-point conversion. Here a failed pass to end Pete Varney was nullified by a pass interference call against John Waldman. Harvard decided to run for it this time and Crim, running behind a block by Tom Jones, scored. Harvard was now within a touchdown, down 29-21.

I was thinking of Red Smith. This was a time when Smith was between his stints with the *World Telegram and Journal* and the *New York Times*, writing for the *Women's Wear Daily*. I was wondering if he was listening to all this on his car radio. I later would try to see his piece in the *Women's Wear Daily* to see how he handled the late dramatics, but I was unsuccessful.

With only 42 seconds left everybody from Cambridge to New Haven knew that Harvard would try an onside kick to maintain possession. Yovicsin said Harvard had practiced the onside kick all season, but never had to try it. Now, Tommy Wynne, the regular kickoff man advanced on the ball as usual, but he veered away at the last moment, and defensive back Ken Thomas sneaked in from the right to deftly squib the ball toward the Yale sideline. The ball bounced and rolled into the chest of Yale guard Brad Lee. For a moment it seemed as if he had it, but the elusive ball squirted out of his hands. A scramble ensued.

Lee was devastated by the play. He couldn't bear to face his teammates and skipped the bus ride back to New Haven, spending the night alone in a Boston hotel room. Years later he would say, "That was the worst feeling of my life. It still hasn't left."

Somehow the ball came out of the pack and Harvard's sophomore safety, Billy Kelly, jumped on it and cradled it on the Yale 49, fending off desperate Yalies. "I thought to myself," Kelly said later, "this is amazing. All I have to do is fall on it."

At this point amidst the pandemonium in the arena, alert observers could see Dowling talking animatedly to coach Cozza. He told the coach that he ought to put him and Hill into the game on defense; he had played safety in high school and the 6-foot-4, 200-pound Hill had been a linebacker. In a memoir published years later, Cozza wrote that he was tempted but "I wouldn't do it because it would have meant taking two players out of the game. I said we would destroy the two young men if I took them out now." Looking back 30 years he said he did not regret the decision because it was a "team game."

Now 42 seconds remained as Champi came back onto the field. No anger now, just fierce desire as he took charge with the ball on the Yale 49.

Here's the sequence that followed:

- Champi scrambles under duress and gains 14 yards around left end. Bouscaren collars him in front of the bench and is called for a facemask penalty. The Yale coaches believe otherwise and scream at the officials.

(32 seconds left)

- From the Yale 20 an incomplete Champi-Freeman pass attempt in the end zone.

(26 seconds left)

- Incomplete pass attempt, Champi to Jim Reynolds.

(20 seconds left)

- Harvard captain Vic Gatto comes hobbling out of the huddle and is a decoy as fullback Gus Crim gains 14 yards to the Yale 6 on a draw play.

(14 seconds left)

- Champi sacked for two-yard loss to Yale 8.
- He calls final time out (three seconds left).
- Coach Yovicsin calls a pass to Varney with banged-up Gatto the secondary receiver. Champi scrambles to the 15, can't find Varney in the clear, plays ring-around-the-rosy eluding more tacklers as the final gun goes off, slithers to the 10, finds Gatto, a dumpy little guy, in a corner of the end zone and hits him with an eight-yard pass. Gatto holds onto the ball as he is tackled in the end zone.

Champi later told Al Silverman:

It was my best scramble of the day because I remember I scrambled and scrambled back there, and found myself in the middle of the field. And at that point I actually stopped for a second. Because I expected to be hit, I really did . . . I had gone this way and that way and didn't know where else to go. Then all of a sudden I didn't see anybody, and nobody hit me. It was like I was being shielded by something. It was almost metaphysical. So I said, 'okay,' and I moved out again and that's when I spotted Gatto. I threw off my wrong foot; I just threw it in his general direction. It was amazing, given our small sizes, [Champi was 5-foot-11, Gatto 5-foot-6] that we saw each other at all.

Champi turned out to be Harvard's Merriwell, with six completions in 15 attempts for 82 yards with some scrambling derring-do that helped produce three touchdowns.

Gatto later recalled the play this way: "I remember just this tunnel of noise, and it was as if time had slowed down. I knew I was free but I didn't want to wave because I didn't want to call attention to the fact that I was open. Then Champi threw to me and the ball came so slow and big."

Hundreds of Harvard fans had been standing 10-deep beyond the end zone behind Gatto. They broke loose and rushed onto the field, some of them delirious, jumping on Gatto, picking him up. Ken Coleman, who was calling the game on New England radio, shouted, "People are all over the field. There is no time left, but they have the right to go for the extra points. They must go for two points. If they get two this will be two undefeated football teams."

For the two-point conversion coach Yovicsin called for "the roll right, curl-in pass" to end Varney. Champi took the snap, half-rolled to his right, then turned to see Varney racing downfield six yards, hooking back inside from the left on a slant pattern. Champi let the ball go, aiming high for the six, foot, three-inch Varney who was guarded by the five-foot, nine-inch defensive back, Ed Franklin. Varney jumped as Franklin desperately clutched at him and gathered the ball in. Touchdown:

Harvard 29, Yale 29.

The film of the game seen over and over again through the years by Harvard alumni shows Varney with his back to us. We see his big number 80, his feet off the ground, a half-yard inside the end zone, his hands high in the air, holding the ball. Franklin has his arms hooked around Varney in vain. The referee, facing the camera, is waving his hands overhead, the signal for a touchdown. Harvard 29, Yale 29. In a screech reminiscent of Russ Hodges' immortal call of Bobby Thomson's 1951 playoff home run, Ken Coleman screams, "It's tied, it's tied. It's bedlam at Harvard Stadium! The crowd pours out on the field. The Yale team is stunned. Harvard team is being mobbed by its fans." And again, "He fires it to Varney, it is tied. The game is tied."

Hordes of Harvard fans charged onto the field again, celebrating what many Crimson fans claim is "the most thrilling tie in the history of college football." I did not rush off to the locker room interviews. I preferred to sit in the press box for a while looking down, enjoying the celebration. The Harvard squad did not rush off to the locker room either, delighted to bask in the adulation of the moment. It took the players an hour to get off the field. They then stood on the lawn outside the field house. They kissed mothers and girlfriends and were pounded on the back by pals. "I'll buy you one," said a dude to rambling Fritz Reed, "at least one."

The Harvard Alumni Bulletin reported, "The stadium exploded. Strangers embraced, full professors danced, and the Yale people put their handkerchiefs to the use they were intended for."

Stunned Yale coach Carmen Cozza did not duck the postgame press conference. He said, "There was no way of it happening; it probably won't happen again in 10,000 years." He would often say later, "It was a tie, but I still regard it as the worst loss of my career." Harvard's Yovicsin sympathized. He said, "I think, so, too. I don't think I'll live long enough to see anything like it again. So I am glad I was here today." Cozza, whom many consider the best football coach in Yale history, retired in 1996 after 32 years, having won 10 Ivy championships.

Many years later Harvard official Will Cloney revealed a startling postscript to that ending. After the game the media was crowded around the coaches in the second-floor lounge at Dillon Field House. "During the press conference," Cloney said, "the door opened and the referee stuck in his head. He waited for a pause in the interviews, then announced, 'Gentlemen, you may have seen a flag on the final play.'"

Then he paused. The gent had a flair for the dramatic. "Talk about sucking the air out of a room," Cloney said, "Everyone was stunned. I doubt anyone had seen a flag because as soon as Varney caught the pass in the end zone, the crowd surged onto the field." He said the room went silent—except for the distant sounds of the Harvard band serenading outside. The prospect was, of course, mind-blowing. If the penalty was against Harvard, the crucial two-point conversion would be nullified and the play repeated.

The shock in the room was palpable. Would the referee demand the teams suit up again? If so, could the teams plow through the celebrating masses to resume play? There would be mass confusion, Cloney suggested, maybe a riot. "All that must have been flashing through everyone's mind, especially the coaches." And then, "finally, the referee said, 'Well, you can ignore the flag. The call was against Yale and I assumed that Harvard would decline.'" It was suggested that of all the sighs of relief none was more audible than from coach Yovicsin, who had had life-threatening heart surgery three years earlier.

The loyal legions who sang "10,000 men of Harvard want victory today" could break into what the *New York Times'* Steve Cady called "the boisterous, if slightly inaccurate, mass singing of 'with Crimson in triumph flashing.'" The tumultuous turn of events inspired this paragraph in Cady's account in the *Times* on Sunday: "Out came the papers in the press-box typewriters, out came articles that had begun, 'Brian Dowling completed a spectacular Yale football career today by passing for two touchdowns and running for two more.'" Cady, of course, was referring to his own never-to-be-used lead.

I didn't have Cady's deadline of the *Times* because *Newsday* did not have a Sunday paper in those days. The beginning of my column on Monday read under the head: "Obviously an Act of God (or the Devil):

Cambridge, Mass—Delicious, delirious, bumbling, fumbling madness took hold of the Harvard stadium Saturday as Harvard came from behind with two touchdowns and a pair of two-point conversions in the last 42 seconds to gain an exhilarating, damn-sight-better-than-kissing-your-sister 29-29 tie with stunned Yale. The partisan Harvard view was that it was one of the great and noble and valiant and heart-warming and poetic-justice come-backs of all time. It was all of that, and it was also enough to make a sobersides roll in the aisles with giggles at the way the generally not-too-ept but ever-willing Harvard boys somehow got The Game turned around and achieved The Tie.

Within five minutes after the game spectators walking out of the stadium were greeted with a special "Extra" edition of the Harvard Crimson that reported the tie. On Monday the Crimson flashed the immortal headline—the most celebrated college newspaper headline of the 20th century I would say—"Harvard beats Yale, 29-29." Nobody truly knew the name of the author. The Crimson photo editor, Tim Carlson, suggested it to the night editor, Bill Kutik, but said he heard it slurred to him by a drunken Harvard undergrad in the end zone during the post-game celebrating.

The game penetrated the rest of the nation to the extent that the taped replay of the Kansas-Missouri game was bumped off network television Sunday morning to show a taped replay of The Game. The CBS Boston affiliate rebroadcast it the next day, garnering some of the highest ratings of the year. Two weeks later the station aired "42 Seconds," a documentary about Harvard's season, topped off by The Game.

A most unkind cut was delivered to The Yalies a few days after the game when the Harvard team invited them to a joint Ivy League championship banquet. The Yale squad refused. "Everyone was a little bitter," center Fred Morris said. "There was no way in hell we would do it . . . When we put it to a team vote, it was an almost unanimous no."

Ten years later The Tie was one of the memorable games chosen for the nationally televised series, "The Way It Was," hosted by Curt Gowdy and Dick Enberg. Vic Gatto, Bruce Freeman and Frank Champi appeared for Harvard, coach Carmen Cozza, Brian Dowling and Bob Levin for Yale.

The participants' reactions were shown on the bottom of the screen as the game action rolled. Gatto displayed an ear-to-ear grin watching himself catching the ball and being mobbed by students. Cozza revealed it was the first time he had seen the game footage since that bleak Nov. 23, 1968 afternoon. Champi, ever the curious one, still seemed to nurse a Rodney Dangerfield grudge that he had not been given respect at the time. He said that he had been a star at Everett High School in Massachusetts and like Dowling had never lost a game in which he started as a freshman and in junior varsity games at Harvard. Champi played two games the next season and suddenly quit football for track. He was an excellent javelin thrower.

When Enberg asked if they felt Harvard won the game, he got an enthusiastic yes from the Harvard people. Dowling admitted that he never met anybody who thought of the game as a tie. Cozza agreed.

This is how the line score read on the black scoreboard at the open end of Harvard Stadium:

Yale	7	15	0	7	—29
Harvard	0	6	7	16	—29

The 1968 game towers over the more-than-100-years of Harvard-Yale football. Ivy League partisans would argue that it ranks with the greatest ever college football games. It enriched the rivalry, the sport, and for me it helped make a mockery of a *Sports Illustrated*'s ranking in 2003 of college athletic rivalries. The magazine put Harvard-Yale sixth behind Auburn-Alabama; Duke-North Carolina; UCLA-USC; Army-Navy; and California-Stanford.

The essence of the deep feeling that exists about The Game may have been captured by the comment of one devoted Harvard loyalist shortly after the game. "I'm terribly sorry I missed it," he said. "Not so much because I didn't see what happened on the field, but because I couldn't look at those people in the Yale stands watching it unfold."

#5

The Princes of New York

If you held your head at the proper angle, squinted a little and looked at the man with just a bit of cockeyed perspective, you might have taken Red Holzman for, say, a crabby biology teacher who wouldn't give any of his pupils a grade of 100 just as a matter of principle. Or a garment center cloak and suitor who would cut velvet two years after it went out of style.

Red Holzman was, of course, none of these. He was the coach of the New York Knicks in the glory days of the early 1970s when they were the princes of New York. There was nothing regal about William (Red) Holzman. This is Holzman on Holzman:

"I'm an average guy. There's nothing special about me. There are people on my block who don't even know who I am, and that's the way I like it. You do your best; you win, you win. You lose, you lose. What are you going to do? You try things the next time, but you're not going to help anybody by worrying or letting the pressure get to you. You know what makes a successful coach? Lots of hard work and being fortunate enough to have good players."

His "good players" in the legendary 1969-70 season were Willis Reed, Dave DeBusschere, Bill Bradley, Walt Frazier and Dick Barnett. All but Barnett would make the basketball Hall of Fame, all would have their numbers retired at Madison Square Garden. And so would Holzman, whose retired number hanging from the ceiling was 613, the number of victories his Knicks teams achieved.

Holzman's guys—abetted by a hustling supporting cast topped by Cazzie Russell and Mike Riordan—produced one of the greatest nights in New York sports history when they defeated the Los Angeles Lakers in the seventh game of the 1970 National Basketball Association championship finals. They shocked the sports world by the way the near-crippled Reed hobbled out of the locker room to inspire the team and overcome the mighty Lakers of Wilt Chamberlain and Jerry West.

Before there would be such a night of glory there was a checkered Knicks history of 24 years without a championship. It all began on June 6, 1946 when Madison Square Garden was granted a charter franchise in the Basketball Association of America, forerunner to the NBA. The name Knickerbockers traced to the Dutch settlers who came to New York in the 1600s. It referred to the style of pants the settlers wore, pants that rolled up just below the knee, which became known as knickerbockers or knickers. Washington Irving solidified the identification of New York with knickerbockers; the more manageable name, Knicks, for newspapers and conversation evolved in the 1960s.

The Knickerbockers debuted on Nov. 1, 1946 on the road, beating the Toronto Huskies, 68-66. Neil Cohalan was the first coach. The starting team for the inaugural game was dominated by New York City collegians. Ossie Schectman, Stan Stutz, Jake

Weber, Ralph Kaplowitz and Leo Gottlieb started. Joe Lapchick took over as coach the second year and the Knicks made the playoffs their first nine seasons. They made the playoffs only once in a 10-year span from the late 1950s to the '60s. At one point they lost 25 regular season games in a row against Boston.

And then came Holzman. He was a star at New York's City College, then moved on to the Rochester Royals of the National Basketball League where he was rookie of the year as the Royals won the 1945 league championship. He joined the Milwaukee Hawks as a player-coach, then was fired in the middle of the 1956-57 season. He moved on to become a scout for the Knicks for 10 years. In that time they had little success under coaches Vince Boryla, Fuzzy Levane, Carl Braun, Eddie Donovan and Harry Gallatin.

When the Knicks floundered under coach Dick McGuire in 1967, Knicks president Ned Irish put in a call to Holzman. Red described the exchange in his book, *The Knicks*.

Mr. Irish said, "We'd like you to be the coach."

What could I say? "I don't think I'd like to do it" I replied.

"Sometimes," he said, "we have to do a lot of things we don't like to do."

I could take a hint.

Holzman worshipped at the shrine of defense. He believed that defense generated offense. Watching him from the press table across the floor, I would note that he stomped his foot when the Knicks made a sloppy defensive play. He rarely showed emotion on a missed shot.

The Knicks had a 15-23 record when he took over in 1967. They lost his first two games as coach, then won 28 and lost only 14 to finish third and make the playoffs, only to lose in six games to the Philadelphia 76ers. They finished third again in the 1968-69 season, winning their first playoff series against Baltimore in four straight, then losing to Boston in six games.

The team that would become New York's darlings had pretty much been assembled by the time Holzman took over in the middle of the 1967–68 season. Willis Reed had been drafted in 1964, Bill Bradley and Dave Stallworth in 1965, Cazzie Russell in 1966, Walt Frazier and Mike Riordan in 1967. Most significantly they pulled off what would become their greatest trade in history on Dec. 19, 1968, bringing in DeBusschere from the Detroit Pistons in exchange for Walt Bellamy and Howie Komives. As much as every Knick was significant to their success, it was the arrival of the 6-foot-6 DeBusschere that rounded out what would become a fabled five.

DeBusschere was 28, a jock's jock who had grown up in Detroit, a star in basketball and baseball. He was signed right out of the University of Detroit by the Pistons and by the Chicago White Sox for a bonus of $75,000. In 1962, when he was only 22, he was playing in two professional sports. He had a record of three victories and four losses pitching for the White Sox in 1963. He gave up baseball for good when he was named player-coach of the Pistons in 1964 at the age of 24, becoming the youngest coach in NBA history.

DeBusschere was recognized as a coach on the floor with the Knicks. He was smart, durable, an outstanding defensive specialist and one of the best ever rebounders as a forward. He took on the opponents' best offensive players and he matched Bradley in hitting shots from the corners. With his presence, Bradley got better and Reed came into his own as a center, not having to play off the departed big guy, Bellamy. DeBusschere earned all NBA defensive honors six times with the Knicks and made the All Star team in each of his full five seasons in New York.

Holzman said, "Dave is the kind of player who plays himself into exhaustion. Some men know how to pace themselves. Dave knows no other way than putting his head through the wall all the time he is out there." Once, DeBusschere limped to the bench and told a teammate, "Hold me, I think I'm going to pass out." His head wobbled as he drank a cup of water. A minute later he was back in the game.

Savvy New York fans know basketball. They took DeBusschere to their hearts immediately. They recognized what he meant to the team. With him they were running better, defending better, hitting the boards better and, Holzman said, "laughing better."

Along with the eight-man core, the squad for the 1969-'70 season included Bill Hosket and Don May, who were drafted in 1968, Nate Bowman purchased from Seattle in 1967, and rookie John Warren from St. John's. The Knicks got off winging with five straight victories. They lost to San Francisco and then started The Streak. They won 18 straight games.

It started with a 116-92 shellacking of the Pistons at Detroit. They then beat Baltimore, and after they routed Atlanta, 128-104, Hawks coach Richie Guerin, a former outstanding Knick, was moved to say, "When they were up by 25, they worked like it was a close game. They applied the pressure on defense and didn't get selfish and played team ball." Walt Frazier scored 43 points in a

13-point victory over San Diego. He got a two-minute ovation from the Garden crowd when he left in the closing minutes. "It was a helluva tribute," Frazier said. "I was going to stand up and start yelling, 'We're No. 1.'"

Frazier was probably the most dazzling, the most colorful of the Knicks. Born in Atlanta, March 29, 1945, he came out of Southern Illinois relatively unheralded, though he had led his school to a National Invitation Tournament victory. Shy at first, he eventually established himself as a terrific defensive player and a brilliant floor leader. By his second season he had broken Dick McGuire's team record of 542 assists by almost 100. He had, as well, a sly sense of humor and was a terrific interview.

Holzman analyzed Frazier's maturation this way:

"I was impressed by the way our players began picking him up. They looked to give him the ball. They trusted him, they had faith in his ability, his leadership.

His ball-hawking was legendary. His steals often came in bunches and lit up the Garden. The line about the 6-foot-4 Frazier was that his hands were so fast he could grab the hubcaps off a moving car. I once had fun with that by telling him I had such fast hands myself that I could catch a fly while the insect was still in the air. Frazier said the he could do that, too. I extended it, saying I could catch two flies in the air at the same time. He wasn't fazed. He said, "I could do that, too, if they came near me. But they have heard about me and they usually stay away from me."

I once played around by naming an all-pro football team made up of pro basketball players. I assumed that the great floor leader, Oscar Robertson, was the obvious choice for quarterback. When I told Frazier I had slotted him for defensive corner back, he surprised me by saying, "I'd like to be the quarterback." I thought he was being a bit presumptuous, but in view of his future success and the fact, which I learned later, that he had been a quarterback in high school, he may have at least deserved to fight Robertson for the quarterback job on my imaginary squad.

Nicknamed "Clyde" by Knick trainer Danny Whelan because he wore the same kind of hat as Clyde Barrow, the gangster in the movie, "Bonnie and Clyde" he became a dashing character around town. His quick wit and colorful way with alliteration later earned him a place as a popular radio broadcaster with the Knicks.

The Knicks beat Milwaukee twice in a row for six straight. At one point Barnett flipped a pass behind his back on the dead run to Frazier who did the same thing up ahead to Russell. The ball never touched the floor from midcourt and Cazzie laid it in. When the Bucks moved to within seven points Reed beat Lew (not yet Kareem Abdul Jabbar) Alcindor for four successive baskets to clinch the victory. "I stunk," Alcindor said afterward.

They beat Phoenix and San Diego for eight straight. Despite an 18-for-18 night on the foul line by Jerry West, they beat Los Angeles, 112-102 as Reed scored 35 points. DeBusschere's nose was broken in the game. He played with an aluminum protection mask taped over his nose the next few games. Bill Bradley, his roommate, was moved to comment, "He sleeps quietly now. He used to snore."

The streak extended to 12 with easy victories over San Francisco, Chicago, and Boston. Their record of 17-1 beat the 16-1 mark of the 1948–49 Washington Caps. Then came Cincinnati and a close encounter with the 76ers in Philadelphia that they won, 98-94, for 14 in a row. Phoenix was next for No. 15.

They then beat Los Angeles, 103-96 despite 41 points by Jerry West. They played a marginally illegal defense that drew two technical fouls from referee Mendy Rudolph. In a 138-108 whomping of Atlanta that tied the record of 17 straight victories, Frazier razzle-dazzled with 15 steals, seven in the final quarter. Three of them came on successive possessions by Atlanta, Frazier flicking the ball out of Walt Hazzard's hands.

They had tied the record of 17 set by Washington in 1946–47 and Boston in 1959–60. Cincinnati was next. The game would be played in what was considered a neutral floor, the Cleveland Arena, before a crowd of 10,438. And for one of the few times Holzman could remember there was tension in the locker room and he kidded them more than usual to make them relax. It didn't work well because the Knicks had trouble with the Royals, not one of the top teams in the league.

They had to contend with Oscar Robertson. He had a good night, scoring 33 points with 10 assists and played well on defense. He fouled out with 1:49 left, and that set up an extraordinary drama. Bob Cousy, the great Boston Celtic and rookie Cincinnati coach, had activated himself at 41 after not playing for seven years. Now he put himself into the lineup with the Royals ahead, 101-98.

Frazier cut the lead to a point by sinking a basket. Then, with the crowd in an uproar, Cousy took his time bringing the ball upcourt and whipped a trademark hook pass of his to Norm Van Lier who hit from the side. Bradley then fouled Cousy and the old guy coolly sank two foul shots to up his team's lead to 105-100 with only 22 seconds left. Here, Reed was fouled and given three shots to make two. He missed the first, then made the next two to make it 105-102. With 16 seconds left.

When Cousy took the ball out, he couldn't find anybody open against the stifling Knicks' press, but was able to call a timeout, Cincy's last. When play resumed from midcourt, Cousy still had trouble getting the ball in. He threw the ball toward Tom Van Arsdale, but Dave DeBusschere cut in front of him, picked off the pass and drove in for a layup that got the Knicks to within a point again at 105-104. Walt Frazier made another steal, then was fouled in a scramble and made two shots to put the Knicks ahead. With two seconds left. Reed then picked off the inbound pass and the scoreboard showed the final: Knicks, 106, Royals 105.

They walked off the court with their record-setting 18th straight victory. "Beautiful, beautiful," Bradley kept saying in a wild dressing room. "How we won it," Holzman said many times, "I'll never know."

Holzman would not say it, but his coaching had more than a little to do with the Knicks' success. A clue. He once said, "I like to do something, almost anything to make the other team change if it is doing things right. There are times when I deliberately create a mismatch and hope it will cause the other team to concentrate on beating it. Basketball is a team game and if you can interrupt the team pattern you have a better chance."

Having set the record of 18 straight victories, the Knicks promptly lost their next game. The Garden fans were a part of the story on this night. Probably all of them—well almost all of them—had seen the Royals game on television, and when the Knicks came out on the Garden floor they were greeted by a four-minute ovation. They were flat from start to finish and were beaten by Detroit, 110-98. As time ran out on their record run, the

19,500 fans expressed their appreciation of the team anew with another standing ovation. The players were moved.

They continued to shine, and when they were 26-2, they were leading the league in just about everything—won-lost, magazine articles and cover stories. Leonard Lewin of the *Post* said, "The next cover for the Knicks may be the Bible."

They had an anniversary on Dec. 19, a year to the day they had gotten DeBusschere from Detroit and were 69-21 since then. Frazier understated the team's appreciation of him by saying, "Look what he's done for Bradley. He has helped Bill to become a good player. He has even taught him how to drink beer."

Bradley was a special case, of course. He was almost a mythical figure when he came out of Princeton. He opted to take a Rhodes scholarship at Oxford rather than play pro ball right away, and commanded a $500,000 contract from the Knicks when he entered pro ball. He was regarded as a white knight, bringing Ivy League class to the league, though for all his erudition, he was at heart a jock who loved basketball.

He grew up in Crystal City, Missouri, the son of a banker. Bradley would often say his father was only a small-town banker, trying to knock down the image that he had come from great wealth. Bradley was a liberal and, given his background, people actually projected him as a President of the United States; his teammates sometimes called him, "President" though "Dollar Bill" was more like it because of his salary and his close-fistedness as a spender. He became a New Jersey senator and had an aborted try for the Democratic nomination for President in 2000, but lacked the fire in the belly to sustain that effort and lost out to Al Gore.

On the court Bradley was almost in perpetual motion. Moving without the ball was his specialty. He would unhinge himself from a crowd, find an open spot on the floor, then do something pivotal. He'd circle the floor, darting here, there, cutting to the baseline or across the key. He would screen a man, then run an opponent off the screen into a pick in order to get free. That often left him open in the corner from where he was deadly or let him sail in for an easy lay-up.

I had a distinct remembrance of Bradley when he was the one-man team who took Princeton to the semi-finals of the NCAA championships in Portland in 1965. He was called for ticky-tack fouls early, then fouled out. His absence for a good part of the game allowed Michigan to win easily. The next night in the consolation game against Wichita State Bradley set a scoring record for the time. For a while he wouldn't shoot, but his teammates, aware of his chance for a record, kept passing the ball back to him and with something of a resigned look, he would shoot and score . . . 58 points.

The game against Detroit at the Garden on Christmas day was special. They pulled off what came to be known as the "one-second play." It was set up by the Pistons' Walt Bellamy scoring a lay-up to give Detroit a 111-110 lead with one second remaining. The Knicks immediately called a time-out and Holzman called for the one-second play. They had worked on it time and time again for just such a situation. It called for Frazier to take the ball out at midcourt. As he slapped the ball, Dick Barnett would swing around to set a screen allowing Reed to get free and take a pass from Frazier.

They had tried it in an overtime game against Atlanta and it hadn't worked because Joe Caldwell foiled them by deflecting the inbound pass. This time Frazier hung the ball about a yard from the basket—it seemed to hang up in the air a long, long time. Barnett came around and picked off Bellamy, Reed took two big steps toward the basket, leaped, caught the ball and then in the same motion banked it off the backboard for the winning basket. The clock didn't start, of course, until the ball was touched by Reed. The finish was so dramatic, the Knicks celebrated as if they had won a playoff game. "A one-in-a-million shot," said the usually cool Holzman.

This was a man who wore a one-dollar watch. He would say such wild things as, "Some guys like to wear their hair short and others long. To each his own. I only wish I had hair to wear, period." The years of playing and scouting and observing had made him a perfectionist about the large and small details of the game. He would say, "One message I wanted to get across was that everything the Knicks did was important. It is just as important for [sub] Mike Riordan to give a foul at the right time as for Reed to score 35 points or grab 30 rebounds."

The Knicks played such smart basketball, team basketball, that Walter Plinge, a devoted Knicks fan, commented, "The Knicks are loaded with so much intelligence, Albert Einstein couldn't make the squad."

They were a varied, colorful crew in many respects. They had expertise in many areas: Cazzie and Barnett on healthy food; Reed on hunting and fishing; Bradley on politics; DeBusschere on beer and stock tables; Bowman on soul music; Riordan on short-order meals; Stallworth on hats; Frazier on sleeping and styles.

Sartorially, Frazier as Clyde commanded the most attention, but Dick Barnett was probably more flamboyant. One night he walked into the locker room with a Chesterfield coat, homburg, striped pants and an umbrella hooked on his arm. He was the first to wear the Nehru jacket, soon copied by Frazier and Nate Bowman. Dave Stallworth and Bowman dabbled in capes. Reed had a closet full of fancy suits; he showed up once with a full-length sealskin coat that he had gotten free along with Frazier as a promotional suit from a shrewd furrier. Reed took his rookie roommate Johnny Warren in hand, as well.

Phil Jackson, the team's hippie, wore crazy, flowered shirts, with huge lapels, fringed vests, wide bell-bottom pants, sometimes with a strand of love beads and beaded Indian belts. The black players regarded the white players as hopeless. DeBusschere wore dark suits, while Bradley was considered a horror show. His shirts were dirty, frayed, often missing buttons. He would at times rely on paper clips to hold his cuffs together. The guys were so offended by the filthy London Fog raincoat he wore almost all the time that they actually trashed it one time and chipped in for a new one.

During the time that the Vietnam war split the country, the Knicks had political discussions but they did not heat up to the extent of interfering with team chemistry. Mike Riordan and Cazzie Russell, who missed games on occasion because they were serving National Guard stints, were hawks. So were Bill Hosket and Don May, DeBusschere less than he might have been if he were not Bradley's roommate. Bradley and Phil Jackson were against the war. Barnett and Bowman believed that the Vietnam War was another example of the black man being sent to fight a white man's war.

Barnett, the oldest of the Knicks at 33, came to the Knicks in 1965 after playing with Syracuse, Cleveland of the American Basketball League and Los Angeles. He gyrated in the air, twisting his body in what was called a "question mark" jump shot. He came into his own with the Knicks as a smart tactician and outstanding defensive player. He had a dry wit, once compiling an NBA "All Ugly" team. He told Holzman, "Red, I don't know if you're conning me or I'm conning you." Barnett later went on to earn a doctorate in education at Fordham University.

When the Knicks record stood at 26-2, there was talk of them threatening the all-time high of 68 victories by the 1966-67 Philadelphia 76ers. They cooled down after that, though. They were 11-8 after the 18-game streak ended, went on to win 34 and lose 20 to finish up at 60-22, a not-too shabby .732 percentage. They clinched first place with a 119-103 victory at San Diego. They were the hot team of the league and big crowds came out wherever they went. And they inspired compliments: Milwaukee coach Larry Costello said, "I have never seen a team move the ball like the Knicks, hit the open man like the Knicks." Even Holzman had some good words, singling out Reed and DeBusschere. "They are perfect team players," he said. "When they aren't rebounding, they are boxing out so Bradley, Barnett or Frazier could clear the board."

The Knicks had to overcome a succession of injuries down the stretch. Reed's kneecap bothered him most of the year, but he was too much the Spartan to complain. He also had stomach problems. Bradley twisted his left ankle and was out for more than two weeks, finally returning on the night they clinched. DeBusschere pulled a muscle in his back and was out for three games. Frazier, who nursed a sore groin at time, was out with the flu and when Donnie May caught an elbow in the mouth, it put three Knicks out of action at the same time. Phil Jackson, the 6-foot-8 defensive attacker with a wingspan that earned him the nickname, "Coat Hangers" never recovered from a bad back and was lost for the season.

The Knicks' depth showed itself on a night they whipped the 76ers, 151-106. Cazzie Rusell, taking over for Bradley, scored 35 points with some sensational shooting. As always he attributed his success to his diet of health food and tea. After a game at home Russell would take a teapot from his locker, brew a cup of tea and offer it to reporters, extolling the virtues of ginseng, eucalyptus and rose hips.

Russell could be spectacular at times, but the Knicks missed Bradley when he was out. Russell was a deadly shooter, but he was too often a defensive liability. One expert said, "Russell scores points, but he doesn't make the players around him better the way Bradley does because of the continuity he gives us."

The Knicks drew the Baltimore Bullets in the first round of the playoffs—again. They had beaten them in four straight in the previous year's playoffs and in five of six this regular season. They were strong favorites to repeat, perhaps easily, but there is no such thing as easy in the NBA. Holzman once remarked, "I sometimes wonder if any lead in the NBA is safe, even after you get into the dressing room and lock the door."

With the usual full house of 19,500 screaming meemies in the Garden, Baltimore got off to a 12-2 lead in the series opener. The Knicks bounced back to take a 14-13 lead, but Baltimore, showing a Knick-like defense, led 52-46 at the half. Fred Carter shadowed Dick Barnett and Earl Monroe did not give Frazier any room to get off his jump shots. Old rivals Bradley and Jack Marin bumped each other, Marin screaming when Bradley was not called for holding him.

Reed and DeBusschere combined for 25 points in the third period, and the Knicks led by three. Monroe, twisting and gyrating, ran off eight straight points and the Bullets led 101-100, then 102-100 with 38 seconds left. Here Bradley drove the baseline for a lay-up to tie the game at 102-all with 27 seconds remaining. Now it was flashy Earl the Pearl making his dazzling moves, trying to get free of Frazier as the Garden erupted with the familiar cry of "dee-fense, dee-fense." At the buzzer he got off one of his anatomically impossible jump shots over Frazier. This time it hit the rim and bounced off. Overtime.

In the overtime the Bullets led by four, then three, then by two. Frazier stole a ball, passed to Barnett who was fouled and made both shots to tie the game at 110. With 23 seconds remaining in overtime, Frazier wowed the crowd anew with his fast hands. He stole the ball from Monroe and passed to Barnett, who looked as if he was putting up the winning lay-up. No. The 6-foot-3 Fred Carter flashed across the floor, leaped to the moon and hit the ball at the backboard. The Knicks screamed "goal-tending" but referee Mendy Rudolph did not agree, and time ran out. Now double overtime.

The teams battled to 117-117, then Reed sank a shovel shot from underneath with less than a minute left and the Knicks held on for a 120-117 gut-wrenching victory, both for the players and the fans. Reed, who played 54 of the 58 minutes of the game on a knee that still smarted, scored 30 points. Monroe, who played with such intensity, constantly bringing the ball up, getting off shots, scored 39 points for Baltimore.

The Knicks won the second game, 106-99, and it was Mike Riordan's turn to shine. Riordan, a 6-foot-4 hard-nosed guard from a working class family in Queens, had been a 12th-round draft choice from Providence College. He was a tenacious defender who fouled out of 20 of the 80 games he played in college. Holzman sicced Riordan on Earl Monroe and he did a good job, even hitting hit two shots that gave the Knicks the lead for good.

Riordan was one of the most open of the Knicks, one of the best interviews. He and Frazier were my favorites. Riordan was known as "Bags" for the award he introduced. This was the "Scumbag Ball." After Knick victories he would take the dirtiest or most lopsided used ball and present it with great fanfare to the Knick who had made the worst shot of the night—an air ball or one off the side of the backboard.

Baltimore won the third game at the Garden, 127-113. Frazier said, "They're like a lion wounded in the grass; we'll have to go in there and kill them." Wes Unseld pulled down 34 rebounds and the Bullets came right back two nights later at home to win 102-92. The sellout crowd of 12,289 emulated Knicks fans with crescendos of noise as the series evened at 2-2. The Knicks rebounded with a 101-80 shellacking at the Garden for a 3-2 lead. The next game in Baltimore was a different story. Reed shot only 2-for-14, DeBusschere 2-for-11 and Bradley 1-for 9. Monroe and Gus Johnson scored 28 of the Bullets' 30 points in the third quarter. Baltimore 96, New York 87.

In the series finale the Knicks put on a shooting clinic, with six men scoring in double figures. Barnett starred with 28 points and did a good job of harassing Monroe even though the Pearl put up 32 points. The Knicks won, 127-114 before a screaming crowd at the Garden relishing a 4-3 series win for their darlings.

Beating Milwaukee in the Eastern Division finals meant dealing with 7-foot-2 Lew Alcindor. He had terrific numbers in most games, but the Knicks dominated and prevailed in five games. When it was over Alcindor remembered more than anything else the two free throws he missed in the last minute of the second game, when the Bucks trailed by a point. In the finals, the Knicks met the Los Angeles Lakers, who had beaten Phoenix in seven games before sweeping Atlanta in four straight. They had Jerry West and Elgin Baylor and the fearsome yet enigmatic Wilt Chamberlain, who had returned from leg injuries 13 days before the end of the regular season. The Lakers had been in the championship series six times in the previous eight years, but hadn't won the title because they could not overcome the Bill Russell-led Boston Celtics. The Knicks had taken the season series from the Lakers, 4-2, but Chamberlain had played in only one of those games.

GAME ONE AT MADISON SQUARE GARDEN: KNICKS WIN 124-112

It was a battle of gimpy-legged big men because both Reed and Chamberlain labored with knee injuries. Chamberlain had some trouble moving around and let Reed shoot from outside for 37 points. Reed also had 16 rebounds, though the Lakers out-rebounded the Knicks, 57-48. Reed jammed his shoulder and a doctor gave him a shot to ease the discomfort. Jerry West scored 33 points in defeat.

GAME TWO AT MSG: LAKERS WIN, 105-103

Chamberlain, probably stung by the questions raised about his timid performance in the first game, dominated the action. He came out to challenge Reed's jumper and stopped him. That changed the nature of the game. With less than a minute to go and the Lakers ahead, 105-103, the Knicks had a final chance. Reed stole a pass. He passed to Barnett, who tried a shot from the top of the key that missed. Chamberlain played 44 minutes and got 24 rebounds. West played all but two minutes and scored 34 points.

GAME THREE AT THE LOS ANGELES FORUM: KNICKS WIN, 111-108 IN OVERTIME

Holzman liked the Forum. He said, "The fans are not noisy and they sit a little removed from the court. It's a nice place to play ball." The arena, designed by the same people who did the Garden, had a Hollywood flavor. The locker rooms were spacious and carpeted. Elgin Baylor supplied the visiting dressing room with fried chicken from the place he owned. Reed limped around the hotel during the afternoon. Trainer Danny Whelan used heat and massages on him and he managed to play through the pain.

Chamberlain had another good night and the Lakers led by 14 points at the half. The Knicks went on a late tear and caught the Lakers at 96-96 with 1:18 left in the game. Here, Barnett, who had spent most of the night hanging all over West, made a basket to put the Knicks ahead, 100-99 with 18 seconds left. Chamberlain, then made one of two shots to tie the game at 100-all. Chamberlain at the foul line was a show all its own. He made only two of 13 foul shot attempts in the first two games of the series. He once made as many as 28 free throw attempts in a game, the night he scored 100 points against the Knicks. He is also the man who once missed 32 foul shots in a game and who missed more than any other player in NBA history. He invariably had a pained look of distaste while at the foul line.

At 100-100 the Knicks worked furiously for a final shot and it went to DeBusschere. He sank a 17-foot jumper with only three seconds left. Now it was all over but the shouting—the shouting of adoration by Los Angeles fans for Jerry West. At this point, Chamberlain took the ball out from under the basket 92-feet away. He flung a pass up to West who took the ball in the middle of the floor just about the top of the key on the Laker side of the court. He took two steps and let the ball go. It sailed straight and true into the basket. The immediate image that registered for me was DeBusschere falling down in a weak faint under the basket.

I wrote "West didn't shoot from the parking lot, but he could have from the way people tried to reconstruct the distance of the desperate heave. There were estimates of 63 feet, then 55 feet, then 57½ feet as the distance of the shot. Most people settled on 55 feet." West said, "When I let it go with an old-fashioned push shot, I thought that it looked good. I felt good about it, I suppose, but . . ."

Laker broadcaster Chick Hearn shouted, "The Lakers tie it, The Lakers tie it, Oh my God." DeBusschere said, "My heart went down into my stomach. I just sank to the floor because it deflated the heart right out of me." Frazier said, "I said to myself, 'He's got a certain look in his eyes as if he knows he's going to make it.' Then it went in, and I said to myself, 'Is he crazy?' " Holzman was ever the coach. The moment the ball went up, he said to Knick publicity man Frank Blauschild, "Did it beat the clock?"

It probably took a few moments for many to realize that the shot had only tied the score and sent the game into overtime. Holzman said, "I had to call all the players off the floor to remind them the game was only tied. Frazier just stood there, staring into space." By any measure of justice the Lakers deserved to win after that. But the Knicks took charge in the overtime, outscored the Lakers, nine to six and won the push-shove-sweat-strain uphill struggle, 111-108. Reed's 38 points helped despite suffering an accidental kick from Chamberlain in the third period that aggravated his knee injury.

There was nothing but sympathy by all, including the Knicks, for West. The multitude in Los Angeles had seen West perform brilliantly year after year, but never on a championship team. They wanted desperately to see him win one, and he underscored the sentimental feeling for him by his unabashedly wistful expressions of hope to play with a champion. Afterward he sat in the trainer's room for a long time with a cold ice pack on the thumb of his right hand. He had jammed it in the first half. There were tears in his eyes, and he suggested to the first people to come over to him that they please give him a few moments and he would talk. He thought less of the shot than the outcome.

GAME FOUR AT THE FORUM: LAKERS WIN, 121-115 IN OVERTIME

There was concern in Los Angeles that West's swollen thumb would keep him out of this game or at least hamper him. Slim chance. He dominated the game, scoring 37 points with 18 assists. Elgin Baylor added 30. Frazier said afterward, "This team without West would be through. They'd be hurting." The Knicks' wounded warrior, Willis Reed, limping on a bad knee, got 23 points. When a reporter pointed to his knee afterward, Reed winced. "Don't touch it," he said. The Knicks returned to New York, and Reed was given ultrasonic and whirlpool treatment for the next game three nights later.

GAME FIVE AT MSG: KNICKS WIN, 107-100

The afternoon of May 4, the nation was stunned by the incident at Kent State in which four students at an anti-Vietnam war rally were gunned down by National Guardsmen. This was of particular note to Cazzie Russell and Mike Riordan who occasionally left the team to pull National Guard duty. It did not distract them, though, for the game that night.

An injury to Reed turned out to be the motivating factor in a tumultuous Knick victory. The big man twisted on the floor, attempting to drive by Chamberlain only eight minutes into the game. The action moved upcourt as he writhed in pain. He hobbled back into action for one more sequence of plays, but couldn't stand the pain in his right hip. He limped out of the arena to an ovation and that set the tone for the evening.

From that point the Knicks were underdogs. They trailed by 10 points when Reed left, 53-40 at the half, then came together late in the third period. They produced whirling-dervish, fast-break basketball forcing errors and panic in the Lakers with their intense defense. To combat the Lakers' disguised zone defense, the Knicks adopted Bradley's suggestion to play a 1-3-1 offense to beat the zone. This opened up the game. Once the Knicks got it going, they were playing like they were back in the midst of their 18-game winning streak, when some suggested they might never lose. They made up for Reed's absence by gambling on defense, overplaying every man, sending two men after the ball.

The Lakers deteriorated under the pressure. They kept trying to dribble the ball and lost it with increasing frequency. They suffered 30 turnovers, 19 in the second half. They couldn't get the ball to Chamberlain, who took only three shots in the second half.

West got off only two, missing both. DeBusschere and Dave Stallworth took turns with Nate Bowman guarding Chamberlain, who towered more than a half-foot over them. They prevented Wilt from getting the ball, and they used their mobility to shoot long shots over him, or, in Stallworth's case, drive around him.

They cut the deficit to 82-75 in the third period, then went ahead, 93-91. They had trailed for almost 42 of the 48 minutes of play. The underdog effect of it all was personified at the opening of the fourth quarter when DeBusschere, 6-foot-6, jumped against Chamberlain 7-foot-2. Chamberlain won the tap—he won all the taps—but the Knicks defense prevented the Lakers from taking advantage of these possessions.

I took note of the tumult in the arena. I wrote, "The crowd? Don't ask. Wild, crazy, sore-headed, ref-baiting, panic-manic; the crowd to end all Garden crowds of this season, if that's possible. At one point a short, young man behind the Knicks bench rushed from his courtside seat to contest a call against the Knicks. The madhatter was actor Dustin Hoffman, a season-long spectator."

The sense of the evening was underscored by a vignette I witnessed on 33rd Street after the game. The street rats spotted DeBusschere coming out of the Garden, ran over to him for autographs or just to be around him, just to be with any New York Knickerbocker. Mobbing DeBusschere, they shouted the shout of New York basketball, "Dee-fense, dee-fense." For that time and place the shout was nothing less than eloquent.

GAME SIX AT THE FORUM: LAKERS WIN, 135-113

Reed did not play: he could hardly walk without help. Chamberlain dominated. Nate Bowman, Bill Hosket, DeBusschere and Stallworth took turns guarding him, trying to lean on him, but couldn't contain him. He scored 45 points with 27 rebounds, West added 33 with 13 assists. Dick Garrett, the rookie who had complained the previous game that he couldn't bring the ball upcourt against Frazier, hit his first eight shots.

GAME SEVEN AT MSG: KNICKS WIN, 113-99

Reed commanded attention immediately after the Knicks' loss in the sixth game. He and trainer Danny Whelan took the red-eye plane from LA and landed in New York at the Garden so early Thursday morning, Whelan said, "the pigeons were on the sidewalk having their breakfast." Dr. James Parker, the young sports medicine specialist, diagnosed Reed's injury as a muscle tear. Reed quickly began a regimen to get himself ready to play the final. He started with whirlpool, massage, hot packs and ultrasonic treatment. Reed would continue the treatments and be given shots to ease the pain just before the game started.

If concern about Reed's health dominated the sports dialogue, other events exploded in the news. Helmeted construction workers broke up a student anti-war demonstration on Wall Street, injuring 70 people. And shortly after the end of the game President Nixon addressed the country, justifying the controversial move into Cambodia.

In New York radio reports during the day kept up running details on Reed. People seized on word that there was a 50-50 chance he would play. Pessimists said it would be typical Knicks bad luck for him to miss the game. Optimists quoted Reed's words that he would play. It had been 24 years without a championship for the Knicks. All the glory of this season, the 18-game winning streak, the sensational "hit-the-open-man" team play, the dancing in the aisles of Knick fans enjoying the greatest show in town would mean little if they didn't win this final. Somewhat surprisingly, the oddsmakers made the Knicks a five-point favorite. They had the home court advantage.

Reed arrived at the Garden early for more treatment and took the court at 6 p.m. They decided he would play after getting some pain-killing shots of carbocaine. The clock went past game time while he was getting the shots. With the fans yelling, "We want Willis," the Knicks kept peeking toward the dressing room, where he would come out. Then he was spotted and section after section in waves joined the standing ovation. Players on both teams stopped their warm-ups to look at him. A later poll would declare that Reed hobbling out on the floor like that was the second greatest moment in the history of New York sports, second only to Bobby Thomson's "Shot Heard 'Round The World" home run.

Then the game started. After Reed did not contest Chamberlain on the tap, Bradley rebounded a missed shot, whipped it to Frazier who passed to Reed at the top of the key. Reed, dragging his bum leg "like Frankenstein's monster" author Bob Spitz would write, sank a one-handed jump shot after only 18 seconds of play. The Garden rocked, people high-fiving their neighbors in seats all the way up to the rafters. After Chamberlain put back a rebound to tie and Bradley made a foul shot, Reed improbably scored another basket, a jump shot from 20 feet. Now it was bedlam again and the Lakers could well have thought this was a special kind of theater: science fiction.

Holzman said, "Willis gave us a tremendous lift out there. He couldn't play his normal game, but he meant a lot to the spirit of the other players."

The Knicks built a 15-6 lead, extended it to 38-24 at the quarter, 69-42 at the half and 94-69 after three quarters before coasting to the 113-99 victory in the insane asylum that was Madison Square Garden. Reed, dragging his leg and trailing every offensive play, occupied Chamberlain enough to keep him in bounds. He played 21 minutes in the first half. The game came back to the inspiration he had provided by sinking those first two shots. After that DeBusschere, Bradley, Barnett and Frazier played like demons, all scoring in double figures. Frazier scintillated anew. He forced many of the Lakers' 23 turnovers, converted almost every one of his steals into a basket, scored 36 points and racked up 19 assists in what was his best-ever game.

During the half, Reed was given another shot and again was late coming onto the floor and again was greeted with a sustained ovation by the nearly hysterical crowd. Reporters are not supposed to cheer, but those of us at the press table on the floor across from the Knicks bench shook our heads with admiration for his remarkable resolve. I sat next to Jeff Denberg, *Newsday*'s enthusiastic young Knicks beat reporter, and I didn't stop him when he stood up and applauded for Reed. The Knicks captain played only six minutes in the second half, took two shots that missed and went out to another ovation. The Lakers outscored the Knicks only in the last quarter, when it was too late. Elgin Baylor wound up with 19 points on 9 for 17 shooting. Chamberlain scored 21 points, mostly on fall-away jumpers that the Knicks were happy to see him take, and had 24 rebounds. Lord Chamberlain was at his royal worst on the foul line, sinking only one of 11 foul attempts.

West, who was given pain-killing injections in both hands before the game, had a relative off-night for him, scoring 28 points on 9 for 19 shooting, 10-for-12 at the foul line and a sub par five assists. He was a valiant figure at the end of the game, at the line sinking two foul shots. The final action had DeBusschere dribbling the ball and killing the last eight seconds. While the seconds ticked away, Holzman was busy keeping Don May from running onto the floor, Bill Hosket was jumping wildly on the sideline, and Bradley was dancing on the court.

When the final buzzer sounded, Holzman, ever the thinking man, grabbed the pockets of his jacket to keep the change from flying out as he hustled off the floor. In the locker room Reed sat near his stall, accepting hugs from his teammates, answering the reporters. The Knicks were a beer team—"I need a beer, man," said Frazier—but somebody got out some champagne and Hosket led the dunking of Holzman. In the arena, the fans rocked.

It had been 24 years. Years of hope, frustration, disappointment. Now there was this season and this tumultuous night. I had always been unhappy with Bill Bradley's cautiousness when talking to me or other reporters. He always seemed on guard lest he say something that, I joked, would hurt his chances when he later ran for President. But he opened up to me and others in the locker room afterwards.

He said, "During the playing of the national anthem I had the chills. I said to myself 'I'd rather be here playing the seventh game of the NBA championships with the Knicks than anywhere else.'"

"But it's only basketball, Bill," I said facetiously.

"It's only basketball," he said, "but this is the top of my profession and how many people can say that at 26 they're at the top of their profession? This team is that. Pro sports are made of conflicts. Conflicts never turned to bitterness on this team."

The head on the "Out of Left Field" column the next day read, "Never Was a Night Like the Night the Knicks Won." They had shocked the sports world.

#4

Ali-Frazier

In his typically understated way Muhammad Ali described his heavyweight championship showdown with Joe Frazier as "The biggest sporting event in the history of the whole planet earth." It came to be known as "The Fight of the Century."

In recognition of the pre-fight excitement I settled on a take-off of the Leo Rosten short story, "The Education of H*Y*M*A*N K*A*P*L*A*N." In my pieces on the fight I inserted asterisks to call the fight a T*I*T*A*N*I*C clash.

Madison Square Garden buzzed with the electricity of anticipation as a crowd of 20,455 spectators came in from snow flurries in midtown on March 8, 1971. As I settled into my seat in the third row from ringside, my stomach tingled with nervousness. I had covered hundreds of big events but it was only at big championship fights—usually heavyweight bouts—that I felt these nerves at the start of an event. As I reviewed my notes, my thoughts invariably went back to the first time I had met the central figure of the evening.

He was Cassius Marcellus Clay then and it was the week of the first Floyd Patterson-Sonny Liston heavyweight championship fight in Chicago, Sept. 25, 1962. Angelo Dundee, his media-hip trainer, brought the brash young man into the press room at hotel headquarters. He burst about the room, spouting poetry, declaiming he was "The Greatest."

Most of the younger writers looked up from their typewriters and smiled at the antics of the outrageous young man. Dundee introduced him around to Larry Merchant, Jack McKinney and me and a few others. He told us that this was the "feller" who had won the light-heavyweight championship at the 1960 Olympics in Rome and that he was compiling an impressive record since turning professional two years earlier.

If the kid's prattling amused some of us, it annoyed some of the veteran reporters on the fight beat. Clay had won 15 fights without a loss at that time and as he continued to win and talk, win and talk, the dislike of him intensified among those older writers. It should be pointed out that this contempt for him preceded the time when he would shuck off his name Cassius Clay and become a Muslim with the name Muhammad Ali.

These walruses disliked him to the extent that for a long time they would not use the name Muhammad Ali. They continued to bait him by calling him Cassius. I was torn by his name change. If he wanted to convert from being a Baptist to a Muslim and wanted to change his name, who was I to say otherwise? But I loved the name Cassius Marcellus Clay. His parents obviously had some sense of history because they chose the name of one of Kentucky's greatest anti-slavery crusaders before the Civil War. Cassius Marcellus Clay, a cousin of Henry Clay, was an emancipationist who served three terms in the Kentucky legislature and helped found the Republican Party.

I thought I could solve the dilemma of how to handle his name by describing the fighter in print as Muhammad (Cassius Marcellus Clay was a grand old name) Ali. That lasted for a time until Muhammad Ali was generally accepted and with some regret, I dropped my obeisance to the emancipationist of old.

Clay won 15 of his first 19 fights by knockouts and correctly predicted the exact round ("They all fall/in the round I call") in some of those fights. At least Dundee said he did. This further infuriated the sizeable anti-Clay people in the populace. This was evident when Clay fought Doug Jones in Madison Square Garden, March 13, 1963. As I recall Clay predicted he would kayo Jones in the fifth or sixth round. He was greeted with considerable booing when he was introduced before the fight and the catcalls intensified when he did not achieve the knockout as predicted. He won a close 10-round decision. Such was the dislike of him that the decision was greeted with a roar of disapproval, many agreeing with Jones that he had won. This was ridiculous. Clay had won even if he didn't achieve the knockout.

Clay had knocked out the ancient one, former light-heavyweight champion Archie Moore, and Charlie Powell before the Jones bout. He then knocked out the Britisher, Henry Cooper, before being matched against the heavyweight champion, the fearsome Sonny Liston, Feb. 25, 1964 in Miami. Off two one-round knockouts of Floyd Patterson, Liston was regarded as a possible all time great. At dinner a few nights before the fight, Dundee and Bill Faversham, one of Clay's managers, expressed concern to me that the irrepressible youngster, 22, had forced a fight with Liston six months earlier than they would have preferred. They were so persuasive in their doubts that I changed my mind about predicting a Clay victory and joined the huge majority of pundits who predicted Liston would win. My colleague, Bob Waters, *Newsday*'s boxing writer, was only one of two reporters who picked Clay to win and he deservedly basked in some adulation afterward.

I had a greater regret about that week. Some time earlier, Dick Schaap, then with the *New York Herald Tribune,* raised the specter of Clay having an association with the Nation of Islam, popularly called the Black Muslims, which was regarded with some dread by the white community. I heard some talk about Malcolm X, the charismatic Muslim leader, being at the Clay camp in Miami. I went over to the motel where Clay was staying. There were many tall, ominous-looking (at least to me) young black men who seemed to be part of the Clay entourage. I have to admit that it was with much trepidation that I inquired about seeing Clay. I actually think I saw a man who looked like Malcolm X through a doorway. In any case I wasn't assertive, and did not gain entry. I retreated, not happy with myself.

Clay scored a technical knockout when Liston quit on his stool after the sixth round. Having been roasted by the establishment reporters and columnists before the fight—even before the specter of his joining the Black Muslims was raised—Clay presided over an uproarious post-fight press session in which he baited the reporters. He railed on about how good he was, how pretty he was, and demanded his due. Looking down from a platform over the media hordes, he shouted, "Who's the greatest?" There was some consternation and hesitation at first. He repeated his demand, "Who's the greatest?" Finally the answer came, even from a few who had castigated him.

"You are" or "Cassius" they shouted back at him. It was, in a word, hilarious.

After the fight, Clay's conversion to the Nation of Islam and name change to Muhammad Ali became public. He defended his title with a controversial one-round knockout of Liston in Lewiston, Maine a little more than a year later. Liston went down from what was regarded as a phantom right-hand punch by Ali. This raised a hullabaloo about a "fix." I sat in the TV truck immediately afterward and watched the punch in slow motion. It was a short-right hand punch that landed flush on Liston's chin. It could well have knocked him down but didn't seem powerful enough to prevent him from getting up. I agreed with Larry Merchant's analysis of Liston's behavior. Merchant said, "I think Sonny was psychologically whipped by Ali, by the kid's taunting, his outrageous behavior."

It was a bizarre night. Robert Goulet, the Canadian crooner, botched the lyrics of the "Star Spangled Banner" and former heavyweight champion Jersey Joe Walcott, the referee, got mixed up in counting Liston out. I think it was Leonard Shecter of the *New York Post* who observed: "There were three men who didn't belong in that ring: Goulet, Walcott and Liston."

Ali successfully defended his title eight more times before he had the championship taken away from him. He refused induction into the U.S. Army on April 28, 1967 in Houston. He had said in 1966 "I ain't got no quarrel with them Viet Cong." The New York State Athletic Commission immediately suspended his boxing license and stripped him of his title. Other boxing commissions followed. After Ali was found guilty of avoiding the draft, he appealed his conviction in a case that went to the Supreme Court. It wasn't until three months after the fight with Frazier that the Supreme Court reversed the conviction.

On Oct. 26, 1970, five months before the Frazier fight, he returned to the ring in Atlanta, which had no boxing commission. He scored a three-round TKO of Jerry Quarry. I was as much struck by the dazzling show of black fashion at the Atlanta fight as I was by the one-sided bout itself. Men outshone the women as they peacocked in Cab Calloway Sportin' Life grandeur at fight headquarters and at the arena. Then, on December 7, Clay had a tough fight with the unorthodox Oscar Bonavena before knocking him out in the 15th round.

While Ali was away from the ring for 43 months, Joe Frazier won the heavyweight title by knocking out Ali's friend, Jimmy Ellis, on February 16, 1970. He came into the Garden ring against Ali with a record of 26 victories, including 23 knockouts. Ali boasted 31 victories with 25 knockouts. It would be the first time in boxing history that two undefeated fighters would vie for the heavyweight championship.

In boxing terms it shaped up as a spectacular match-up. Frazier, the left-hooking brawler, ever coming in, willing to take punches to land punches. Ali, the fancy dan, the fastest heavyweight in history, who saw himself as a bigger Sugar Ray Robinson. He had lived up to the description, "float like a butterfly, sting like a bee," which had been coined by his alter ego, Drew Bundini Brown, by cutting down Liston, Henry Cooper, Cleveland Williams and Zora Folley. I was dismayed by the way he punished former champion Floyd Patterson.

The ramifications of the bout overshadowed the basics of two highly regarded, unbeaten prizefighters settling the heavyweight championship in the ring. Because of Ali it was more than that. He was the political martyr, the slacker, the black hero, one of the five most well-known figures in the world. He was the man many wanted to see win—or beaten to a pulp. It almost came down to this: if you were against U.S. involvement in the war in Vietnam, you were for Ali. If you saw yourself as a patriotic American alienated by war protestors, you were for Frazier.

I had mixed feelings. I wanted Ali to win because of the injustice he'd suffered, for his stand against the Vietnam War. I was among a small coterie of sportswriters—including Bud Collins, Larry Merchant, John Crittenden, Jack McKinney—who denounced the stripping of his title. We derided the fanatics who hated him for avoiding the draft, for being a Muslim. Howard Cosell, the TV blowhard, made a reputation for himself defending Ali, but, in his bluster, he made it appear that he was the only one to support the banished champion.

On the other hand, I was disenchanted by Ali's actions in the ring against Floyd Patterson, Nov. 22, 1965. It was painful to watch him punishing the fawn-like Patterson, taunting him, mocking him, making him suffer. He carried Patterson into the 12th round when he could have knocked him out earlier. He punished Ernie Terrell the same way, belaboring him for 15 rounds on Feb. 6, 1967 because Terrell called him, "Clay." Gradually, I found his histrionics less amusing than I had when he first burst like a Roman candle upon the boxing world. I admired Frazier as an honest workman who behaved honorably in not scorning Ali for being a Muslim or avoiding the draft.

About that time I spoke to a class of Columbia University journalism students about sports. I talked about sports as "the opiate of the masses" in the United States. I soon began to get the sense that these high-status students were agreeing with me a little too much, so I asked how many were interested in the approaching Ali-Frazier fight. When only about a half of the students—male as well as female—expressed interest, I reacted. I called them supercilious. I told them that if they didn't have an interest in an event that transcended sports, they shouldn't think about going into journalism. They protested. The professor complimented me afterward for shaking up their sense of superiority about sports.

I thought the build-up labeling the bout "The Fight of the Century" was a bit of an overstatement, because the second Joe Louis-Max Schmeling fight in 1938 had world-wide significance beyond Ali's controversial status. With Schmeling seen as the representative of anti-Semitic Nazi Germany, the fight underscored race relations and the prestige of two great nations.

Hyperbole floated above this promotion. Garden publicist John Condon said, "That night was like a combination of New Year's Eve and the Easter Parade." Gil Clancy, the veteran trainer who would work in Frazier's corner, called it, "The greatest sporting event of all time." As mentioned previously, I had fun with that by pilfering the asterisk gimmick from Leo Rosten's short story "The Education of H*Y*M*A*N K*A*P*L*A*N" to call it a T*I*T*A*N*I*C clash. I mined the general interest by gathering predictions from celebrities.

A sample from the pages of *Newsday*:

Bill Moyers, Texan: "Frazier's going to go down because Cassius Clay lived in Houston before he became Muhammad Ali, and that put a lot of meanness in him."

Arthur Ashe, tennis ace who keeps fighting to break through the South Africa apartheid line: "I love the guy, but I don't think Ali is ready mentally. He needs more fights . . . Frazier comes out smoking like he says, and I don't think Ali can stay with him. Frazier by a TKO in the 11th or 12th."

Erma Bombeck, mother: "After 21 years of marriage and three kids, I've seen enough fighting to last me a long time. I go with Ali because he seems so virile and confident."

Joe Farmer, assistant principal at Roosevelt High who was named after Joe Louis because he was born June 22, 1938, the night Louis knocked out Max Schmeling: "As an ex-athlete (college wrestling champion) I appreciate Frazier's skill, but it's beyond that; it's an emotional and spiritual thing that many black people feel for Ali and we have to believe he can't lose. Ali."

The two fighters each were guaranteed a then record $2.5 million. The Garden was a sellout, but there was talk the closed-circuit theater sales were lagging. Ali did his bit by trumpeting himself at Frazier's expense. Angry that the Frazier camp, like Floyd Patterson, called him, "Cassius Clay," not "Muhammad Ali," he mocked Frazier as he had Patterson. He called him an "Uncle Tom," "a gorilla."

This infuriated Frazier, the hard-working blue-collar figure in the drama, particularly because Frazier had lent money to Ali during the time of his banishment from boxing. It was also bizarre because the previous August, Frazier drove Ali up to New York from Philadelphia to tape record a conversation for a book about Ali. Most of the way they jabbered about what each was going to do to the other. "Later, as we got to New York," Frazier said, "he got more serious. He was acting like a veteran fighter handing out the benefit of his experience to the new guy on the block, which I appreciated: tips on how to handle my money . . . on how to dress so as to make a good impression . . ."

Frazier had his own word in response to Ali. He called him a "scamboogah."

And of course Ali had a poem for the occasion. He sing-songed:

Joe's gonna come out smokin'
but I ain't gonna be jokin'
I'll be pickin' and pokin'
pouring water on his smokin'
this might shock and amaze ya
But I'm gonna destroy Joe Frazier

When Clay first arrived on the scene spouting poetry, cynics noted his lack of education and declared that the poems were being written for him. An incident with Ira Berkow, the fine *New York Times* writer, proved otherwise. At the end of a one-on-one interview Berkow, however embarrassed that he was being a bit unprofessional, asked Ali for an autograph for the young sons of friends. Berkow told him, "Their mother has trouble making them clean their room"

Ali took a pen and on the spot wrote:

To Timmy and Ricky, from Muhammad Ali.
Clean up that room
or I will seal your doom.

Berkow was taken by this, and was curious to see how Frazier would handle the same request. Berkow wrote that Frazier told him, "If their mother didn't have trouble making them clean their room, they wouldn't be boys . . . Best wishes, Joe Frazier." It was in a way a reflection of the "float like a butterfly" style of Ali and the down-to-earth honesty of Frazier.

The air in the Garden crackled. People rubber-necked to spot the many celebrities in the joint. The fight drew a dazzling Hollywoord to Harlem audience. The old champs, Jack Dempsey, Gene Tunney, James Braddock, Joe Louis, Willie Pep and Sugar Ray Robinson climbed into the ring for introductions. Arthur Mercante, the referee, said afterward that he was awed being in their presence. Frank Sinatra somehow wrangled an assignment to shoot pictures for *Life Magazine*, and his photo appeared on the cover of the magazine. I was sitting in the third row of the press section across the ring from Burt Lancaster, who worked the closed-circuit telecast of the fight with veteran blow-by-blow announcers Don Dunphy and Archie Moore, another former champion.

I was too busy trying to settle myself, gathering my notes, to notice them, but I read afterward about others in the crowd: The civil rights figures—Coretta Scott King, Jesse Jackson, Julian Bond, Ralph Abernathy and Andrew Young. Count Basie. Miles Davis. Barbra Streisand, Dustin Hoffman. New York City mayor John Lindsay. Senator Ted Kennedy. Former Vice President Hubert Humphrey couldn't do better than a seat in the balcony.

The fight was witnessed by 20,455 at the Garden. It was televised via closed-circuit and satellite TV to 350 theaters and arenas in the United States and Canada and to 35 other nations. Scalpers ran rampant outside the Garden. One Garden executive turned down an offer of $20,000 for 20 ringside seats, $1,000 for each ticket. One scalper gave a rundown on his ticket sales: the most expensive seats, $150 for ringside, went for $400 to $600; the $100 tickets went for $200 to $300. The $75, $50, $40 and $20 seats were going for twice to two-and-a-half times the value. A Garden executive said, "We could have sold out Yankee Stadium twice for this fight."

Ali, whose plight made him a world-wide figure, said the people would be in the streets of Africa and Asia waiting for word of what happened. There was undoubtedly an aura about him. Harry Markson, the Garden's boxing head, recalled a moment after the weigh-in when Ali was walking across the Garden floor. "There was a basketball team practicing," he said "and one of the players threw a ball to him. He was at mid-court and he took a shot, just flung the ball toward the basket. And I'll be damned if it didn't go in. Swish. Everyone just stared in awe, but that was the kind of luck I figured followed Ali."

The crowd stopped milling and the celebrities stopped preening a few minutes before 11:00 p.m. Ali moved down the aisle toward the ring surrounded by his retinue. The self-professed "dancing master" stabbed the air with jabs and hooks. His chocolate body glistened in the ring lights as he removed his scarlet and white robe. He sported red velvet trunks, red tassels bobbing on white shoes. With him were his reputed manager Herbert Muhammad, the son of Muslim leader Elijah Muhammad; the peerless, alert trainer, Angelo Dundee; his cut-man, Chickie Ferrara and the ever-present ominous-looking body guards from the Nation of Islam. Drew Bundini Brown, Ali's court jester, was stationed in Frazier's corner.

Frazier strode out into the arena on the opposite side of the Garden from Ali, closer to where I was. He was darker than Ali, wearing a green- and-gold brocade mini robe on which the names of his five children were printed. He glowered as he walked along, his manager Yank Durham shouting, "Make room, make room" to clear the path. He recalled later that he heard fans shout, "Go get him, Joe," "Kill that mutha, Joe." He bounced on his soles as handlers removed his robe, revealing green satin brocade trunks decorated with flowers. With Durham was the highly-regarded corner man, Eddie Futch, who had sparred with Joe Louis as a young man. There were also cut-men and New York City detectives guarding Frazier against death threats he had received before the fight. Gil Clancy, who had trained several champions, worked Ali's corner.

The crowd chanted: "Fray-zer, Fray-zer." "Ah-lee, Ah-lee."

When the two fighters moved toward announcer Johnny Addie, the contrast between them was striking. Ali had an 80-inch reach, six-and-a-half inches longer than Frazier's. Ali stood four inches taller, and it seemed more than that as he looked down at Frazier, five-foot eleven, 205½ pounds. He seemed even taller than that during the action in the ring as Frazier burrowed with his head down toward him. Ali used his reach advantage to ward off the ever-pressing smaller man.

As Addie, in a tuxedo with a blue shirt, prepared to announce them, Ali danced along the ropes, playing to the crowd. With his little boy's smile he brushed up against Frazier and said, "Chump." Frazier rapped him on the back, as intent as Ali to pile up points in the psychological hijinxing.

Addie pulled down on the microphone to make the introductions: "Ladies and gentlemen, in this corner wearing red trunks and weighing 215 pounds from Cherry Hill, New Jersey, the return of the champ, Muhammad Ali." Cheers and a chorus of, "Ah-lee, Ah-lee." Then, "And in this corner, wearing green-and-gold trunks, weighing 205½ pounds, from Philadelphia, the heavyweight champion of the world, Joe Frazier." The Frazier fans chanted, "Fray-zer, Frayzer."

Mostly because of Ali's 43–month layoff, Frazier was the 7-5 betting favorite. It would be the 17th heavyweight championship in a Madison Square Garden (This was the fourth Garden.)

The fight would be judged by Artie Aidala and Bill Recht. The referee was the veteran Arthur Mercante, a public relations man for a beer company. He was paid $750 and said later he would have been happy to work this fight for nothing. "I knew I was taking part in a historical event," he said. "Afterward I didn't go to any post-fight parties. I was at my desk at 8 o'clock the next morning as usual."

The bell clanged several times and Mercante called the fighters to the center of the ring for their final instructions. Ali shook his head back and forth, teasing, "Look out, niggah, I'm gonna kill ya." Frazier said later that he couldn't hear the referee's words because of Ali's jabbering. He glared at his opponent, the anger festering inside him. Back in his corner, his manager, Yank Durham said, "Get on his ass. Work him 'til he don't want no more."

* * * * *

Joe Frazier was born January 12, 1944, the 11th child of Rubin and Dolly Frazier in Beaufort, South Carolina. He said, "I was poor but happy." His father was a sharecropper who had lost one arm in a shooting over a woman. Joe was raised in Philadelphia, left school at twelve, worked in the New York garment center, then went back to Philadelphia to work as a butcher's apprentice in a slaughterhouse where he punched sides of beef (the inspiration for a scene in the movie *Rocky*).

He migrated to a Philadelphia Police Athletic League gym where he hooked up with manager Yank Durham. He worked hard, learned things from Durham, and developed a mighty left hook that became his trademark. He won the Golden Glove heavyweight championship in 1962, 1963 and 1964, and won the heavyweight championship gold medal at the 1964 Olympics in Tokyo.

Durham, noting that a syndicate of white businessmen had financed Ali's early career, got 270 white and black citizens from Philadelphia to form Cloverlay. Each put up $250 to provide Frazier with a bankroll of $20,000. Frazier tuned pro on Aug. 16, 1965 with a one-round knockout of Woody Goss. He won his first 11 fights by knockouts until running into the unorthodox Argentinian, Oscar Bonavena. Frazier got up from two knockdowns in the second round to win a split decision.

Before that he had scored an 11-round knockout of Buster Mathis to win the New York State heavyweight title. During Ali's absence from the ring he became the undisputed world heavyweight champion by knocking out Jimmy Ellis in the fifth round on February 16, 1970, almost a year before his showdown with Ali.

* * * * *

A roar of anticipation filled the Garden as Frazier came out quickly for round one to throw the first punch. It was a right meant for the head and it just missed, Ali bending back out of the way. Frazier's strategy was to stay in close, bobbing and weaving, to neutralize Ali's 6-3 to 5-11½ height advantage. He would concentrate on the body and then go to the head. Durham always said, "Kill the body and the head will die." At one point when Frazier landed a left hook to the jaw, Ali shook his head to tell the crowd and Frazier "it didn't hurt me." Frazier responded by sticking out his chin, inviting Ali to take a free shot. Frazier was willing to take three or four punches to land one. He even expected Ali to be sharp at the beginning and take an early lead. Dundee thought Ali came close to knocking Frazier out in the first round, yet one of the judges, Bill Recht, gave the round to Frazier. As the fight developed the officials' saw eye-to-eye on only eight of the 15 rounds.

Ali won the second round on all three cards. He peppered Frazier with jabs. Frazier continued to take the lighter punches, trying to land left-hook haymakers. He landed one hard right to the jaw, but Ali danced away, shooting jabs. At the end of the round Ali waved his hand in disdain at Frazier's corner. He mouthed across the ring, "You gonna get whupped." He stayed on his feet in his corner, playing to the crowd.

Ali's tremendous ego was on display all evening. It was as if he felt that a fight of this magnitude, with all the celebrities in the audience and all the world watching—(he always mentioned Pakistan when he named countries)—deserved more than just a fight. So he was the mad mad mad Muhammad putting on another of the circuses that had established him as the most madcap fighter of all time. He did most of the talking. A few times Mercante told him to stop talking; he would stop for awhile and then start up again.

Frazier landed more in the third round. He blocked Ali's uppercuts and continued digging into his body. He drove Ali into the ropes with body punches. Ali kept tying him up, leaning on Frazier. Toward the end of the round Frazier delivered a battery of punches to Ali's face without a return. This undoubtedly impressed the officials. For the first time Frazier won the round on all three cards. At the end of the round Mercante warned both, Ali for holding, Frazier for having too much Vaseline on his face.

Frazier's strategy was laid out by Eddie Futch, one of the most respected trainers in boxing. He would work Frazier's corner in all three fights against Ali and later was with Ken Norton for his three fights against Ali, one of which Norton won, then two defeats, one of them highly questionable. Unlike others in Frazier's camp who referred to Ali as Clay, the 59-year-old Futch, a soft-spoken kindly man, called him, "Ali." He said, "I saw flaws in Ali's style that could be exploited. When he was on the ropes he would pull his head back from punches in a way that left his body exposed. Most fighters would immediately go to the head when they fought Ali. We told Joe when Ali was on the ropes to work the body with both hands. We knew that eventually, instead of pulling back to avoid shots to the head, Ali would bring his head forward to protect his body. And it worked. Joe pounded his body all night."

The pattern developed in the fourth, Frazier scoring to the body, occasionally to the head. Near the end of the round a left hook sent a trickle of blood from Ali's nose. Frazier said, "I sent a powerful message in the fourth round when I nailed him on the jaw with a left and could see by the look on his face that it shook him. Ali said later, "Frazier had what I was vulnerable to—a good, in-close left hook. Joe stayed on me, always on my chest, and from out of nowhere he'd throw the hook. If I was young I'd have danced for fifteen rounds and Joe wouldn't ever have caught me. But I was 3½ years out of shape. He punched hard and he pressured me good." Frazier won the fourth round on all three cards.

Frazier upset his corner in the fifth round when he showboated, Ali style. He dropped his arms in the middle of the ring, inviting Ali to bop him. Ali responded with two jabs and Frazier laughed. Yank Durham scolded him. "Don't go jivin' him. He gets a rest when you do that. Keep the pressure on him." Dundee didn't like what he saw, either. He yelled at Ali, "He's conning you, go after him." At the end of the round, Ali sat down on his stool. He was in the corner to my right and I could hear him shouting to the crowd, "No contest, nooooo contest." He stopped that now.

The judges, Recht and Aidala awarded the fifth to Frazier; Mercante voted for Ali. At the end of five rounds, a third through the fight, these were the cards:

Mercante: Frazier, three rounds to two.

Aidala: in full agreement with Mercante, Frazier, three rounds to two.

Recht: also Frazier three rounds to two, but not the same ones as the other two.

Ali had made his usual fight prediction. He wanted to read his prediction in the ring just before the fight started, but the New York Boxing Commission refused to allow that. The prediction he scrawled on a piece of paper was shown to the closed-circuit audience of 300 million just before the bout started. The prediction: "Frazier falls in six."

Frazier somehow got wind of the prediction because as the bell rang for round six, he sprang out of his stool to meet Ali. He shouted, "Come on, sucker. This is the round. Let's go." He bobbed and weaved under right-hand leads Ali leveled at him. Ali never liked to fight inside; he waited for the referee to break them out of clinches. Mercante, who was praised for the work he did all night, said, "Ali was basically a clean fighter. If I said, 'clinch' he wouldn't attempt to hit on the break. He did a few things inside that were illegal, mainly pushing an opponent's head down as part of tying him up." The electricity never left the building. Dave Kindred, the respected columnist for Ali's hometown paper, the *Louisville Courier Journal,* told me , "I don't remember breathing all night."

Ali fought in flurries, retreating to the ropes. Dundee hated this. Frazier did not "fall in six." He won the round on the cards of the two judges.

The seventh round, like most of the others, was close. I found it a hard round to judge. Ali landed more punches, but Frazier's punches were more punishing. He kept bobbing and weaving, taking punches, but getting under the taller man, leveling shots at the body. Ali coasted more, staying on the ropes. At one point he held out his hand, sneering at Frazier. His supporters in the crowd couldn't help but be worried by his lack of action. He did manage to land a left hook that rocked Frazier. It was the best punch of the round, but both judges gave the round to Frazier.

In the eighth round Frazier won on all three cards for the third time. The officials were not impressed by Ali's showboating on the ropes, gesturing and mouthing insults at Frazier. At one point in the round Mercante cautioned Ali to fight. He said later, "There were some parts of the fight I couldn't understand. When Ali lay along the ropes just throwing pitty-pat punches, allowing Frazier to put it to him."

I kept recalling scenes in Dundee's Fifth Street Gym, when I saw Ali training for the first Liston fight. He would stand in a corner and allow sparring partners to bang away. Though he was wearing headgear, it was a little scary to see punch after punch land on his head as the sparring partners whaled away at him. In the later years when Parkinson's disease had made Ali a pitiful shell of his former self, I thought about those punches he needlessly took in the gym and from Frazier in their three fights.

Between rounds Dundee tried to caution Ali, urging him to keep moving. But he could see that the speed, Ali's trademark before the exile, was not there.

* * * * *

Muhammad Ali was born Jan. 17, 1942 in Louisville, Kentucky. When he was twelve, somebody stole his bicycle. In his desire for revenge, he met up with a policeman, Joe Martin, who ran a gym where the boy learned to box. He was a natural from the start and went on to win two national Golden Gloves middleweight championships and an AAU national light-heavyweight title. Soon after graduating from high school he won the light-heavyweight gold medal at the 1960 Olympics in Rome. One of the myths that grew up about him was that he was so disgusted by the racist treatment he received when he returned to the United States, he threw his gold medal off a bridge into the Ohio River. His friend and official photographer Howard Bingham revealed later that he simply had lost it.

A group of ten Louisville businessmen took him under their wing and the shrewd Angelo Dundee settled in as his trainer. Working out of Dundee's Fifth Street Gym in Miami Beach, he fought his first professional fight, Oct. 29, 1960, winning a six-round decision over Tunney Hunsaker. He showed dazzling speed and quick hands. He won his next five fights on knockouts by wearing down his opponents with a flurry of punches; he was never a one-punch knockout guy like Joe Louis or Frazier.

Nicknamed "The Louisville Lip," he was brash from the get-go and adopted the flamboyant wrestler Gorgeous George as a role model, declaring himself "The Greatest." He said, "When you are as great as I am, it's hard to be humble." One of his pet lines was, "you are not as stupid as you look." He said that to the Beatles when they came to the Fifth Street gym to help publicize the upcoming fight with Liston. I happened to be alone in the dressing room with Ali and Dundee when the Beatles were hustled in. John Lennon answered, "You aren't as stupid as you look, either." Later, Clay said the Beatles were the greatest but he was the "prettiest."

A product of the racist Louisville schools in the 1950s, Ali had trouble reading: I once saw him mouthing with some effort the words of an article he was reading. But he was a keen observer and reader of people. He had street smarts. I recall a boxing dinner at which Ali was one of the fighters honored, all of them seated at the dais. Ali noted that the faces of the people who did the fighting were all black and that the faces of the promoters and the managers in the room were all white.

* * * * *

Just when it looked as if Frazier had taken charge of the fight, Ali rallied in the ninth round. He raked Frazier repeatedly with right hands. Frazier bled from the mouth and his face was beginning to lump up. All of a sudden he was looking like a tired fighter. Ali supporters in the crowd chanted anew, "Ah-lee, Ah-lee." Still, Frazier took no backward steps; he bobbed and weaved and tried to keep up the pressure on the opponent who had mocked him for so long. For only the second time Ali won the round on all three officials' cards.

Though each had their moments, Ali had another one of his better rounds in the 10th. At one point he actually shouted, "He's out." Dundee said later that he was beginning to feel good again. There was an incident involving the referee and Frazier. In separating the fighters at one point the little finger of Mercante's right hand poked the bottom of Frazier's right-eye socket. Frazier cursed him. At the end of the round, Mercante said, "I went over to his corner to apologize. Durham bawled me out. I felt relieved that Frazier didn't seem to suffer any eye problem in the next round."

Mercante and Aidala gave Ali the 10th round. After two-thirds of the fight these were the cards:

Mercante had Ali ahead, six rounds to four.
Aidala had Frazier ahead, six rounds to four.
Recht had Frazier ahead, seven rounds to three.

In the 11th Ali grabbed through most of the round, flicking jabs and then holding onto Frazier. "Let go of me," Frazier yelled at one point. Coming out of a clinch, Frazier caught him with a booming left hook to the head, followed by a shot to the heart. Ali was sent reeling into what seemed like dream sequence. He staggered like a boat about to keel into the sea. But he didn't go down. Then, as some strength ebbed back into him, he clowned to indicate that he wasn't hurt. It seemed to me he was playing possum, as if he were putting a double-psych on Frazier. It probably fooled Frazier because he hesitated somewhat in coming after Ali again.

Futch said later that "Joe should have knocked him out in the 11th. Ali conned him out of it. We teased Joe about that later because he didn't realize at the time that he was being conned. Ali gave him exaggerated moves and Joe didn't press him immediately. It gave Ali extra time and kept Joe from scoring a knockout."

Frazier came off his stool for the 12th throwing punches. He whacked Ali with successive bombs to the belly and head. Frazier later likened his punches to "wrecking balls that could take down a building. The guy surprised me. He stood and traded with me. And what he was throwing wasn't pitty-pat." Some ringside wondered what was holding Ali up. When he rallied to throw a left-right combination to Frazier's head, Frazier laughed at him. Durham didn't find it funny. "In the body, in the body," he shouted.

I think officials tend to even things out in their cards in the later rounds if they think their round-to-round scoring wasn't matching their overall sense of the action. Mercante, who had Ali ahead, 6-5 going into the 12, called the round even, while both judges lengthened their lead for Frazier, giving him the round.

Ali got up on his toes and started dancing again in the 13th. "The butterfly got his wings again," Frazier said afterward. Ali danced and shot jabs at Frazier and then lay on him until Mercante broke them up. In his corner Bundini screamed himself hoarse with "You got God in your corner, champ." Mercante and Recht voted for Frazier, Aidala for Ali.

Before the 14th and next-to-last round, Durham took a leaf out of Dundee's book when he lied to Frazier about the round. When Frazier asked what round it was, he said "three to go." Dundee was busy trying to rally his man. "Dance, goddamit," he shouted. "You're blowing the fight." Ali responded, with jabs and a series of left-right combinations to the head. When he rested by laying on Frazier, Joe shook him off, looking for a chance to land a knockout punch. Some of his punches whistled by Ali's head.

Both judges gave the round to Ali, Mercante awarded it to Frazier. Going into the last round, Ali couldn't win on either judge's card unless he scored a knockout. He could get only a draw from Mercante if he won the 15th.

The crowd roared with the clanging of the bell for the 15th round. It would be a cliché to say everybody was up on his/her seat, yet there couldn't have been many outside the press row who did not get up. When the fighters came out, Mercante had to take their hands and force them to touch gloves, one of the rituals of the sport. Less than a minute into the ring as Ali maneuvered to find an opening, Frazier threw a left hook that caught Ali on his right forearm. As Ali stepped forward, Frazier dipped down and threw a tremendous left hook, leaving his feet to launch the punch. It landed against the right side of Ali's face and knocked him flat on his back. Ali fell, his body stretched like a stiff on a slab, his feet pointing to the ceiling. He rolled onto his left elbow, got up at the count of three and stood in the corner, pained and perplexed—as if this couldn't have happened to him—until it was time to fight again.

At this point Ali, who had walked the ghettos to become one of the foremost black heroes in America, was walking on the most famous thoroughfare in boxing: Queer Street. He came back and held Frazier off for the entire round. He reeled and held on, and absorbed a few more of the roundhouse hooks that Frazier aimed at him all night. His capacity to take those punches illustrated the kind of courage that many cynical boxing people said he lacked.

Ferdie Pacheco, his doctor friend, said, "It looked like he was out cold. I didn't think he could possibly get up. But he got up almost as fast as he went down. That night he was the most courageous fighter I'd ever seen. He was going to get up if he was dead." Mercante said, "That round showed me Muhammad Ali was the most valiant fighter I'd ever seen. Frazier hit him as hard as a man can be hit. He was up in three seconds. I motioned Frazier to a neutral corner and when I turned to face Ali, he was already on his feet. I didn't have time to pick up the count."

These were the judges' cards at the end of fifteen rounds:

Mercante: Frazier eight rounds, Ali six, one even.
Aidala: Frazier nine rounds, Ali six.
Recht: Frazier 11 rounds, Ali four.

I had Ali the winner 10 rounds to five, but wrote that if I were an official judge of the fight I would have voted for Frazier.

How could that be? I would have erased some of the marginal rounds I awarded to Ali and given them to Frazier to make sure I turned in a card for Frazier. I would have done this because I felt that though Ali won more rounds, Frazier won the two most meaningful rounds by such big, impressive margins that I thought Frazier deserved the victory. In his excellent post-fight report my colleague Bob Waters said he preferred the "Brooklyn method" of scoring where you choose the man who "beat up" the other guy. I agreed.

Neither fighter heard the final bell. Mercante had to step in and grab both of them. Ali had said he would crawl across the ring and kiss Frazier's feet if he lost. He didn't. He patted Frazier on his shoulder. Frazier raised his hands in victory and told Ali, "I kicked your ass." He said afterward, "I was 27 years old and there would never be another night like it in my life." The front page of the *Philadelphia Daily News* the next day headlined: "Joe's The Greatest" with a photo of Ali lying on his back and Frazier turning to go to the neutral corner.

The closed-circuit telecast of the bout replayed the knockdown punch fifteen times. The fighters suffered considerable damage. Both of their faces were misshapen afterward. Ali's face no longer was round. Frazier's was all lumped up. He was in a lot of pain. He said at one point, "Can't somebody do something about this? It hurts." At the press conference Frazier answered questions through puffed lips while one of his handlers held an ice pack to his face. When he was asked what he would like from Ali now, he said, "I want Clay to come to me and apologize for all the rotten things he said about me." And with the plaintive plea of a man asking for the recognition finally due him as the undisputed heavyweight champion, he said, "I can read, you know. What are you going to say now?" After a few days, he was in such bad shape that he was admitted into a hospital in Philadelphia.

After the fight Ali was taken to Flower Fifth Ave. hospital. The right side of his jaw was puffed up, though the x-rays were negative. Pacheco wanted him to be kept overnight for observation.

Ali said no, he didn't want anyone to say Frazier had put him in the hospital. He did not show up to face the press he had once taunted to tell him he was "the greatest." In the dressing room Diana Ross, the singer, put an ice bag to his face. She said, "It's okay, champ." The man who for once did not float like a butterfly and sting like a bee, said, "I ain't the champ no mo'."

* * * * *

They fought two more times. Ali won both. He won a 12-round decision at the Garden, January 28, 1974 that was, by Ali-Frazier standards, unmemorable. Then came the tumultuous "Thrilla in Manila" on October 1, 1975 when both men showed remarkable courage until Eddie Futch wouldn't let the badly beaten Frazier off the stool for the 14th round. After that fight Ali said, "That fight was as close to dying as I've ever come."

#3

The Jets Upset the Colts

This was the lead paragraph in my "Out of Left Field" column about Super Bowl III:

Youth is mighty and shall prevail.

And Joe Namath, the outrageous kid of the moment, pulled off one of the most cocky and daring personal triumphs of this sporting time. He flew in the face of all the sober values and then led the New York Jets to a 16-7 victory over the Baltimore Colts yesterday. He did it in the premier sports showcase of the 1960s—the Super Bowl. Call him Super Joe . . .

A 25-year-old brash, strong-armed quarterback who guaranteed victory and pulled it off. A roly-poly, cuddly, 61-year-old gent who stands as the winning coach of what arguably could be regarded as the two most significant games in pro football history. Joe Namath and Weeb Ewbank, an unlikely pair, achieved the upset that shocked the sports world.

Namath led the 18-point underdog Jets over the Colts in Super Bowl III on January 12, 1969 at the Orange Bowl in Miami. Jets coach Ewbank, who nobody ever called a genius, had coached the Baltimore Colts team that had beaten the New York Giants, 23-17, in the sudden death 1958 National Football League championship game that was called, "The Greatest Game Ever Played." (Ewbank called it, "The Great Bowl.")

Namath thrust himself into the role of central character of Super Bowl III when he responded to a heckler at a Miami Touchdown Club dinner three nights before the game. With a double scotch in his hand, he said, "We're going to win Sunday, I guarantee you." At that time no athlete was so bold as to make such a public declaration. It later became a routine thing for athletes to make that guarantee, such a cliché that people didn't really respond whether the boast came through or not. But such was the tenor of the times in 1969 and the awe for the Colts so great that he risked public mockery if he didn't back up his words.

He had himself an eventful week. And because he and the Jets won the game, he emerged as colorful Broadway Joe, a non-conformist, a rogue, a ladies man about town who people almost believed could walk out on the field with a bottle of gin in one hand while throwing a pigskin around with his other. His swinging bachelor persona, his anti-establishment shaggy hair, moustache, white shoes and endorsement of panty hose made him a symbol of the social change in the country. Though he had no particular political beliefs, some mistakenly made him a symbol of the political upheaval in the country. He was, though, color blind; he would make it a point to hang out with blacks as well as whites on the team.

One night he ran into the Colts' Lou Michaels at a bar in Miami. One thing led to another, there were needling words and it got so heated that Michaels at one point threatened to take Namath outside. The Namath charm prevailed and before long they were buddy-buddy. When the evening was over Namath put down a hundred-dollar bill to pay for the whole tab.

Not only did Namath guarantee a victory, he had the gall to demean the Colts. He said there were five quarterbacks in the American Football League who were better than the Colts' Earl Morrall. He dared say the Colt defensive line was of dubious quality. These were the Colts who were called by some analysts "the best team ever." They had a 13-1 record. They scored 402 points while yielding only 144, and eleven of their 13 victories could be described as routs. They avenged their only loss, to Cleveland, by crushing the Browns, 34-0, in the NFL championship game. When Johnny Unitas was injured, Earl Morrall stepped in at quarterback and earned the league's Most Valuable Player award. Left end Bubba Smith, 6-7, 285 pounds, loomed almost like a mythical giant and Billy Ray Smith, Fred Miller and Ordell Braase completed a vaunted defensive line.

Defenders of the old league were shocked at the nerve of this kid, this beatnik. Former NFL star and coach Norm Van Brocklin was typical. He said before the game, "This will be Namath's first professional football game." The Jets were coming into the game as the champion of a league that had yet to prove it belonged in the company of the old league. After the merger of the AFL with the NFL and the creation of the Super Bowl (not officially carrying that name until Super Bowl III) the NFL's Green Bay Packers had beaten the AFL's Kansas City Chiefs, 35-10 and the Oakland Raiders, 33-14.

I never pretended to be the keenest analyst on the block but it occurred to me that Namath's talk was in the tradition of Green

Bay coach Vince Lombardi, the most exalted figure in proper football circles. "Lombardi's approach to football was to run at the opponent's strength," I wrote. "He would take the battle to the enemy's stronger battlements on the theory that if you weakened that, you weakened the whole team. So Namath has knocked the Colt defensive line, the pride of Baltimore and all NFL outposts. It's a far more interesting tack than trying to justify the AFL's right to play on the same field with the NFL." I joked that the Jets were "the most overconfident 18-point underdogs in football history."

At least one key Baltimore figure, coach Don Shula, took Namath's baiting in stride. He said, "Any time you have a colorful personality like Namath, you create interest. We've had a little fun with the affair that was reported between Joe and Lou Michaels. If it's true that Lou threatened Namath, then Joe is the 827th guy Michaels has threatened to deck." And Shula agreed with Namath's comment that if the Colts needed to put newspaper clips of his remarks on the wall to get them up for this game, they were in bad shape. "We're adults," Shula said. "The players know the magnitude of this game."

Shula, 39, an Ohioan like Ewbank, had succeeded Weeb as head coach of the Colts in 1963. He was the youngest coach in the league at the time. He would leave Baltimore at the end of the 1969 season and go on to coach the Miami Dolphins, the team he'd lead to two Super Bowl victories and to the NFL's only perfect season, 14-0, in 1972.

Namath was born on May 31, 1943, the fifth child of a Hungarian steelmaker, in Beaver Falls, Pennsylvania, a steel mill town located 28 miles northwest of Pittsburgh. He excelled in football and basketball. He reportedly received offers from major league baseball teams, too. He opted to play football at the University of Maryland but was rejected because his college-board scores were below the school's requirements. Alabama had more suitable academic requirements.

At Alabama Namath played under the famed Bear Bryant from 1962 through 1964. A year after being suspended the last two games of the 1963 season for breaking curfew, he led the Crimson Tide to a national championship. Alabama went 29-4 with Namath at quarterback, and Bryant called him "the greatest athlete I ever coached."

Namath was selected by the St. Louis Cardinals 12th overall in the NFL draft; the Jets selected him with the AFL's first pick. Jets owner Sonny Werblin scored a publicity coup by awarding Namath a stunning three-year $427,000 contract and a Lincoln Continental. Werblin lauded him as a personality over and above football. "Namath has the presence of a star," he said. His signing was one of the major factors triggering a recruiting war between the two leagues.

In college Namath suffered a serious injury to his right knee that would plague him throughout his pro career. As a visitor to the Jets dressing room before games, I was awed at the careful time-consuming procedure of a Jets trainer encasing Namath in what was described as "Lenox Hill hospital derotation knee braces." He became the AFL Rookie of the Year in 1965 and in 1967 the first professional quarterback to pass for 4,000 yards in one season.

The Jets advanced to the Super Bowl out of a 1968 AFL championship game in which Namath threw three touchdown passes to overcome a 23-20 fourth quarter deficit and beat the defending champion Oakland Raiders, 27-23. These were the same Raiders to whom the Jets had lost six weeks earlier in what came to be known as the notorious "Heidi" game. The Raiders trailed, 32-29 with 65 seconds remaining when NBC goofed by switching most of the country to the children's classic. TV viewers missed a 43-yard touchdown pass from Daryle Lamonica and a two-yard fumble return on the ensuing kickoff for a 43-32 Oakland victory.

Despite all the publicity heaped on Namath as "the $400,000 quarterback," Weeb Ewbank brought him along slowly. When I went down to Houston for the Jets' opener I was stunned that Ewbank started journeyman quarterback Mike Taliaferro over the celebrated rookie, Namath. He didn't make Namath his starting quarterback until close to mid-season. Namath gave Ewbank fits during his early years. While Sonny Werblin was encouraging Namath to be seen around town, Joe was missing bed checks at training camp and being fined.

Ewbank was born, May 6, 1907 in Richmond, Indiana. He played football at Miami University of Ohio behind Paul Brown, who would become a legendary coach with his Cleveland Browns. He coached in high school, served as a coach at the Naval Station Great Lakes during World War II; coached at Washington University of St. Louis; and coached the Baltimore Colts from 1954 to 1962.

Though his Colts won "The Greatest Game Ever Played" in 1958, repeated as NFL champions in 1959, Baltimore owner Carroll Rosenbloom fired him after the 1962 season. When Werblin bought the New York Titans franchise in 1963, he changed both the team's name to the Jets and its coach. Ewbank took over a team that had not had a winning record in its three years and made them into a force to be reckoned with.

Ewbank was a likeable, unassuming man, almost cuddly. Nobody regarded him as anything more than a good football coach, a good organizer, a man who paid attention to detail. He came across as quite human, a relief from some of the so-called genius coaches of NFL lore. His players made jokes about him. Once, he asked Don Maynard, the outstanding end, not to tell teammates about his new contract. "Don't worry," Maynard replied, "I'm just as embarrassed as you are."

I loved his name; it inspired me to offer this eminently forgettable ditty:

It has me puzzled
I must be frank;
Ought Weeb Ewbank's name
Be Ewb Weebank?

Ewbank delighted the assembled press on the Wednesday before the game when he told us how he might get his boys ready in their locker room before a game. He said, "Sometimes I even tell them dirty jokes."

Dirty jokes?

"Sure, I even heard a good one the other day."

To a man the assembled press said, "Tell it, tell it."

Ewbank frowned."Well, I don't tell jokes really well."

"Tell it, tell it."

Just as he got set to tell it—"I know I'll mess it up," he said—he interrupted himself when he saw a waitress who was working the press eating room. "Madam, would you mind leaving the room for a few minutes," he said. The waitress tittered, and left . . . reluctantly.

Ewbank told the joke. It wasn't particularly funny, though too blue for family newspapers, and it faded from memory a long time ago. But it was right for the moment. It drew a big laugh because Ewbank had warmed up his audience; almost anything he said would have drawn a big laugh—and affection. It seemed right for Ewbank, so human, to be enjoying himself in the midst of pre-game Super Bowl excess. He would be voted into the Pro Football Hall of Fame in 1978.

It was of note that there was a Jet who had played under Ewbank in that 1958 "Greatest Game." He was the colorful cornerback, Johnny Sample, whose mouth was bigger than his talent. He was a dirty player, age 31, in his 11th season, an intimidator who got away with illegal hits. He had been eaten up by Oakland's Fred Biletnikoff in the AFL championship game. He was considered a weak link in the Jets defense whom the Colts might exploit.

Five years earlier in the same city, Cassius (soon to become Muhammad Ali) Clay shocked the sports world by overcoming much ridicule for his boasting before he knocked out Sonny Liston to win the world heavyweight championship. Having covered that fight and being exposed to the derision directed at the Jets before this game, I couldn't help but wonder about the irony of another upset here.

It inspired me to write a piece of whimsy, waking up the echoes of one of the classic upsets of all time: David over Goliath. I wrote that I had come into the possession of an undiscovered transcript of the post-battle press conference with the victorious David. I played the Bible off the football press conference talk of the moment.

Some excerpts:

Scribe: Congratulations, David.

David: Thank you. But I'd like to point out that I couldn't have done it without the help of all the Israelites. It was a team victory.

Scribe: When did you first think you had it won?

David: When I had Goliath down on the ground, pulled the sword out of its sheath and cut off his head.

Scribe: What went on in your mind while you were doing it?

David: When the Philistine arose and drew near to me, I figured the best defense was a good offense. So I ran to meet him. The old element of surprise you know.

Scribe: Goliath was six cubits and a span. [Ed note: nine feet, eight inches] Were you very nervous looking up at him?

David: I was all right once the battle started. I've always been a cocky little guy. Let's face it, some people say I'm too cocky. They don't like my popping off about how good I am and what I am going to do to my opponent.

Scribe: What happens now, David?

David: They say that King Saul will reward the man who kills Goliath, that he will give great riches and will give him his daughter and make his father's house free in Israel. I also have a lot of offers to speak at banquets and there are some slingshot firms that want me to endorse their products . . .

I was pleased to read in an account in *The New York Times* after the game a comment by a psychiatrist, Dr. Arthur Wachtel of Scarsdale. He said, "The common man always identifies with David."

The Super Bowl was being played in Miami's Orange Bowl, the same arena for the second successive year, something that would never occur again. The weather came up a mild and breezy 73 degrees, overcast with the threat of rain that never developed. A crowd of 75,389 was on hand for a game that would be watched by an estimated 60 million viewers of the NBC telecast. Curt Gowdy, Al DeRogatis and Kyle Rote worked the game out of the press box, complemented by Jim Simpson and Pat Summerall for interviews and sideline reports.

When the Jets came onto the field to warm up, Namath did not come out with them. A few moments later he came out by himself, the only one wearing a helmet. The delay probably stemmed from all the time he needed to have his brace adjusted, but the effect was that of a great entrance befitting a prima donna; this was just the kind of thing Sonny Werblin envisioned for Namath when he signed him and projected him as a star of stars.

When Namath started warming up, he stationed himself on the five-yard line and lofted passes. He pantomimed taking a snap from an imaginary center and with graceful ease, threw long, high spirals that floated down past midfield to the 40-yard line, 55 yards away. Those passes supposedly were the get-rich-quick bombs that critics argued made up the only potent weapons in the Jets arsenal.

After Anita Bryant warbled the Star Spangled Banner, referee Tom Bell conducted the coin toss. The Jets won the toss and chose to receive. Lou Michaels kicked two yards into the end zone and Earl Christy returned the ball to the Jets 23. Super Bowl III was under way.

Matt Snell ran off tackle for three yards on the first of his 30 carries. He then picked up a first down, gaining nine yards again off tackle. Emerson Boozer lost four yards trying to run around right end and then Namath completed his first pass, good for nine yards to George Sauer. The drive stalled when Snell was stopped for a two-yard loss trying to run up the middle, brought down by right tackle Fred Miller. After a five-yard penalty against Baltimore, Curly Johnson punted and Tim Brown returned the ball nine yards to the Baltimore 27.

The Colts started off well. Earl Morrall completed a 19-yard pass to tight end John Mackey. Tom Matte swept 10 yards around right end for a first down at the Jets 44 before being tackled by linebacker Ralph Baker. Jets defensive coach Walt Michaels, the brother of Colts kicker Lou, had said about Baker, "He is not the most outstanding linebacker, but he gets the job done." Baker did not contest that. He told me before the game, "I would be satisfied to play well, not make any mistakes, and help us win."

Runs by Jerry Hill and Matte picked up another first down to the Jets 31. Despite a 15-yard Morrall-Tom Mitchell completion, the first Colts drive stalled at the Jets 19 yard line. Willie Richardson dropped a pass, Morrall overthrew Mitchell, then was stopped for no gain trying to evade the Jets' pass rush. Don Shula sent out Michaels to kick a field goal. His try from the 27-yard line skittered wide right.

A team favored by 18 points is not supposed to miss such opportunities. Reporters are supposed to be non-partisan, but that is often a fiction. The writers who had covered the established NFL teams were in the forefront of those ridiculing the Jets before the game. As the action developed and the Jets momentum continued, there was more than a little gloating by AFL types and underdog rooters. Larry Fox, who had covered the AFL from its inception, wrote, "I had never seen a press section so polarized."

The Colts went into the game determined to stop Namath. Baltimore coach Don Shula said, "The Jets must be respected because they "can strike long to get the easy touchdown." In the next sequence the Jets' offense consisted of nothing but Namath passes. He threw six. One was a 13-yard completion to Bill Mathis for a first down to the Jets 35, another went to George Sauer for six yards. Three of the others were incomplete, but one of them had impact anyway. From the Jets 35, Namath threw one of his celebrated bombs downfield to Don Maynard, the adept, stringbean flanker. The ball sailed beyond him, sure evidence of Namath's celebrated ability to throw long. Maynard, hampered somewhat by a pulled hamstring, did not catch a pass the entire game, but he kept the Colts defense wary. Namath said later that this helped keep Sauer open for short passes. Sauer caught eight for 133 yards. These combined with Snell's running enabled the Jets to control the game.

The Colts didn't make a first down on their next sequence. Neither did the Jets, but the first big break of the game went to the Colts. Sauer caught a three-yard sideline pass, was tackled by Leonard Lyles and fumbled. Linebacker Ron Porter recovered for the Colts on the Jets 12, possibly missing a chance to run the ball into the end zone. On the last play of the scoreless first quarter, Jets left end Gerry Philbin stopped Jerry Hill for a one-yard loss.

Tom Matte then opened the second quarter with a seven-yard sweep to put the ball on the Jets 6. The first key play of the game ensued. Morrall fired a quick, hard pass toward substitute end Tom Mitchell. Jets linebacker Al Atkinson got a fingernail on it, altering the trajectory. The ball bounced off Mitchell's shoulder pad high into the air where it was snatched by Jets cornerback Randy Beverly, who had been outmaneuvered by Mitchell.

Shula's comment that the Jets had to be respected because they could strike long reflected the feeling by many NFL people that the Jets' only chance was to score on big plays, while the Colts, a superior team, could grind out touchdowns. The Jets ground this piece of reasoning to dust in their next offensive sequence after Beverly's interception. Starting on their own 20, they moved 80 yards in 12 plays, a five-minute drive whose longest play measured no longer than 14 yards.

Namath beat the Baltimore blitz by unloading the ball quickly to George Sauer before the defenders could reach him. Ewbank had told his receivers, "Find the dead spots in the zone, hook up and Joe will hit you." Namath foiled the Colts' feared blitz by checking off under pressure to Snell or Emerson Boozer.

The drive started with four successive running plays by Snell aimed at the Colts' right side. End Ordell Braase and linebacker Don Shinnick were victimized for a total of 26 yards. Namath, whose long dark hair stuck out from the back of his white helmet, his neck jutting out from the front of his No. 12 jersey like an egret, ambled to the line of scrimmage in his distinctive round-shouldered way. From the Jets 46, he threw incomplete to George Sauer, then six yards to Bill Mathis. On third down, Namath hit Sauer with the biggest gain of the drive, a 14-yard completion, and came right back with an 11-yarder to Sauer to move to the Colt 23. He alternated a two-yard run by Boozer with a 12-yard pass to Snell and a five-yard burst off right tackle by Snell to the four-yard line. Snell then swept off left tackle for a touchdown. Jim Turner's kick gave the Jets a 7-0 lead.

Two sequences followed in which each team was able to move the ball, then fall short. Both tried field goals that failed. After a 30-yard pass by Morrall to Tom Matte penetrated Jet territory, Michaels missed a 46-yard attempt. A 35-yard Namath-Sauer pass moved the Jets into field goal territory setting up a 41-yard try by Turner. It failed. Ewbank was a wreck on the sideline. He chewed ice cubes and spit out pieces.

Jets cornerback Johnny Sample inserted himself into the game as an ogre for the Colts, a sweetheart for the Jets. On the next Colt drive Tom Matte ran 58-yards around right end before he was tackled by safety Bill Baird. Sample, trailing the play, "accidentally on purpose" stepped on Tom Matte while he was on the ground. The infuriated Colt back charged at Sample and his facemask accidentally knocked out one of the official's teeth. No penalty was charged to Sample—or Matte.

One play later, from the Jet 15, Morrall threw to wide receiver Willie Richardson who appeared to be open at the goal line. Sample cut over, however, and intercepted the pass at the two-yard line. Another missed opportunity for the Colts.

Morrall's worst mistake followed soon after that on the last play of the first half. At the Jet 41, Matte took a handoff from Morrall, seemingly ran harmlessly to his right, then threw a lateral pass back to Morrall. A flea-flicker gambit. Split end Jimmy Orr got behind Randy Beverly and was twenty yards clear of any Jet in the left side of the end zone. Morrall said later that he never saw Orr. He threw instead toward fullback Jerry Hill, who was in front of the goal post. Safety Jim Hudson spotted him and picked off the pass at the 12.

As the Florida A&M band performed at the half, we looked at the half-time statistics passed out in the press sections. The Colts out-rushed the Jets, 91 to 72. The Jets led in passing yardage, 103 to 71. The Jets had escaped damage from a fumble, while the Colts were victimized by three interceptions. I had a seat in the auxiliary press rows below the main press box. The buzz was that this would be a close game after all.

The third quarter belonged to the Jets. At the start, Baltimore returned the kickoff to its 25. On the first play from scrimmage, Matte gained eight yards only to have the ball stripped from him by Ralph Baker. The Jets took over on the Colt 33. Eight plays that consisted of five runs, one pass completion, one incompletion and a 9-yard sack of Namath by Bubba Smith gained only eight yards. That set up Jim Turner for a 32-yard field goal and the Jets increased their lead to 10-0.

The Colts then went three-and-out after starting from their 26. On the first play tight end John Mackey broke clear of defenders but Morrall overthrew him. The Jets took over on their 32. Namath completed three passes and missed three throws to Maynard. They went 45 yards in 10 plays to the Colt 23-yard line. Colts tackle Fred Miller threw a scare into the Jets when he crashed into Namath on the drive. Namath suffered an injury to his thumb on his throwing hand and 38-year-old reserve quarterback Babe Parilli tried a third-down pass which fell incomplete before Turner kicked a 30-yard field goal for a 13-0 lead.

The Jets offensive line, Winston Hill, Bob Talamini, center John Schmitt, Randy Rasmussen and Dave Herman provided Namath with outstanding protection, holding off the line anchored by 6-foot-7 Bubba Smith, considered the NFL's best pass rusher.

With four minutes remaining in the third quarter, Baltimore coach Don Shula replaced Morrall with the legendary Johnny Unitas. The Baltimore fans in the Orange Bowl had visions of more heroics by the 35-year-old Johnny U, the hero of the sudden-death drive that won "The Greatest Game Ever Played" in 1958. Bothered by the sore shoulder that kept him out most of the season, he misfired on two passes to Matte and Jimmy Orr. The Colts had to punt. The Jets controlled the ball for all of three minutes in the third quarter. The Colts were limited to only eight plays, including two punts.

The Jets were in the midst of a scoring drive as the third quarter ended. Their longest gain of the day, a 39-yard pass from Namath to Sauer put them on the Colt 10-yard line. The drive sputtered here and Turner came on for a chip-shot nine-yard field goal. They led, 16-0. On one play when Colt safety Rick Volk tackled Snell for no gain, the impact was so great, Volk limped off the field and spent the night in the hospital.

The Colts put on a mild threat in their next possession. Five-yard completions by Unitas to Mackey and Richardson along with runs of seven and 19 yards by Matte and 12 more by Jerry Hill moved the ball to the Jets 25. Unitas then overthrew a pass to Richardson and was victimized when Beverly outwrestled Jimmy Orr in the end zone for his second interception of the game.

The Jets played ball control after that, draining the clock. They tried seven straight running plays, setting up a 42-yard field goal attempt by Jim Turner. It missed.

The Colts made late bids to pull the game out. With a little more than six minutes remaining, they drove for a touchdown. It started with three incomplete passes before Unitas connected on a 17-yard pass to Orr. After two more incompletions he hit Mackey for 11 yards; Richardson, 21 yards; and Orr 11 yards. Two offsides penalties against the Jets helped set up a one-yard buck by Jerry Hill for a touchdown. The Colts trailed by nine points with three minutes and 19 seconds remaining.

The momentum continued to shift for a time. A Colts onside kick succeeded when Tom Mitchell recovered Lou Michaels' bouncing boot on the Jets 44. Unitas completed a 14-yard pass to Orr and then a five-yarder to Richardson. But he failed on three more passes. The ever-taunting Sample broke up a pass to Richardson and the tender-armed Unitas underthrew Orr twice.

The Jets ate up more than two minutes on their final drive, again not throwing a pass. The game ended on two desperate passes by Unitas, the last a 15-yard completion to Richardson, who was tackled on the Colts 49-yard line by Sample.

Jets 16, Colts 7. The victory meant $15,000 for each Jet player. It also meant the coming of age of the American Football League. It would no longer be sneered at as a "Mickey Mouse" League.

Namath was voted the game's most valuable player. He directed the team with poise and confidence. Don Shula said, "He beat our blitz three or four times and we beat him only once. He was all we heard, a fine football player." Billy Ray Smith, the veteran defensive tackle, said, "He did it all. He threw the ball short a little. He threw the ball long a little. He ran the ball a little. I just couldn't quite get to him."

Namath turned out to be the only one of 22 MVP Super Bowl quarterbacks who didn't throw a touchdown pass. Dave Anderson wrote in *The New York Times* that Snell, who carried a big load with 30 carries for 121 yards and four pass receptions for 40 yards, "appeared to be equally deserving" of MVP honors.

Jets defensive coach Walt Michaels credited "great play by our safeties. And I can't say enough about our linebackers. We sacrificed by letting the linebackers help out against passes. We didn't think their runners could go all the way."

Statistics on the game were deceiving. The Colts had a 143-142 yards edge in rushing, the Jets passed for 195 yards to the Colts' 181. Each lost one fumble. Namath completed 17 of 28 passes for 206 yards and was sacked twice. Morrall had just six completions for 71 yards, Unitas finished with 11 completions for 110 yards. Neither was sacked but the four Jet interceptions were crucial.

The line score:

New York Jets	0	7	6	3 =16
Baltimore Colts	0	0	0	7 = 7

At the finish Namath ran off the field with a forefinger pointed in the air, the signature TV image of the game. Snell said, "Leaving the field, I saw the Colts were exhausted and in a state of shock. I don't remember any Colt coming over to congratulate me."

Afterward Namath stood up on a bench in the locker room to say his piece. As he looked over his audience, he conjured up the image of another outrageous fellow who shook the sports world in a similar way in the same city five years earlier. At that time, after Cassius Clay, an 8-1 underdog, whipped Sonny Liston, Clay taunted a press corps that had pilloried him for boastfulness. "All right," Clay shouted, "who's the greatest?" Grown men who knew this was a kid they would have to deal with as the heavyweight champion mouthed back the words, "You're the greatest."

Namath was more subdued than Clay. But he did not choose to be a phony and come on with what he called "the humble bit." He said he never regretted saying all those audacious things about how the Jets would beat the Colts. He said, "I always have confidence. . . . A guy who doesn't have confidence just doesn't come from a good family." He said he was sorry only about saying Earl Morrall was not one of the better quarterbacks in the league. Quarterbacks generally respect each other.

A poignant image for me after the game was seeing Pat Summerall, longtime NFL player and announcer, in tears while trying to go about his work of interviewing players. Johnny Unitas was unemotional about it all. "Yeah, I felt sorry for him," he said of Morrall, "but that's the nature of the game. He'll bounce back."

Sample, who was so overwrought going into the game that he threw up blood, luxuriated in victory. He gloated, he made jokes at the NFL's expense. He said, "The NFL will catch up with us in two years." His comments infuriated people and inspired such reactions as this from an NFL partisan:

The worst part of the Colts' shocking downfall that humiliated the entire NFL was the aftermath in which the Jets proved such ungracious, bad-mouthing winners. It could not have been often that members of a supposedly big-time organization in a major sport had shown themselves to be blatantly and viciously unsportsmanlike in downgrading their beaten opponents in a close championship match that was in doubt almost to the last moment. The mean [mouthed Jets] have upset two institutions at once—the NFL's cherished prestige and the sports tradition in all fields that it is the worst possible bad manner to crow and jeer loutishly at those you have beaten.

There was no reference in that to the ridicule the 18-point underdog Jets had been subjected to *before* the game.

Namath's Super Bowl experience, the boasting, the backing up of the boasting—the winning—combined with his air of devil-may-care insouciance about him made him a superstar. He nurtured a playboy image, talking about ladies, attracting groupies, even providing a prostitute for his buddies at one party. He was photographed more often than he liked with a drink in his hand.

I had met Namath one day in his rookie season after a workout at Hofstra. He struck me as a wise guy, a likeable wise guy, with an accent—Alabama drawl overriding milltown Pennsylvania slurring—that I found irritating when he became a TV analyst. He was not Intelligence Quotient smart—a pro scout once measured him for a score of 104 on an IQ test—but he was quarterback smart. He could spot defenses, beat blitzes with his famed quick-release passes. I think what made him was that he, like two other non-introspective stars—quarterback Joe Montana and baseball great Joe DiMaggio—had singleness of purpose on the playing field.

He played with the Jets from 1965 through 1976, his skills fading through the years. He retired after an undistinguished single season with the Los Angeles Rams in 1977. He did TV commercials. He settled into a minor career as an actor. On television he did charity work, he traded on his celebrity status to appear as a guest and to host his own TV shows. He was out of his element as an analyst on Sunday afternoon and Monday Night Football.

The Playboy of the Western World drank too much and his alcoholism became evident on an ESPN game telecast in 2003 when he drunkenly told interviewer Suzy Kolber, "I want to kiss you." He entered an outpatient alcoholism program shortly after.

Namath was voted into the Pro Football Hall of Fame in 1985. He had a mediocre 50 percent career completion percentage and threw almost fifty more interceptions than touchdowns. But he had that magic day on Jan. 12, 1969 when he acquired legendary status as the symbol of American Football League's legitimacy. He made good with the guarantee that the Jets would win the Super Bowl, and in doing so he shocked the sports world.

#2

"The Shot Heard 'Round the World"

I am in the Polo Grounds, the fabled, much-beloved, much-maligned Polo Grounds. It is October 3, 1951, an overcast day for the epic third and deciding game of the National League playoffs between the New York Giants and the Brooklyn Dodgers.

My assignment as a 22-year-old reporter for the *New York Daily Compass* is to cover the Giants clubhouse after the game. Usually, in such a situation, a reporter will make his way out of the old press box extended from the second deck behind home plate at the Polo Grounds in the top of the ninth inning; he will inch toward the clubhouse area in distant centerfield to be ready to enter the locker room complex when it is opened to the press a few moments after the end of the game. But I am at this time a fan as much as I am a reporter. I am a Giant fan, a long-suffering one. The Giants hadn't won a pennant in 14 years and I had only a faint remembrance as an eight-year-old of the last time they won the National League pennant in 1937.

I want to see this game to the bitter end, hoping against hope, but with too much awareness of the Giants' failings of the past decade to think the Giants would actually perform any heroics. I leave the press box with the Dodgers ahead, 4-1, going down in 1-2-3 order to Larry Jansen in the top of the ninth. I walk from the press box along the front row of the upper first base stands and descend an aisle to a ramp in right field. This was the runway fans walked, moving out of the shadows into the light where they would get their first view of the old, oval-shaped ballpark's lush greensward.

I stop at a point where I can see the field in the gap between the upper and lower stands in right field. For some two decades it would have been a good spot to view, from the rear, my hero, Mel Ott, in his position in right field. I join a chocolate-complexioned middle-aged man with a pork pie hat, kneeling at a rail, getting his view of the game. In a moment or two, we recognize we are kindred spirits, hoping against hope that the Giants would do something.

We watch together the events leading up to Bobby Thomson facing Ralph Branca with men on second and third, one out and the Giants behind, 4-2. I am of little faith because I had memories of many other Giant failures, two in particular.

There was the day in the early 1940s when my father and I jousted with Dodger fans in Ebbets Field during the opening game of a doubleheader in which the teams took turns holding the lead. The Giants broke a tie in the top of the tenth inning with a two-run homer by Johnny Mize. In the bottom of the tenth, the Dodgers loaded the bases off Hal Schumacher on a walk and two hits. Here, Manager Mel Ott brought in Harry Feldman to face Dolph Camilli, the Dodgers' first-baseman slugger. On the first pitch, Camilli hit the ball over the right-field screen onto Bedford Ave. for a grand-slam homer. Dodger fans around us razzed us to a faretheewell. My father took me by the hand and we left; he wouldn't stay for the second game.

There was also the game at Ebbets Field that any Giant or Dodger fan of that era would recognize as the Mead-Rucker game during the World War II years. The Giants led into the ninth and, with two out, one of the Dodgers lifted a soft fly into short right-center field that should have been the final out. Both right fielder Charley Mead and center fielder Johnny Rucker pursued the ball. Either could have caught it. Instead they collided, the ball dropped to the grass, the Dodgers ran merrily around the bases and the Dodgers won the game.

The Giants lost so often and with such epic futility at Ebbets Field in those years—10-of-11 games one season—that Giants owner Horace Stoneham couldn't stand it any longer. He would not go to Ebbets Field for any of the games between the arch rivals.

Ott, the Giants Hall of Famer who failed as a manager from 1942 to 1948, was overmatched in those years by Leo Durocher. So it was as if a thunderbolt had crashed on New York in the middle of the 1948 season when Durocher was let go by the Dodgers and named the Giants' manager. Many Giants fans objected to the hated Durocher, but I had seen him outwit Ott so many times, I was delighted. I rushed out and bought all eight New York City papers the next day to relish the details.

Durocher's move from the Dodgers to the rival Giants deepened the greatest rivalry in sports that went back to the World War I days of John McGraw and Wilbert Robinson. It was so intense that players on both teams actually would say they hated each other. Monte Irvin of the Giants said the World Series "was nothing compared to the tension of Giant-Dodger games." When the Dodgers won, their fans would enjoy mocking their friends who were Giant fans. And vice versa. Pee Wee Reese said, "There were times we stopped playing to watch fights in the stands." The rivalry would blossom anew, though with somewhat less heat, when the two teams moved west and were natural sparring partners for longtime rival cities, San Francisco and Los Angeles.

Once Durocher took over, the Giants morphed from heavy-legged, home-run happy sluggards to scrappy, resourceful players with an emphasis on speed and pitching. He jettisoned sluggers Walker Cooper and Johnny Mize. He got his kind of guys when he acquired Alvin Dark and Eddie Stanky from the Boston Braves. Stanky (The Brat) was almost as foul-mouthed and intense as Durocher. They finished fifth in 1949, Durocher's first full season, and third the next year before making the miracle run in 1951.

The Giants had outstanding talent, managed with craft and daring by Durocher. Along with Dark (No. 19) at shortstop and the pesky (127 walks) Stanky (No. 12), at second base, the Giants had Wes Westrum (No. 9) a good handler of pitchers, catching, Whitey Lockman (No. 25) in left field, Bobby Thomson (No. 23) in center field and in right field, Don Mueller (No. 22), called Mandrake because he handled the bat like a magic wand. The team wouldn't really gel until Willie Mays (No. 24) came up from the minor leagues in May to take over centerfield, which moved Thomson to third base. And Monte Irvin (No. 20 in left field) started hitting.

When the pitching staff started to come around in July, it produced the best team-earned run average in the league. The ace of the staff was Sal Maglie (No. 35). He won 23 games. He was named "The Barber" by *Daily News* reporter Jim McCulley because he gave the batters a close shave with his high, inside fast balls. Larry Jansen (No. 46) also won 23 games and managed to stay in Durocher's good graces even though he wouldn't throw at hitters. Jim Hearn (No. 21), who had come into his own the previous year, won 17 games.

The Dodgers had a solid group that would play together for almost a decade. The heart and soul of the team were Pee Wee Reese (No. 1), the captain, and Jackie Robinson (No. 42). In 1951 Reese hit .286, and played a smooth shortstop. He teamed with the mercurial Robinson to give the Dodgers the strongest up-the-middle defense in the league. Catcher Roy Campanella (No. 39) was voted the Most Valuable Player that year and Duke Snider (No. 4) performed admirably as the third best of what would come to be known as a great trio of New York center fielders along with Mays and Mickey Mantle of the Yankees. Pennsylvanian Carl Furillo (No. 6) was called the "Reading Rifle" because of his strong throws from right field. As smooth as silk at third base was Billy Cox (No. 3) who often looked at the ball a few mini-seconds before throwing out a runner. Gil Hodges (No. 14) ranked with the greatest fielding first basemen of all time and hit 40 homers with 103 runs batted in that year.

Robinson, the first black player in baseball, had achieved the monumental task of holding his temper his first two years. Once integration was established, he could be his natural self: a brilliant, fiery, obscene competitor who infuriated opponents while lighting up Ebbets Field with his daring. I recall a time when an opposing batter hit what would be an extra-base hit into right-center field.

He rounded second and tried for third. When he slid in, the umpire called the runner safe. Dodger third-baseman Billy Cox and manager Charlie Dressen argued for a few moments. The Dodger cause soon was taken up by Robinson, who came over from second base. He argued vehemently.

Afterward I approached Robinson in the clubhouse. I said, "Jack, with all you have to contend with as the first black player in baseball, with all the burdens you carry on your own, why would you get so agitated about a play at third base that didn't involve you?" Robinson looked at me as if I was an idiot and said heatedly, "But he was out, he was out."

Steve Jacobson of *Newsday* wrote that "Robinson invented more ways of winning games than perhaps any man who ever played." His brilliance never was more evident than in an August 8 night game, the second game of the first two-admission doubleheader conceived by Branch Rickey. The Dodgers won the day game, 7-2, without incident. In the second game, Robinson faced Sal Maglie with whom he had a history of knockdown pitches, collisions on the basepaths, obscene shouts and near fisticuffs. The first time up Maglie threw at him to knock him down. Robinson took a few steps toward the mound, screaming. Maglie answered with an obscene gesture. Robinson then doubled off the center field wall. He stole third and continued home when the throw by catcher Sal Yvars' (7) sailed over third base. He cackled at Maglie as he sauntered home.

His next time up he dropped a bunt down toward first base. He had done this in an earlier game and run up Maglie's back as the pitcher tried to field it. This time Maglie backed off, allowing first baseman Whitey Lockman to field the ball too late to catch Robinson. Robinson then danced off first, daring Maglie. He jiggled to and fro in his inimitable style that has never been matched for excitement by any base stealer. On one of Maglie's tosses to first, Robinson took off and beat the throw to second for a stolen base. Roy Campanella then doubled over Mays' head in centerfield and Robinson addressed more abuse at Maglie as he trotted home.

Robinson came up again in the sixth inning with men on second and third and two out and the Dodgers leading, 3-2. He lashed a single to right field for two runs. He then stole second and third. Scampering off third, he shouted "going home on the next one" at Maglie. Rattled, Maglie threw a wild pitch and Robinson came home, running slowly in the hope Maglie would try to cover the plate. The pitcher never moved.

The Giants tied at 6-6 and the game went into extra innings. The Dodgers finally won in the tenth inning on Billy Cox' single with the bases loaded. Who scored the winning run? Robinson. He had scored four runs and knocked in two to account for six of the Dodgers' runs. Afterward Robinson gloated and banged on the Giants' clubhouse door with a bat. Bill Rigney recalled that this infuriated the Giants and finally, Eddie Stanky yelled out, "Stick that bat up your ass, you black cocksucker." The Giants realized that Monte Irvin, their black teammate, was there. Such was the intensity of the desire to beat the Dodgers, he looked over at Stanky and said, "That's okay with me, Eddie."

The Dodgers had a solid foursome of pitchers. Don Newcombe (No. 36), the workhorse, had a 20-9 record, Carl Erskine (No. 17), only 24 years old, won 16 games and Ralph Branca (No. 13) a veteran at 25, won 13. Preacher Roe (No. 28) set a record for winning percentage with a 22-3 mark. He would later admit that a spitball was his best friend.

The Dodgers' Reese, Robinson, Campanella and Snider would all make the Hall of Fame, but only Mays for the Giants. A constant campaign to earn Hodges a place in Cooperstown emerged after his retirement. Hodges would go on to manage the Senators and Mets; six Giants would also become managers: Dark, Lockman, Stanky, Westrum, Rigney and coach Herman Franks.

Off a solid finish and a climb to third in 1950, the Giants figured as a pre-season favorite along with the Dodgers in 1951. But they stumbled early. They won their opener, lost, won again and then lost eleven in a row. And the Dodgers won the first five games between the teams. The low point was reached on August 11. The Giants fell 13 ½ games behind first when they were shut out by Robin Roberts of the Phillies. They had 44 games remaining.

The next day they started a 16-game winning streak. It stemmed from excellent pitching, two good moves by Durocher and the presence of Willie Mays. Monte Irvin, who was floundering at first base, was moved to left field where he was more comfortable. He would lead the league in runs batted in. Whitey Lockman made a smooth transition from left field to first base and Bobby Thomson took over at third base on July 20. He more than made up for occasional lapses in the field as he became the best hitter for average on the team.

In mid-May Giants' owner Horace Stoneham finally acceded to Durocher's pleas to bring up 20-year-old Willie Mays from Minneapolis where he was tearing up the league. He hit .477 in 35 games. Mays debuted in Philadelphia and got off to a poor start, hitless in his first 12 times at bat. I was a spectator in the upper left field stands in late May for his first game at the Polo Grounds when he got his first hit. He belted a home run over the section I was sitting in and over the roof off the Braves' Warren Spahn. He had only that hit in his first 26 times at bat before settling down. He would go on to hit .274 with 20 home runs, winning a few games with his offense.

His defense was sensational. It seemed as if he was born to roam the spacious center field at the Polo Grounds. I covered the Giants at home that year and it seemed that he made an outstanding play almost every day during July and August. People talked about him carrying the team. History looks back on Mays' over-the-shoulder catch of Vic Wertz' long drive at the Polo Grounds in the 1954 World Series as his highlight catch. Mays, however, picks a different one—the catch he made off a drive by the Dodgers' Bobby Morgan with the bases loaded at Ebbets Field in July, 1951. From the press box I watched as he ran to left-centerfield, dove and caught the Morgan's drive as he hit the ground and bounced off the wall. He lay there for a few moments after showing that he had held the ball.

There will, I'll wager, never be another play like the one he executed on August 15 at the Polo Grounds. With one out, the score tied, 1-1, in the top of the eighth inning, and Billy Cox, no slowpoke, on third base, Carl Furillo hit a fly ball into right-centerfield. Mays, shading Furillo to his right, had a long run to reach the ball. He sprinted on a diagonal toward the right field line and caught the ball in right-center. He then made a 360-degree turn to his left and, with his hat spinning off, unleashed a dead-on throw to home plate. Wes Westrum was so surprised he didn't take off his mask. He caught the ball with plenty of time to put a tag on an astonished Cox sliding into home. Westrum estimated that the throw had sailed some 325 feet on the fly. Mays then singled to lead off the Giants' half of the inning and Westrum homered for an exhilarating 3-1 victory.

Afterward, the often buffoonish Dodger manager, Charlie Dressen, uttered a classic line about Mays' catch. He said, "I'd like to see the guy do it again."

The Mays catch-and-throw game was one of the highlights of the Giants' 16-game winning streak in August. The string ended on Aug. 28 with a 2-0 loss to the Pirates. During that streak the Giants gained eight games on the Dodgers. At the start of September they were behind by seven games and for the next two weeks the Dodgers' advantage fluctuated between five and seven games. Bill Rigney (No. 18), a Giants reserve, said, "That last month we lived or died every night. It seemed that when we lost, the Dodgers lost. We'd get to thinking we were going to catch them and then we lost a game on the road and they won. 'Oh, now the momentum is gong to shift,' we thought, but then it started all over again."

September began with the Giants beating the Dodgers two straight games in the Polo Grounds. On Saturday Don Mueller hit three home runs, and Dark and Stanky collaborated on a triple play. On Sunday Mueller hit two more home runs in an 11-2 laugher behind Jim Hearn. Beanballs flew throughout the series and in the Sunday game umpire Al Barlick ejected five Dodgers, including Branca and Robinson.

The Giants had lapses. On Aug. 30, they blew an 8-1 lead and lost to Pittsburgh, 10-9. In a Labor Day game against the Phillies, they had a few chances to put Robin Roberts away, but failed. Willie Mays committed the gaffe of forgetting to touch third base, nullifying an inside-the-park home run. On Sept. 8, Newcombe won his 21st victory. Robinson had three hits, scored three runs and enraged the Giants anew by squeezing home the last run in a 9-0 victory. The Giants got their revenge the next day. They led 2-0 in the eighth when Duke Snider doubled and Robinson tripled with one out to narrow the score to 2-1. Andy Pafko then hit a hard grounder to third base. Bobby Thomson snagged the ball at the bag, reached out to tag the surprised Robinson off the base and threw on to first base for the third out. Maglie beat Branca, 2-1.

As the last six days of play began on Tuesday, Sept. 25 these were the standings:

	W	L	GB
Dodgers	93	54	—
Giants	92	58	2½

On "Black Tuesday," (the 1929 Depression term resurrected by author Ray Robinson) the Dodgers lost a doubleheader to the Braves in Boston while the Giants won in Philadelphia. Both teams won on Wednesday. While the Giants were off Thursday and Friday, the Dodgers lost on both days. The teams now were tied at 94-58 with two weekend games left. The Giants would wind up winning 37 of their last 44 games, 12 of their final 13. The Dodgers would win a respectable 26 of 48, but only four of their last 10.

Both teams won on Saturday. Maglie pitched a five-hit shutout over the Braves for his 23rd victory. Newcombe shut out the Phillies on seven hits to win his 20th. It came down to what turned out to be a momentous final day of the regular season.

First, the Giants. In a game moved up a half-hour by the umpires because of threatening weather in Boston, the Braves scored a run in the first inning. The Giants tied on Bobby Thomson's 30th home run in the second. The Giants scored another run in the third and took a 3-1 lead in the fifth when Monte Irvin singled Alvin Dark home from second. Larry Jansen pitched smoothly into the ninth inning and got the first two Braves out. Here, after they scored a run and had men on first and second, Durocher walked out to talk to Jansen. He went against the lefty-righty percentages and stayed with Jansen against ex-Giant Willard Marshall. After a long foul fly, Marshall lifted a soft fly to Irvin in left field and Jansen gained his 22nd victory.

The Giants had clinched first place. Immediately after the game the Giants heard a false report that the Dodgers had lost. But the celebration was short-lived. They dressed and listened to Red Barber reporting the Dodgers game from Philadelphia as they got ready to take the train home.

The Dodgers trailed 8-5, batting in the eighth. First Gil Hodges and Billy Cox singled and Rube Walker doubled them home. Philadelphia manager Eddie Sawyer (who would quit on Opening Day the next season) called on Robin Roberts, his ace 21-game winner. Carl Furillo singled home the tying run, 8-8. It would be the only hit off Roberts for the next five innings. The game was tied when the Giants entrained for New York. There was no radio reception on the train, so Russ Hodges, the Giants' broadcaster, got in touch with radio station WMCA in New York and relayed via a phone the developments in Philadelphia.

Charlie Dressen called on Newcombe, who had beaten Roberts the day before. Both of them pitched scoreless ball through the ninth, tenth and eleventh, the pennant seemingly riding on every pitch. In the twelfth Newcombe walked Roberts, got an out, but then Eddie Pellagrini, a non-descript veteran, beat out a bunt and Willie "Puddin' Head" Jones was walked intentionally to load the bases. Del Ennis took a third strike. That left it up to Eddie Waitkus with two out, the bases loaded (two summers before, Waitkus had been the unwitting gunshot victim of a crazed 19-year-old groupie in a Chicago hotel room).

The count went to 3-and-2. Waitkus then smashed what the *Herald Tribune* report called "a malevolent drive toward center field." The ball was a blur passing second base. As it headed toward the outfield Jackie Robinson flashed to his right. He flung himself headlong at a right angle to the flight of the ball. For an instant his body seemed suspended in midair, then somehow the outstretched glove intercepted the ball inches off the ground. He fell heavily. The crash drove an elbow into his side and he collapsed. Dodger trainer Doc Wendler rushed out onto the field, not sure what was wrong because Robinson couldn't talk. He could only point to his stomach. He lay still for several moments while his teammates gathered around him. Finally he arose groggily and walked uncertainly to the Dodger dugout. He had saved the Dodgers for the moment; this play would come to be regarded as the single most brilliant heroic on the field of his legendary career.

Tied, 8-8 in the 14th as a sense of darkness descended on the stadium, Roberts retired Reese and Snider on pop-ups. Another chance for Robinson of whom Newcombe once said, "The man refused to lose." Off a one-one count Robinson lashed a home run into the left field stands. The Dodgers won, 9-8 to qualify for a two-out-of-three playoff against the Giants to decide the pennant.

An editorial in *The New York Times* was both eloquent and prescient on the eve of the final showdown. It said in part:

For the next few days, just as in the past few weeks, even the grimmest of world-wide news will have an overshadowing rival for attention in the whirl and clash of the great American game. This is as it should be. It is not thoughtless or careless to turn away from time to time to the drama of fine sport, and what we have witnessed and, one hopes, will be privileged to continue witnessing for at least two more days is the highest and most inspirational drama we could hope for.

The Korean War, which had started in 1950, was raging in 1951, not to end until 1953. It was a time of McCarthyism and the red scare, so much so that for a while the Cincinnati Reds wanted to change their name to the Redlegs. Lew Smith, a crusty Cincinnati scribe harrumphed, "Let the Commies change; we had it first." Baseball teams traveled largely by train. Bacon was 49 cents a pound, candy bars and Philly cigars cost a nickel. Americans read *From Here to Eternity* and *Catcher in the Rye*. Movie-goers watched *A Streetcar Named Desire* and *A Place in the Sun*. Arthur Godfrey and Perry Como were television stars. The 1951 playoffs would be the first to be telecast from coast to coast, on the Liberty television network.

The Dodgers won the toss to determine the playoff sites. Manager Charlie Dressen chose to play the first game at home at Ebbets Field, ceding the last two to the Giants at the Polo Grounds. In the only previous two-of-three games playoff in 1946, Durocher chose for his Dodgers to play the first game at the St. Louis Cardinals' Sportsman's Park. The Cardinals won two straight.

The playoff opened in Ebbets Field on Monday, Oct. 1 the very next day after the end of the regular season. The ballpark, named for owner Charley Ebbets when it opened in 1913, was called a "funky little bandbox" by George Vecsey in the *Times*. Casey Stengel hit the first home run there on April 26, 1913. The park was rung by Sullivan Place along the first base line, Bedford Avenue behind right field, Montgomery Street behind left field and McKeever Place (originally Cedar Street) along the third base line. With a seating capacity of 32,000 it was compact and seemed to be constantly in tumult. It had a colorful set of characters. Hilda Chester, the bell ringer in the bleachers, harangued Dodger and enemy players alike; The madcap musical group named "The Dodger Sym-Phony" serenaded the crowd, playing, "the worms crawl in, the worms crawl out" to accompany a retired opposing player returning to the dugout, finishing him off with a bass drum when his butt touched the bench.

Left field—348 feet down the line, only 384 in the power alley—was a home run haven. Right field, 297 feet down the foul line, was unique. Home runs into Bedford Avenue had to clear a 40-foot barrier consisting of a wire screen atop a base of fifteen feet of concrete sloped at the bottom, making for tricky bounces. There was the celebrated "Hit Sign, Win Suit" sign at the base of the scoreboard in right-center field. Only a line drive to that sector could hit that sign, and Dodger right-fielder Carl Furillo was a noted sentinel guarding against many hitters winning one of clothier Abe Stark's suits. Once, Furillo complained that he had saved Stark from giving away so many suits he deserved something for it. His cause was taken up by Bill Roeder of the *World-Telegram*; Furillo was placated with a pair of pants.

I landed a job as a candy butcher at Ebbets one year as a teenager. I was alarmed to find myself caring more about selling scorecards and peanuts than watching the games; I quit after one weekend.

On a beautiful Indian summer day with the temperature in the low 70s a crowd of 30,707 wended into Ebbets Field for the first game of the playoff. In Stamford, Connecticut the library invited the public to come in and watch the game on its television set: by the fourth inning, the librarian noted, "we had a full house." The Dodgers, who had won the season series from the Giants, 13 to 9, managed only five hits off Jim Hearn, the Giants' No. 3 pitcher. A home run by Andy Pafko put them ahead in the second inning, but they collected only four singles after that. They hit into four double plays, the last one ending the game in the ninth inning. Ralph Branca pitched creditably but not well enough. He gave up a two-run homer to Bobby Thomson in the fourth inning. The Giants added a run in the eighth on Monte Irvin's fifth homer of the year off Branca for a 3-1 victory. Hearn felt so strong, he told Durocher he'd love to pitch again on Tuesday when the playoff shifted to the Polo Grounds.

Polo was never played at the Polo Grounds—at least at this Polo Grounds. The team started playing at what had been a polo field on 110th Street and Fifth Avenue, then moved in 1889 to the site under Coogan's Bluff adjoining the Harlem River at 157th Street and Eighth Avenue. Many outstanding events were held there, including the Jack Dempsey-Luis Firpo fight before 82,000 spectators in 1923. The Notre Dame victory over Army in 1924 served as the vehicle for Grantland Rice's famous lead: "Outlined against a blue-gray October sky, the Four Horsemen rode again . . ." The final score: 13-7. Earlier in the 1951 season Ray Robinson regained his middleweight title at the Polo Grounds, knocking out Britain's Randy Turpin in the 10th round.

John McGraw, Christy Mathewson, Bill Terry, Mel Ott and Carl Hubbell were part of its rich history. The 55,000 seat capacity Polo Grounds was a notoriously misshapen horseshoe of a field, more suited for football than baseball. Center field measured 483 feet from home plate, almost 20 feet more than that to the base of the clubhouse. Many a fly ball died in that distant acreage, covered so magnificently by Willie Mays. As long as the Giants were there, only Joe Adcock hit a homer into the center field bleachers. (When the Mets later played there their first two years, Lou Brock and Henry Aaron also reached those distant seats.) Cheap home runs—"Polo Grounds home runs"—cleared the short fences down the line. Right field measured a paltry 257 feet at the foul line with a fence less than 12 feet high. Left field was worse because, though it measured 279 feet-plus at the foul line, the upper deck hung over the field 23 feet closer. I recall watching Cardinal shortstop Marty Marion settling under a pop fly to left field only to see it scrape the upper deck façade for a home run on its way down.

Other features of the park in the 1950s were the huge Chesterfield cigarette packs hanging from the facades in left and right field and the large Chesterfield sign attached to the centerfield clubhouse. The "h" indicated a hit, the "e" an error as judged by the official scorer. When the Giants won, a blue flag flew from the clubhouse pole; a red-and-white pennant informed passers-by if the Giants lost.

The Polo Grounds rang with the Giants' theme song in the early moments of the great final day there. Any loyal Giant fan could sing along to these heart-felt, if not profound, lyrics:

Come on you ball fans, all you Giant ball fans
Come watch the home team going places around the bases
We're for you Giants, out at Coogan's Bluff,
Come watch those Giant players do their stuff.

Durocher chose to start Sheldon (Available) Jones (No. 37), saving the tired Sal Maglie for another day. With a crowd of 38,609 on hand the game started in sunshine, but the weather darkened and in the sixth inning the game was held up by rain for 41 minutes.

Jackie Robinson hit a two-run homer in the first, sending the Dodgers on their merry way to a 10-0 cakewalk. Clem Labine, the 25-year-old slick curve-baller who won four games and lost one after coming up to the Dodgers in mid-season from St. Paul, scattered six hits. He came through his only tough moment by striking out Bobby Thomson on a 3-2 count with the bases loaded in the third inning. Afterward, Thomson was told he swung at a bad pitch. He looked over to Whitey Lockman at the next locker who nodded. "Well then I wish I could do it over again," he said. Gil Hodges, Andy Pafko and Rube Walker, subbing for the ailing Roy Campanella, all homered. Campanella had suffered a hamstring injury in the season finale on Sunday and didn't play in the two playoff games at the Polo Grounds.

Durocher's last words to newsmen on Tuesday were, "The Barber will be shavin' tomorrow." Maglie was a 34-year-old tough competitor who had jumped from the Giants in 1946 to the Mexican League for a larger salary, then returned to them in 1950 after a ban against jumpers was lifted. He had mastered his curveball in Mexico under ex-Giant Dolph Luque and became the ace of the staff once Durocher made him a starting pitcher in the middle of 1950.

It was Maglie, 23-6, against Don Newcombe, 20-9, the 25-year-old workhorse who had pitched 14 2/3 innings in the two final games of the regular season. The weather came up threatening and in the low 60s for the finale. That has been the explanation for the non-sellout crowd of 34,320, ("22,000 empty seats" noted some cynics) but that figure came to be contested over the years. Careful study of photographs and film of the event show the ballpark was nearly full. And on his national broadcast of the game on Liberty Network, announcer Gordon McLendon commented a few times about a large crowd.

The game also was televised locally on the Giants' station, Channel 11 WPIX, by Ernie Harwell. On radio the Dodgers' WMGM had Red Barber, Connie Desmond and Vin Scully, then in his second year. WMCA, the Giants radio station, had Russ Hodges who, as it would turn out, made the most memorable call of all.

Maglie, a notoriously slow starter, retired Carl Furillo to start the game, but then walked Reese and Snider. This brought up Robinson, always a marked man for Maglie. On one occasion Maglie had repeatedly shaken off his catcher wanting him to throw his curve on a 2-2 pitch to Robinson. Finally, Sal Yvars came to the mound and found out Maglie wanted to throw a fast ball. "I feel like knocking him on his ass," he said. This time Robinson, with that characteristic whiplash swing, ripped the first pitch into left field for a single, driving in the first run of the game. With Larry Jansen and Dave Koslo throwing in the bullpen in right-centerfield, Maglie settled down to retire Pafko on a ground out and Hodges on a pop fly.

The Giants made a move on Newcombe in the second. With one out, Whitey Lockman singled. Bobby Thomson then lined a ball down the left line. It ordinarily would have been a double, but Andy Pafko made a good play on the ball, and quickly threw to Bill Cox at third. This kept Lockman from trying for third. Thomson, running with his head down, approached second as Lockman retreated to the base. Cox threw to Robinson who tagged Thomson for the second out. The Giant stalwart retreated to the dugout, flopping down on the bench away from his teammates with his head in his hands.

Maglie was bone tired, but he kept the Dodgers scoreless from the second inning to the eighth. Newcombe, dead tired himself, held the Giants without a run the first six innings. In the third inning just after the lights were turned on, a groundout by Eddie Stanky that was turned into a double play by Billy Cox in the third inning helped Newcombe. A couple of times the Dodgers infielders gathered around him for support. When Newcombe wondered if he should come out, Robinson scolded him, and told him to keep throwing his fastball at the Giants. Meanwhile, Charlie Dressen kept checking with bullpen coach Clyde Sukeforth about Ralph Branca, Carl Erskine and Clem Labine working in the bullpen. Sukeforth did not like the way Erskine was bouncing his curve, and didn't think Labine should come back after Tuesday's performance. Jansen and Koslo were ready in the Giants' bullpen.

The Dodgers led 1-0 into the seventh inning, a sense of doom in the gloom pervading the atmosphere for pessimist rooters of both sides. Monte Irvin led off the Giants seventh with a double off the left field wall. Lockman laid down a bunt to move Irvin to third and when Rube Walker threw late to third, Irvin slid in safely and the Giants had two men on base with none out. Here, Reese and Robinson gathered around Newcombe again. Reese recalled later that, "Newcombe was exhausted. He said, 'I can't make it.' Jackie and I talked him into staying in."

The Giants tied, 1-1, as Irvin scored on Thomson's long fly to center field. Newcombe then settled down to get Mays to hit into a double play.

The dugouts were screaming at each other most of the game, particularly Dressen and Alvin Dark. Dressen yelled at Dark, "You'll boot it when it counts." Dark reacted in kind. Thomson later recalled, "I had never heard Alvin swear before."

Dark, 29, a Louisiana resident who had been born in Oklahoma, was a great competitor. He was named captain by Durocher shortly after he came to the Giants with Stanky in a 1949 trade with the Boston Braves. An outstanding hit-and-run hitter to the opposite field, he surprised me one day when he repeated something I had been told by Luke Appling, another expert opposite-field hitter in his time. He said it was easier for him, a righty batter, to hit an inside pitch to right field than an outside pitch. Dark, a likeable man, was a devout Christian who had a condescending racist attitude toward minorities. That emerged in a long conversation I quoted him on when he was a manager of the San Francisco Giants, and was bedeviled by the mistakes of some of his black and Latin players. Dark at first denied making the comments, threatening to sue, but then settled into saying that I had taken the comments out of context.

The Giants did not enjoy the sanctuary of a tie too long. The Dodgers took charge of the game with a three-run rally in the eighth. After Maglie retired Carl Furillo, Reese singled over third and went to third on a single to right-center by Duke Snider. With Robinson up, Maglie threw two balls and then broke off a big curve that bounced in front of the plate away from Wes Westrum. It was only his third wild pitch of the season. Reese scored and Snider moved to second. Here Durocher ordered an intentional walk to Robinson after getting assurance from Maglie, backed up by Westrum, that he was still strong. Andy Pafko then bounced a ball off Thomson's glove into left field that was scored a hit, enabling Snider to score and Robinson to reach third. Hodges struck out. With Robinson jiggling off third base—nobody ever dared a pitcher the way Robinson did—Billy Cox whacked a grounder under Thomson's glove and Robinson scored the third run of the inning for a 4-1 lead. Maglie got Rube Walker for the final out. The crowd, realizing that Maglie would be out of the game for a pinch-hitter in the Giants' half, gave him an ovation as he trudged off the mound.

Years later, after Maglie had joined the Dodgers to play more than a season with Robinson, Jackie said, "I gave Sal a hard time, sure, but for all the crap between us, I had a great deal of respect for Sal as a pitcher. There wasn't a better pitcher in baseball that [1951] season. He didn't pitch badly those first eight innings and you know, he was pitching on pure guts."

The three runs bolstered Newcombe. He said later, "After we got those three runs we were going wild in the dugout. I was really charged up when I came out to pitch the eighth. All my tiredness left me." He said he didn't think he ever threw the ball harder in his life. Bill Rigney, pinch-hitting for Westrum, struck out on three pitches. Hank Thompson, pinch-hitting for Maglie, swung hesitantly on an 0-2 pitch and grounded out weakly, Hodges to Newcombe. The hulking Dodger then retired Stanky on a foul pop to Reese.

Larry Jansen came in for Maglie. He ignored some heckling from the Dodgers—"Jansen you can go home now"—and retired three Dodgers, starting with Newcombe. The way Newcombe had blistered fastballs past the Giants in the eighth, there was no thought by Dressen to pinch-hit for him. He had given up only four hits, and looked untouchable going into the ninth.

He would face Dark, Mueller and Irvin. Before the Giants went out to face Newcombe, Durocher addressed his guys. He rested a hand on the dugout roof and said, "We've gone this far, so let's not give up now." He clapped his hands, added an obscenity and said with a wave, "We got three big outs left, let's go," and trotted out to take his position in the third-base coach's box.

Dark waved his black bat as he stepped in against Newcombe. Later, he recalled that he took two strikes. "To this day," he said, "I don't know why I took those strikes. I can only figure it was God guiding me. I wasn't fooled, there was just something that kept me from going for them." Dark did not think Newcombe would waste the next pitch. "That wasn't Newcombe's style . . . I figured he would go for the outside corner . . . I was always able to handle that pitch. I got my bat out there and pushed it down the right side." The grounder shot between Gil Hodges and Jackie Robinson, tantalizingly close to Hodges's outstretched mitt, into right field.

Then "Mandrake" Mueller faced Newcombe with Hodges holding Dark on the first-base bag. This led to criticism of the Dodgers. By playing close to the base, Hodges left an opening for Mueller, the artful lefty, to bang the ball into right field. Mueller did precisely that, a hard grounder which Hodges couldn't reach, sending Dark to third base. Mueller heard this criticism over the years and rejected it. "I saw that hole and I went for it," he said. "I always tried to hit the ball where the biggest hole was. If Hodges was playing off the bag instead of tight behind Alvin, I would have tried to go up the middle with the ball. That's where I hit it best anyway."

Now, Newcombe, tired, but game, faced Monte Irvin, the league runs batted in leader, a clutch hitter. Irvin, overanxious, lifted a harmless pop fly to first base, gathered in by Hodges. Now there was one out, with men still on first and third. Lockman a .280 contact hitter, was next. He had hit only 12 home runs all year, but he said later that he had home run on his mind. "When Newcombe threw me a high pitch on the outside, muscle control took over and I sliced the ball to left field," he said. "There was no question in my mind that the ball would be fair."

The ball landed a yard fair inside the left field foul line. As Pafko chased the ball to the high green wall in left field, Dark scored and Mueller made third, while Lockman reached second. Mueller slid into the base awkwardly and sprawled on the ground in pain. "It was a half-slide," Mueller said later. "I was thinking I might go home if Pafko mishandled the ball. I pulled the ligaments and tendons on both sides of my ankle. The swelling was as big as a softball." Mueller was carried off on a stretcher to the clubhouse in center field and Clint Hartung (No. 26) came in to run for him. A popular trivia question over the years has been to ask who ran for Mueller in that situation.

It was Charlie Dressen's move now. He came out to the mound, surrounded by Reese, Robinson, and Hodges. Cox usually stayed out of these meetings. Newcombe had pitched those 14 and two-thirds innings over the tumultuous final weekend and had added eight and one-third innings now. He was done and there was no attempt by Robinson to goad him into continuing. Dressen had to choose among Ralph Branca, Carl Erskine and Clem Labine all throwing in the distant left-center field bullpen. Clyde Sukeforth told him Branca was "throwing the hardest" and that persuaded Dressen. He said, "Gimme Branca." Nobody tried to influence his decision. "We couldn't have," Reese said. "He wouldn't have listened."

Branca, 6-foot-3, was born in Mount Vernon, New York in 1926, where he grew up a Giant fan. He started the first game of the Dodgers' 1946 playoff against the Cardinals. The next year, at the age of 21, he won 21 games. He made the All Star game and started the World Series against the Yankees, retiring the first 12 hitters, five on strikeouts, before being routed in a five-run Yankee fifth. He didn't realize his potential after that. He had sore arm problems and was in the bullpen in 1951. He became a starter again in May and pitched well, just missing a no-hitter against the Pirates.

As he trudged to the mound on the long walk from the bullpen in deep left-center field, he was met by Dressen, Reese and Robinson. Branca, who had New York wit, reportedly said, "Anyone here have butterflies?" Dressen handed him the ball and said, "Get this guy out." There was no serious thought about giving Bobby Thomson an intentional walk. That would have loaded the bases and set up a double play, but that would have also put the winning run on base. Dressen chose to be conservative and have the right-handed Branca pitch to the right-handed Thomson. The 20-year-old Willie Mays, on deck, later expressed relief many times over that they didn't choose to walk Thomson and pitch to him.

The mood in the Giants dugout was subdued as they waited for Mueller to be taken off the field out of the game, out of the World Series. Thomson came back from the on-deck circle and sat down. Dark said later, "He was just sort of gazing out at the field. I went over and told him to concentrate. I don't think he heard me." As Thomson moved toward the batter's box, Durocher came up behind him, put his arm around him and said, "If you've ever hit one, hit one now."

Bobby Thomson was born Robert Brown Thomson on Oct. 25, 1923 in Glasgow. He grew up on Staten Island. He was 6-foot-2, a fast runner who sometimes overran balls hit at him in centerfield before he was moved to third base. He was nicknamed "The Hawk" and also "Hoot Mon" for his Scottish ancestry. He came to the Giants in 1946. His .309 average in 1949 was his only year above .300. He hit less than .250 in 1951 before the move to third base in mid-July. On July 31 his two homers beat the Cubs, 4-3. On Sept. 7 he went 5-for-5 to beat the Braves. From September 15 to the finish he hit .449. Up until his last surge he was considered something of a disappointment in his career. He was a pleasant man, shy, diffident, self-deprecating.

Thomson came up to the plate at this crucial moment having hit two homers previously off Branca, one the big blow in the first playoff game. He had struck out with the bases loaded against Labine in the second game. He had made a base-running goof earlier in this game; and he was not happy about letting two hits get by him in the eighth inning. Later, he said that Mueller's injury and the delay to get him off the field may have helped him a bit because it took his mind off the situation for a few moments.

When Thomson heard Durocher tell him to hit a home run, he thought, "You're out of your mind. A home run? I was just thinking about getting a hit someplace."

He stepped into the batter's box after Branca had thrown his eight warm-up pitches. Branca's first pitch was a fastball right down the middle of the plate. Thomson took it. He knew that he should have swung at it and cursed to psych himself before the next pitch. Lockman, looking in from second base, said, "That pitch had been perfect for Bobby, the kind he could knock out of the park. When he took it for a strike, my heart sank."

Branca threw his next pitch high and inside, a good pitch to throw to Thomson. This time Bobby, who had quick hands, got his bat around and connected. He sent the ball on a line toward the left field stands. As I watched it on the runway in right field, it looked to me as if it would land in the upper left field stands. Then, as it missed the upper deck, I had the sinking feeling it would not even make the left field fence and would be caught by Andy Pafko. The ball sliced under the façade of the upper deck and then just cleared the green left field wall into the first row a little to the right of the 315-foot sign. A final image: Pakfo looking up forlornly.

From this came Russ Hodges' call for the ages:

. . . Hartung down the line, not taking any chances. Lockman with not too big a lead at second, but he'll be running like the wind if Thomson hits one. Branca throws. Thomson hits a long drive. It's going to be, I believe . . . the Giants win the pennant! The Giants win the pennant! The Giants win the pennant! Bobby Thomson hits one into the lower deck of the left field stands. The Giants win the pennant! They're going crazy. They are going crazy. Whooooo boy!

Red Barber on WMGM gave the action a subdued call. He said, "It's in there for the pennant," stopped for crowd noise and turned the microphone over to Connie Desmond. He would insist ever afterward that Hodges' call, a partisan rooter's call, was unprofessional. Hodges' call was wrong for any normal situation, but it was right for this moment and that is why it has been replayed thousands of times over the years. The station didn't tape calls in those days so it was a weird stroke of luck that the call was taped. A Brooklynite, a Dodger fan, taped the last few innings because he wanted to be able to play it back to taunt a Giant fan who was a friend of his.

This was the walk-off homer of all walk-off homers at a time when that phrase hadn't yet come into being. Thomson remembered that he danced and jumped around the bases. Eddie Stanky rushed out of the dugout to tackle Durocher coming toward home plate and Durocher near climbed on Thomson's back as he moved toward home. Thomson was met by a gaggle of teammates and he jumped into the mob onto home plate. It was 3:58 p.m.

In centerfield Duke Snider dropped to his knees and pounded his fist into his glove. Pee Wee Reese stood there watching Thomson pass him. He said, "I couldn't believe we had lost." There is a disagreement over the years about Robinson's actions. Some said he stood behind second base, watching to make sure Thomson touched the base. I talked about this later with Reese. He shook his head. "I know Jackie was a great competitor," Reese said. "But I doubt that he did that."

My immediate reaction watching it all was to realize, "I am covering the Giants dressing room, the winning dressing room," and I raced down the runway some 100 yards to the Giants clubhouse. Reporters were admitted almost immediately. We were let in to a scene of players dancing, singing, yelling and kissing each other. Thomson seemed dazed as he was surrounded by reporters.

"You gotta be lucky," he said, "I don't know if we live right or what, but you gotta be lucky. I'm a lucky man tonight."

Carl Hubbell, the Giants immortal who was in three World Series and struck out Babe Ruth, Lou Gehrig, Jimmie Foxx, Al Simmons and Joe Cronin in succession in the 1934 All Star game at the Polo Grounds, called this the greatest moment in his baseball life. Around him corks popped, flashbulbs kept popping and players ran from teammate to teammate.

Giant fans wanted a part of it. They gathered in the well outside the clubhouse. One by one the players came out onto the center field steps and waved to the cheering throng. In the Dodgers' gloomy clubhouse, the central figure was Branca. I saw him lying prone across several steps, a solitary dejected figure. Barney Stein, the *New York Post* photographer, immortalized this image and another of Branca sitting on the steps with his head in his hands. Teammates could only tiptoe around their distraught teammate.

After awhile Reese went over to the Giants clubhouse to congratulate Durocher and his men. And so did Robinson. Durocher would write in his autobiography, "I know Jackie was bleeding inside. I know he'd rather have been congratulating anybody in the world but me. And he had come in smiling."

People reacted all over the city and maybe points West: Giant fans in ecstasy; Dodger fans in shock. Many Giant fans sought out Dodger fans to mock them.

Branca learned to live with the notoriety of giving up "The Shot Heard 'Round the World." He was married less than a month after October 3 and was a good sport at the New York Baseball Writers dinner that winter, joining with Thomson singing a parody of the popular song, "Because of You." Branca sang these lyrics while looking at Thomson:

Because of you, I should never have been born.
Because of you, Dodger fans are forlorn.
Because of you, they yell drop dead.
And several millions want my head.
To sever, forever, in scorn
One lovely bird had a word for my ear.
The only girl, what a pearl, of good cheer
I lost the game, but wound up with the dame
She took my name
In spite of you.

For a time Branca stiffened when the subject came up. He soon came to see he was the party of the second part who made money by appearing at memorabilia signings with Thomson. And there was his reaction to the laughable promotion in 2002 by the MasterCard people to select "The greatest moment in baseball history." Most knowledgeable people would surely have put "The Shot . . ." No. 1, but it didn't even make the Top Ten, because most of the voters were relative youths voting for more recent events.

As the contest drew to an end, Branca and Thomson were at Shea Stadium picking up a few bucks on a round of radio talks to promote the contest. I was in the Mets clubhouse, and I eyed Branca, a regular visitor to the Mets because his son-in-law, Bobby Valentine, was the manager. He led Thomson around, introducing him to people. The talk got around to the MasterCard promotion and Branca vented his anger. "It's ridiculous that our moment is not high in the running," he said. He ridiculed votes for Ichiro Suzuki's rookie season and for Cal Ripken's consecutive game streak: "Were they moments? Bah."

Here was Branca, the victim of the day that has lived in infamy for him, for the Brooklyn Dodgers, for their fans, angry that his "moment" was not being properly rewarded.

An epilogue to "The Shot . . ." was a charge—taken seriously because it was made outside sports precincts, in the *Wall Street Journal*—that Thomson hit the home run because he was tipped off by Giants' stealing the Dodgers' signs. The writer revealed that the Giants had an operative in the clubhouse with field glasses picking up signs, who then relayed them to the batter via a signal from a player sitting in the Giants' bullpen in right-centerfield.

Branca seized on this as the reason for his demise, but this is, at best, poppycock. Some facts:

The Giants played better on the road in the final days of the season.

They won on improved pitching rather than hitting.

Batters usually don't hit home runs—or get safe hits for that matter—in batting practice when they know what soft pitches are coming.

The Giants were shutout the day before and had scored only one run going into the fatal ninth.

Thomson denied getting any signs. He had let a fat pitch for a strike go by him just before the homer. And of course, he had hit a homer off Branca in the opening game of the playoff at Ebbets Field.

People of my generation know where they were at three historical times: the attack on Pearl Harbor in 1941; Franklin Delano

Roosevelt's death in 1945; and "The Shot Heard 'Round the World" in 1951. A few decades later, I wrote a column asking people where they had been on the day of Thomson's home run. One of the recollections was from a man who said, "I was listening to the game while in the Navy. I was at Pearl Harbor."

#1

The Munich Olympics

Two days before the start of the 1972 Olympics, a young tour guide drove me through the streets of Munich to give me a sense of the city that was about to host the 20th Olympiad. Munich was a bustling city, the third largest in Germany, the capital of Bavaria. It had a population of 1,400,000. It had been rebuilt from the 55 percent ruins that were left from World War II bombing raids. It was an attractive, efficient, prosperous, beer, tourist and industrial town.

My guide pointed out the sights of Munich, the cultural high spots and places of historical interest. She did not shirk from talking about Hitler. She said, "Munich was Hitler's city. He started his movement here and came back here often, even when he was in Berlin. It's been a long time since then, and we are not proud of it, but we can't try to hide it."

Thirty-six years earlier, the 11th Olympiad had been staged in Berlin. They came to be known as the Hitler Games because the

Nazi leader used the Games as a respectable cover for a regime that would bring the devastation of World War II upon the world. Now, as the guide, Olga Schmidt, a pretty young woman with a guileless manner, drove me through Munich, the shadow of the Hitler Games and Nazi atrocities loomed over the city and these Olympics.

The Germans wouldn't try to hide it, but they hoped to erase the stain of Berlin by staging an Olympic Games of sweetness and light, with *Gemütlichkeit* and good-fellowship. The official motto of the event. "The Happy Games," was intended to present a new democratic and optimistic Germany. More popularly, the German officials referred to it as "The Games of Joy."

The mixed feelings about the site were expressed by Dr. Shaul Ladany, a 36-year-old Yugoslavian-born Israeli walker. He told me, "I would say I am a little guilty of being arrogant when Germans congratulate me on how well I speak German. I tell them, 'I learned it well when I spent a year at Bergen-Belsen after my family was taken from Yugoslavia.' "

The Munich Olympics evolved into the Games of Hell. They were blackened by the massacre of eleven Israeli athletes and one German police officer by a band of Palestinian terrorists. The world watched in horror on television in an excruciating nearly 24-hour standoff between the Arabs and German officials.

Beyond that, less significant, but a stain upon the athletic aspect of the Games were numerous instances of man's inhumanity to man that occurred on the playing fields and the board rooms and by bumbling, stuffed-shirt officials. Incredibly, the Munich Olympics transcended the evil of the Nazi Olympics.

* * * * *

To prepare for the Olympics I had traveled out to Chicago to interview the man known as Mr. Olympics, Avery Brundage. He was 84, a walrus of a man, who worshipped the Olympics as more important than religions, countries, and political systems. He would retire as chairman of the International Olympic Committee at the conclusion of these Olympics, having been a dominant force for almost four decades. Brundage's idol was the founder of the modern Olympics, the French Baron Pierre de Coubertin. His own ideals were shaped in 1912 in Stockholm when he finished 16th in the Olympic decathlon won by Jim Thorpe.

I talked to Brundage in the suite of the Hotel LaSalle, a hotel he once owned. He looked, as somebody said, "like Oliver Cromwell's idea of God." I found him cordial, ready to parry all the questions about the controversies he had endured and survived. I interviewed him for more than an hour on tape. To my dismay I found when I returned home that I had erased one entire side of the tape. However fretful, I managed to put together a 2,500 word essay relying on memory as well as his comments that survived the tape.

I arrived in Munich a few days before the Olympics after traveling through Europe in a camper with my wife and three teenage daughters. They stayed at a campsite on the outskirts of town while I lived at the huge new apartment complex set aside for the press during the Olympics, and which would house German families afterward. When I settled into my small, comfortable room on the 12th floor of the building I found an unsealed letter which a previous occupant had written to his wife, but had apparently forgotten to mail.

I am no less curious than the next fellow. I read it. It turned out to be a letter from Roger Bannister, the British runner who had become the first to break the four-minute mile barrier in 1954. I surmised that Bannister, a physician now, had attended a pre-Olympic meeting of doctors. I was impressed by the thoughtfulness and erudition of Bannister's writing; he was eloquent. I mailed the letter for him.

I immediately walked the Olympic grounds. The Germans had spent three-quarters of a billion dollars to erect the impressive Olympic complex. Walking from the training fields past the many souvenir and snack booths was not unlike promenading through a World's Fair grounds. The roof of the main 80,000 spectator Olympic Stadium was the centerpiece. It looked like a giant cobweb held up by dinosaur cranes. There was a feeling of grace to it. Like Paris' Eiffel Tower—an eyesore of ironwork—it would become the easily recognizable symbol of Munich.

The Olympic Village housing the athletes was no more than a few hundred yards from the main venues. I enjoyed walking through the Olympic Village because it represented the essence of good feeling—beautiful young men and women living together, enjoying the mixture of cultures. Al Oerter, the great discus thrower who won four successive Olympics, once told me, "I have more in common with a Czech discus thrower than, say, an American sprinter."

Early on, the press had difficulty gaining admission to the Olympic Village. Officious guards seemed overly demanding of credentials. Press passes were limited, though it appeared that many officials and commercial representatives had easy access. Later, I had bitter recollections of this when I learned that the terrorists gained admission to the grounds without being confronted by security. On my visits to the Olympic Village I ambled about, noting the spacious cafeterias, the signs in several languages, the recreation centers where spirited table tennis games attracted kibitzers. I watched athletes and officials surmounting language barriers to trade Olympic pins. And one afternoon I chatted on the walkways with some of those in the 43-person Israeli delegation—athletes, coaches and officials. I would never be sure, but I think I talked with Andre Spitzer, the fencing coach, and, judging by their builds, wrestlers and/or weightlifters.

The impressive opening ceremonies assumed something of the atmosphere of a folk festival. As some 10,000 athletes and officials marched joyfully for two hours into the 80,000-seat *Olympiastadion*, row and row of colorfully clad people, I entertained an odd thought: imagine what it would be like if the exalted leaders of nations were made to strip down to short pants and parade around an arena with both friends and enemies. Notably, the two German teams, who competed separately, marched together under the Olympic flag.

The first week of Olympic action was dominated by Mark Spitz, the American swimmer; Olga Korbut, the elfin Russian gymnast; and the track and field contretemps surrounding the American sprinters.

Spitz, a brash, 22-year-old pre-dental student at Indiana University came into the 1972 competition on a mission. He had gone into the 1968 Games in Mexico City boasting he would win six gold medals. He had set the bar so high he was disappointed, even ridiculed by some, for winning only four medals: two gold, one silver and one bronze. He alienated some of his teammates with his boasting and his standoffishness.

Spitz got off to a quick start in the brilliantly-lit *Schwimmhalle* in Munich by capturing the gold in his strongest event, the 200-meter butterfly. He had finished last in this event at Mexico City. An hour later he captured his second gold in the 4 x 100-meter freestyle. He went on to also win gold in the 200-meter freestyle, the 100-meter butterfly, the 4 × 200-meter freestyle relay, the 100-meter freestyle and the 4 × 100-meter medley relay. The addition of a relay race to the ever-expanding swimming program gave him a chance at an additional medal. All in all, he won seven medals, four individual and three in relays, with world records in all of these events. He set a record for the most gold medals by an individual in one Olympics.

Spitz frequently said things in a heavy-handed way so that coaches hovered around him, and shuttled him from press conferences in a hurry. Spitz dutifully played the respectful, abashed hero with such transparent artificiality that the press grew impatient with him. He lost me at the press conference shortly after we had learned that the terrorists were in the Olympic Village holding the Israelis hostage. He had come to the press conference from the athletes' quarters to talk about his record performance, but now the emphasis was on the terrorists and the Jews. Spitz was asked what he saw and knew about the hostage situation at the village. He looked blank. He said, "No comment." This upset many of us. As I recall, Paul Zimmerman, then of the *World Telegram*, said something like, "But you are a Jew and those are Jews being held over there. Can't you tell us anything?" Spitz responded with another blank look. He was spirited away from the village lest he, the most famous Jew at the Games, become a terrorist target.

ABC-TV played Spitz' swimming performances to the hilt. "Mark really made our coverage," said Donna de Varona, a network reporter at the Games. "We'd build his story every night. Is he going to win?" Every night for a week. There was much talk about the endorsement and appearance riches that awaited him when he returned to the United States. After a quick, short burst of exposure, the seven gold medal man faded from the limelight. His dull personality didn't endear him to the public, though he occasionally was called upon by the networks to be an analyst at Olympic swimming competitions. He became a dentist.

By its astute planning ABC came up with another bonanza in the bubbling 17-year old gymnast from Belarussia, Olga Korbut. ABC won the right to bring some of its own cameras to supplement the German feed for the overall gymnastic competition. It placed one of its cameras near the balance-beam exercises. American viewers saw close-ups of the charming, diminutive Korbut as she slowly progressed in the gymnastic floor exercises. Korbut, all four feet, 11 inches of her, was made for television, a pixie with bright eyes and an infectious smile. Her acrobatics and open display of emotion were in contrast with the stereotypically unemotional eastern bloc athletes. She captivated the Munich audiences as well as billions of TV viewers. All this came as a surprise to me because I was covering more traditional events like track and field and swimming, and didn't know that ABC was making gymnastics one of the star attractions of the Olympics—then and ever since.

Korbut became the first person ever to do a backward somersault on bars and back somersault to swingdown (the Korbut Flip) on the balance beam. "When Olga missed on the bars and started to cry, people in the stands started to cry," said Olympic filmmaker Bud Greenspan. "And ABC played her to the hilt." Americans fell in love with her.

Korbut had such a presence, unsophisticated viewers didn't realize that she was not the top Russian gymnast. She fell from bars. The all-around title went to her teammate Ludmilla Tourischeva, though Korbut ended up winning three gold medals—for the balance beam, floor exercise and team competition, and one silver medal in the uneven bars. Her routine on the uneven parallel balance bars stood out.

ABC voted her the "Athlete of the Games." She later visited the White House where President Nixon reportedly commented that she had done more to defuse the Cold War than all the meetings in Washington and Moscow combined.

Before the Israeli tragedy, I was dismayed with the stupidity, boorishness and downright sore-headedness of American losers. This started with the debacle of the American sprinters who did not show up on time for their 100-meter trial heat race. In the first morning of the competition Eddie Hart, Reynaud Robinson and Robert Taylor, all potential medalists, easily won their first-round heats and qualified for the quarter-finals later in the day.

Assistant track coach Stan Wright's time schedule indicated they would not run again before 7 PM. At 4:17 PM, relaxing in the Village, they saw on television what appeared to be a replay of the morning races. When they realized it was really the quarter-finals, they rushed to the track. Hart and Robinson were disqualified because their races had already been run; Taylor got there just in the nick of time and finished second to advance to the semi-finals.

Just about everybody but the American track people seemed to know the correct time for the race. It had been printed in the *U.S. Track and Field News* two weeks earlier and in the *International Herald Tribune* and *Stars and Stripes* that were posted outside the track dormitory in the morning. The American officials infuriated just about everybody by not admitting they were at fault. They gave out this line of gobbledygook: "The USA track and field staff has conscientiously made every effort to obtain all information from the proper source—the Village information center. However, for some unexplainable reason, information pertaining to the second round of heats in the 100 meters was not received and disseminated to the coaching staff, and an erroneous schedule was followed."

The "erroneous schedule" was a year-and-a-half old. No other country failed to show up for the heats in time, though some American apologists noted that other nations missed races in three other events because of time changes they were not told about. Track coach Stan Wright took the blame for the mistake and carried it to his grave. As liable as the coaches were, the athletes deserved little sympathy for not making sure to be on time for the most important races of their lives. A distraught Wright said, "I am deeply grieved for these boys."

Valery Borzov, the rapid Russian, won the 100-meter event easily. The absence of Hart, the favorite, and Robinson tainted the victory, of course, but Borzov had a logical answer. "I beat the men who were there." It is the custom in track parlance to label the winner of the Olympic 100-meter dash "The Fastest Man in the World." The Americans wouldn't concede that to Borzov because of the freak absence of their two top countrymen.

Americans had another crack at Borzov in the 200-meter race, not regarded as his best event. No matter. Borzov repeated his 100-meter efforts, winning all the heats easily and then beating the Americans in the final. He was surely "The Fastest Man in the World." The Americans still wouldn't acknowledge that. Larry Black, who finished second, said the Americans in the 200 all were affected by the 100-meter incident and weren't at their best in the 200. He said Borzov hadn't set world records in his finals and had looked back while winning those races. "What world class runner would do that," he bleated. He called Borzov a clown. The legendary Jesse Owens, who had won both the 100 and 200-meters at Berlin in 1936, was an observer. He called Borzov, "Sensational." I asked him which runner Borzov reminded him of. He answered, "Me."

A few days after the Israeli tragedy and memorial, Americans Vince Matthews and Wayne Collett made fools of themselves after finishing one-two in the 400 meters. Matthews and Collett slouched and chatted on the victory stand during the playing of the Star Spangled Banner, an action that neither was a protest or a non-protest as far as anybody could figure out. Matthews said he did this because he was "unhappy." And why was he unhappy? Because, he said, *Track and Field News*, the bible of the sport, had picked him to finish sixth in the 400. He said, "That is a slap in the face to me. I have more ability than that." And he said he was unhappy because kids like him from the east coast didn't have the advantages of the athletes on the west coast where all the track action is.

Could he possibly be making a political protest? No. He said he was not making a black power gesture like Tommie Smith and

John Carlos at the 1968 Mexico City Games. He surely wasn't striking a blow for high intelligence, either.

The United States swimming officials matched the track people for buffoonery. Rick DeMont, a 16-year-old Californian, won the 400-meter freestyle only to be disqualified for failing a urine test. He was penalized for taking the prescription drug Marex which was illegal because it contained an amphetamine. DeMont, who long had used the medicine to treat his asthma, dutifully listed the special medication on his pre-Olympic entry form. The American doctors, however, failed to clear the prescription with the International Olympic Committee. Afterward, no American official could be found who would admit to being at fault in not alerting DeMont to stay off the drug during the Olympics. An international swimming official said some American officials should be punished, but none were. DeMont's stunned mother said, "But he's been taking the medicine since he was a little boy."

Some 29 years later the U.S. Olympic Committee recognized DeMont's achievement, but this action did not result in the restoration of his lost gold medal. That could be done only by the International Olympic Committee. It refused, however, to award him the medal.

The Israeli team came to Munich with mixed feelings. It was only 27 years after the end of World War II. Many members of the Israeli team had lost relatives in the Holocaust, but many looked at the Games as a way to forge a new Israeli image and show the resilience of the Israeli people. As if visitors needed any reminder of the Nazi era, the Olympic facilities were less than ten miles from the site of the Dachau concentration camp. Traffic signs noting "Dachau" couldn't be missed anywhere in the city. The Israeli team visited Dachau before the opening of the Games and fencing coach Andre Spitzer lay a wreath at the concentration camp.

The Israeli aggregation enjoyed a night out on Monday, September 4. They watched a performance of "Fiddler on the Roof." At 4:30 the next morning, five Arab terrorists, looking like athletes in their track suits, climbed the fence surrounding the Olympic Village. Some reports said that they were assisted by unsuspecting American athletes who were also sneaking into the Village. Once inside they were met by three others who had gained entrance with credentials. They used stolen keys to enter two apartments being used by the Israeli team at 31 Connollystrasse.

According to some reports they entered Apartment 1 just before 5:00 a.m. and were accosted by Yossef Gutfreund, a wrestling referee. His warning to others enabled his roommate, weightlifting coach Tuvia Sokolovsky, to escape through a smashed window. Wrestling coach Moshe Weinberg fought back against the intruders, who shot him through his cheek. The terrorists moved to Apartment 3 where they corralled six wrestlers and weightlifters as additional hostages. Weinberg and weightlifter Yossef Romano engaged the terrorists again and were shot and killed.

Several Israelis were able to escape, but at 9:30 a.m., the terrorists announced they were Palestinian Arabs, and demanded that Israel release 234 Palestinians and non-Arabs jailed in Israel, along with two terrorist German prisoners imprisoned in Frankfurt. They threw Weinberg's body out the front door of the building to show their resolve.

The Israeli government responded immediately, rejecting the terms. The Germans were caught in the middle. They had to respect the Israeli position while knowing the hostage situation presented a difficult dilemma because the hostages were Jewish. The irony of Jews coming to such a tragic death in a country where they had suffered tragic deaths en masse was not lost on anyone. According to one report the Germans offered the Palestinians an unlimited amount of money for the release of the hostages as well as the substitution of high-ranking Germans. The terrorists refused all offers. The hours passed.

The stand-off drew the attention of the entire world. TV filmed the action of the police, and broadcast live images on television. This enabled the terrorists to watch the police as they took positions around the building. There was a weird fascination in watching the terrorist known as Issa, clad in a white hood with sunglasses, darting in and out of the building and onto the balcony for the entire world to see as he conducted negotiations with authorities. It seemed that though the event had never been put on the official program, the world was waiting for the first televised Olympic shootout.

I first found out about the hostage situation at about 9:00 a.m. when I came down from my room to the press center to attend what was supposed to be a session with Spitz, who had won his seven medals. There was consternation all around and the only questions asked of Spitz were about the scene at the Village. His relative unresponsiveness was frustrating to say the least.

There was an eerie silence at the Village while the negotiations took place. American soccer goalie from Harvard, Shep Messing, told us, "I slept late. I didn't find out about the Arabs until noon. I could see a big X on a cleared area for a helicopter outside the Israeli building. But things were so relaxed in the Village away from that building it seemed unreal." Rick DeMont, the swimmer, said, "I walked around the Village wondering why it was so quiet, seeing tanks outside the village and armored vehicles. Most of us in the Village really didn't know what was happening."

I shuttled between the press center and an athlete's entrance gate outside the Village where people had congregated. The strains of the song, "Exodus" sounded from a portable radio. People shook their heads with the surrealism of it all. Some Israeli tourists sang "Shalom." One of them said, "If this was Israel, we would break into the building, but we are in Germany."

On German television there was the vignette of the Israeli TV man and the German announcer.

The Israeli said, "It is a real shock."

The German said, "It is a real shock for us, too."

And the Israeli said, "But it is the Israelis who are dead."

Athletes were allowed to go in and out of the Village all afternoon. Messing, a Jew from Long Island, was assured that his folks would know he was not in danger. And because there was something of a war zone atmosphere in such a situation, he was dispatched as a special courier behind the lines into the Village to report the mood of the athletes.

He said, "There are three reactions here. The athletes are angry with the Arabs because they know the Israeli wrestlers and weightlifters as individuals and fear for them. There is frustration that so many outside things keep getting in the way of the athletes and the competition—which is what the Olympics are supposed to be about. And the athletes are puzzled and worried they might call off the Games for good."

The morning and afternoon events went off on schedule. A British and Algerian boxer flailed away. Late in the afternoon word got through to the Germans that it didn't look good to have people playing games while Israelis were laying dead or being held hostage. Avery Brundage and Willi Daume, the bedeviled German Olympic head, announced that the Games would be called off that evening and there would be a memorial service for the Israelis the next day.

After more than half a day of intense negotiations, deadlines set by the terrorists were extended time and again. They demanded transportation to Cairo. The authorities feigned agreement and shortly after 10:00 p.m. a bus carried the terrorists and their hostages from 31 Connollystrasse to two military helicopters to transport them to a nearby NATO airbase, Furstenfeldbruck. The German authorities planned an armed assault on the Arabs at the airport. They never intended to let the terrorists escape on a Boeing 727 jet positioned on the tarmac.

The rescue plan was botched. The terrorists suspected an ambush. A bloody firefight between the Germans and the Palestinians followed, ending at 3:00 a.m. when the Palestinians set off a grenade in one helicopter, killing all aboard, and the terrorists in the second helicopter shot to death the remaining, blindfolded Israeli hostages. Nine Israelis were killed at the airport, 11 in all counting Weinberg and Romano who had been murdered in the Israeli compound. Five terrorists were killed at the airport; three were captured alive and held in Germany. The final victim: a German policeman.

To compound the tragedy, initial reports, published all over the world, indicated that all the hostages were alive, and that all the militants had been killed in the firefight at the airport. Only later did the horrid word come through that "initial reports were overly optimistic." Jim McKay, who did a splendid job as the lead ABC-TV voice during the hostage situation, came on the air after the botched attempt and said, "Our worst fears have been realized tonight. They've now said there were eleven hostages; two were killed in their rooms yesterday morning, nine were killed at the airport tonight. They're all gone."

During the late evening hours, press headquarters were in an uproar as one conflicting report followed another—and in three different languages. At first it was said that some hostages had been killed, then it was said they all were safe, then came the word that probably all had been killed. Men who had covered the toy wars of sports all their lives were now involved with the real thing, and a sense of near-panic gripped the press center.

On a BBC television interview the question was raised about the Israeli policy of not releasing prisoners to save hostages. An Israeli TV man said, "No, we would never release the prisoners in answer to their demands. Nobody can submit to force."

I kept thinking back to the visit I had at the Olympic village with members of the Israeli team. They were real flesh and blood people to me. I could not comprehend the Israeli argument that they would not give in to terrorists because it might encourage more such actions. We didn't know much about terrorists at that time, but it seemed fairly obvious that fanatics would continue to stage terrorist actions whether they were successful or not. Was it worth risking one Israeli life rather than giving in to the fanatics? I didn't think so. Would an American government in that position risk the life of Mark Spitz rather than turn over 200 prisoners?

In future situations we learned that the Israelis did bow to terrorists' demands in order to save their people. And a month after the Olympics a Lufthansa jet was hijacked by Palestinians who demanded that the three Munich survivors be released. The Germans capitulated and the imprisoned terrorists were freed. The Israelis eventually tracked down and killed two of them and others associated with the Munich incident. One of the released terrorists subsequently appeared in disguise in a documentary on the Munich tragedy, "One Day in September."

Willi Daume, the German Olympic head, initially sought to cancel the remainder of the Games, but Avery Brundage and the others who wished to continue the Games prevailed. Brundage believed the Olympics transcended peoples and nations; he said, "The Games must go on." I had mixed feelings about this. On the one hand many people, including esteemed columnist Red Smith, felt that games weren't important in the wake of the tragedy. On the other hand, to call off the Olympics was to give the terrorists a final victory. This was the Israeli position; it endorsed the decision to resume the Games.

I was not particularly happy that in this one instance I was in agreement with Brundage. It was acknowledged, at least, that the Games should not continue in the midst of the hostage situation. The officials called off Tuesday's evening action and scheduled the memorial to the Israelis for Wednesday. The memorial service was attended by 80,000 spectators and 3,000 athletes in the Olympic Stadium. Brundage outdid himself with a speech in which he barely showed a shred of concern for the Israelis. He was more dismayed that people had dared interfere with his precious Olympic Games. He hurled himself at the microphone, and with Olympian gall, paired the struggle to keep the Rhodesians out of the Games (a pre-Olympic controversy) with the murder of the Israelis. Ever one to inflame a troubled situation, he babbled on with a pronunciamento dripping with hypocrisy. He said, "The Games must go on and we must continue our efforts to keep them clean, pure and honest and try to extend the sportsmanship of the athletic field into other arenas."

He said this in the midst of the petty wrangling among nations as well as the lack of sportsmanship that inevitably is a part of the Olympics.

The memorial was more of a show-business tribute staged like a Hollywood spectacular than a proper solemn coming together. West German president Willy Brandt ordered flags flown at half-mast, but accepted the demand of ten Arab nations and the Soviet Union that their flags remain at full-staff. The grief-stricken Israelis were front and center, but more like extras in a cast of thousands. They straggled out of the stadium to search for a bus and had to avoid getting knocked over by officious attendants marshalling limousines for the VIPs. The next day when several spectators at a West Germany-Hungary soccer match unfurled a banner reading, "17 dead, already forgotten," security officers removed the sign and expelled the offenders.

It was not uplifting that in the wake of the Israeli tragedy there were only a few Americans who showed up at the memorial and that only one black athlete, triple jumper Art Walker, was present. This was of a piece with a black-white thing among the Americans at Munich. American blacks rooted for Kenya's black Kipchoge Keino over Jim Ryun, the publicized white American in the 1500 meter run. There was some resentment by blacks against white heavyweight Duane Bobick because he was getting much attention in the press. Heavyweight fighters like Joe Frazier, Floyd

Patterson and George Foreman, all black, had been the center of attention in their time. And there was glee as well by some white track people when the black American sprinters failed to win early events.

Ryun was another casualty. In the 1500 meters an administrative error matched defending champion Keino against Ryun, the world record holder in the mile in the opening round. The long-awaited showdown ended badly for Ryun. He tripped while squeezed in the early running and fell hard, lying dazed on the track. Keino won the heat and eventually the silver medal.

America did have some success. Dan Gable won a wrestling gold medal in the 149-pound freestyle without having a single point scored against him. Dave Wottle's victory in the Olympic 800 meters had a comic element to it. Wottle, who ran wearing a painter's cap, trailed the field the first 600 meters, then came from behind to grab the lead in the final strides and win by three seconds over the favorite, the Soviet Yevgeny Arzhanov. At the victory ceremony Wottle did not remove his cap. This was taken as a form of protest by some, until Wottle revealed he did not know he still was wearing the cap. He apologized profusely.

And there was Frank Shorter in the marathon. I had long been a marathon fan, having covered Boston Marathons in the 1950s before marathoning became a big thing in the major cities of the world. On Sunday, September 10, an added day of competition to make up for day dedicated to the memorial to the Israelis, I scored a ride and squeezed myself into the back of a German TV van that followed the runners throughout Munich.

As the runners moved, twisting and turning through the streets of the city, it soon became evident that Shorter, wearing

No. 1014, would be a factor in the race. The Yale senior took the lead at the nine-mile mark and increased it as the race progressed. By the time we reached the streets leading to the Olympic Stadium there was no doubt that Shorter would win the marathon, the first American to do so since 1908.

We were surprised, though, when we went through the tunnel leading into the stadium, to be greeted by a chorus of boos. We didn't realize that an imposter had inserted himself into the race at the last moment and was being booed by the crowd that realized he was not a legitimate leader. Finally, Shorter moved onto the track and was accorded the ovation he deserved. Erich Segal, the novelist who did analysis for ABC because of his background as a marathoner, almost jumped out of the booth with rage when he realized that the hoaxer had deprived Shorter of the conquering hero welcome he deserved when he entered the stadium.

Shorter's heroics gained less attention back home than merited because of the raging controversy over the U.S.-Soviet Union basketball game that had ended in the wee hours at Munich that morning. The highest pitch of American hysteria was reached as a result of the United States' first Olympic basketball defeat ever. The U.S., which had dominated basketball since Prof. James Naismith put up a couple of peach baskets in Springfield, Massachusetts at the turn of the century, had won every basketball gold medal starting in 1936. The team went into the game with a 62-game winning streak. Against the tragic backdrop of the Israeli massacre, the Cold War played a role, too. It was capitalism vs. communism, the basketball court transformed into a political arena.

Both the U.S. and the Soviets went into the final that was played late in the evening of September 9 with 8-0 records. The

U.S. had whipped every team but Brazil easily, and had routed Egypt, 96-31. Despite warnings that the Russians were talented, the Americans were fairly strong favorites.

The U.S. played the slow game preferred by coach Henry Iba, which allowed the Soviets to dictate the pace of the action. The USSR took a 7-0 lead and led 26-21 at the half. Dwight Jones, the USA' top scorer and rebounder was ejected from the game after a loose scuffle and 6-9 Jim Brewer suffered a concussion after being knocked to the floor. The U.S. finally narrowed the gap when it went into an full-court press that befuddled the Soviets. It reduced the margin to one point, 49-48, on a jump shot by Jim Forbes.

The Soviets worked the clock down to 10 seconds when Tom McMillen blocked Aleksander Belov's shot. Doug Collins (of Illlinois State, later a pro coach) intercepted a pass and drove to the basket. He was undercut as he attempted a layup with three seconds left. Collins, groggy, sank two foul shots to put the USA ahead, 50-49, with three seconds remaining on the clock.

There are two versions of what happened next: a) the highway robbery claimed by Americans and b) what actually took place. A remarkable HBO documentary in 2002 relived the incident with replays and taped interviews with the principals involved. It should have pinned down once and for all what happened in those wild last moments.

After Collins sank his foul shot, the Soviets took the ball out, threw a futile, long pass downcourt and the horn sounded, ending the game. Astoundingly, that play was disallowed and the Soviets had another chance, still with three seconds remaining. They threw another long, futile pass downcourt and the horn sounded, apparently ending the game again. But again for some nefarious reason, that play, too was disallowed and the Soviets had another chance, still with three seconds.

This time, the long pass went to Alexsander Belov, who caught the ball as the two Americans guarding him, Kevin Joyce and Jim Forbes, went sprawling while trying to intercept the pass. Belov then drove for a layup and sank the basket that gave the Soviets a 51-50 victory as time ran out.

Madness. Insanity. Shouts of Foul. Robbery. Shame. Cries of a Communist Plot. Coach Iba stormed the referees, cursed the timekeeper. He even contemplated taking his team off the floor and out of the game. And in the midst of it he had his watch pick-pocketed.

It was learned afterward that the Soviet bench called for a timeout when Collins was on the foul line. This should have been called after he made his first foul shot. The referee was Renato Righetto of Brazil, who spoke Portugese and couldn't communicate with Artenik Arabadjian, the referee from Bulgaria who spoke French. Because Righetto had not heard the Soviet call for the timeout, he allowed Collins to take his second shot. They then gave the ball to the Soviets, who put it into play. But here an off-court official interceded. R. William Jones, the secretary general of the International Basketball Federation, came onto the court to rule that the Soviets should have been give a timeout. The resumption of play with the futile long pass was cancelled and the Soviets had their timeout.

The second long futile pass then was cancelled, too. Why? Because this time the clock had not been reset to three seconds—and a horn that blew from the timekeeper's table before the Soviets made that pass was not heard. So the clock was reset and the Soviets made their third long pass. This one led to the winning basket by Belov.

Pandemonium.

Once the referees made the mistake of not giving the Soviets their timeout, nobody should have interceded. But William Jones saw an injustice when they did not get a timeout. He stepped in. He should not have according to the rules, but he did. The subsequent resumption of play before the clock was reset was another bumbling mistake.

All these were, of course, a series of monumental gaffes. There is little doubt that the officials, who did not speak each other's language, lost control of the game. The Americans deserved to win. But basketball, everyone knows, is an impossible game to officiate. Fallibility by basketball officials is almost an integral part of the sport. Just about everybody who has played the game knows that. The Americans became vulnerable to the officials' incompetence when they allowed the game to be so close.

The basketball controversy stoked the fuel of the Cold War. Because of the injustice of the basketball finish, many Americans saw conspiracy in the developments. There were wild charges that William Jones, an Australian, was a Communist sympathizer. It turned out that he fought with the Poles against the Russians during World War II. He studied at Springfield College. An Olympic official said, "He was not a particular lover of the Russians."

Afterward the Americans made an official protest. When their protest was denied by a 3-2 vote, it was seen as another Communist plot because three of the five officials were from Communist countries. The three, Cuba, Poland and Hungary, voted against the

Americans, while Italy and Puerto Rico of the western bloc voted to uphold the protest.

An Olympic official interviewed on the HBO film responded by saying the Hungarian official was a man who hated the Russians. His family had been killed by the Russians and there had been such hostility between Hungary and the Soviets that they bloodied each other in an Olympic water polo game of that era.

I was as confused as anybody watching those events unfold. I waited a long, long time afterward to gain entrance to the USA locker room. We saw a group of heartbroken, hostile youths sitting in despair. They railed at the world. We could sympathize with them up to a point, but some of their charges could be laid only to their bitterness at having lost a game they knew they should have won.

They complained: "The Soviets played a brutal game . . . they purposefully put the American star, Dwight Jones, out of the game . . . the Soviet who threw the last long pass downcourt had illegally stepped over the inbounds line."

The HBO film disproved all such complaints.

The Americans would not accept the silver medal for finishing second. Olympic history is rife with examples of screw-ups in judging and miscarriages of justice no less severe. But only these Americans wouldn't accept a medal. There is a poignant moment in the film showing the medals in their vault in the Olympic museum in Lausanne, Switzerland. Every year, one American player notes that he is called to see if he wants to accept the medal. He doesn't.

I feel that if any group ever earned a gold medal for sore losing, it was the entire U.S. basketball contingent. The postscript to it all that infuriated the Cold War chauvinists was the final standings:

Country	Gold	Silver	Bronze
USSR	50	27	22
USA	33	31	30
East Germany	20	23	23
West Germany	13	11	16

Using the traditional 3-2-1 method of scoring, the USSR amassed 226 points; the United States 191; East Germany 129; and West Germany 77 points. By my calculations of measuring medals won in relation to total population, tiny Denmark (population less than five million) won the Olympics for its gold medal won by cyclist Niels Fredborg.

In retrospect HBO's ":03 from Gold" showed that the basketball farce was not a plot, not a conspiracy against Americans, but a monumental basketball screw-up—the sport known for officiating screw-ups.

Note: a later ranking by ESPN of the 10 greatest sports upsets of all time listed as No. 1 the young American hockey team's dramatic victory over the Russians in the 1980 Winter Olympics. The Russians' infliction of the first ever Olympic basketball loss on the Americans did not make the Top Ten.

A Russian journalist in the film says, "It is 30 years later. Maybe they should all get together, argue it out, have the Americans accept the silver medal and then have a party." To that, Mike Bantom of Philadelphia says, "We are not going to accept it. There is no way they beat us. I'll go to my grave with that." And Kenny

Davis and Doug Collins have it written into their wills that their families never accept their medals.

The 1972 Games were the largest Olympics to that point. One-hundred twenty three athletes from 121 nations competed in 23 sports. They were the most televised ever; ABC broadcasted more than 60 hours back to the United States. The lasting impression was of the massacre of the Israelis— and the basketball farce remained for many a wound that wouldn't stop festering. The $650 billion "Games of Joy" turned into the greatest sports debacle of all time. I wrote that the five Olympic rings stood for Terrorism, Fanaticism, Hypocrisy, Incompetence and Arrogance.

The final ceremony underscored it all. After Avery Brundage spoke the traditional words closing the Olympics, he retired to the VIP stand. The words, "Thank you, Mr. Brundage" appeared on the scoreboards, and the Armed Forces band played, "For He's a Jolly Good Fellow."

Acknowledgments

Though this book is based on personal memories covering the ten memorable events, I was helped by the kindness and support of many people. I am indebted to Iris Quigley, the demon researcher at the *Newsday* library. Soleen Chandry of the Pro Football Hall of Fame in Canton provided running detail of the two pro football games. Invaluable was the computer wizardry of Nancy Reznick and the fact-checking of Ken Samelson. "I couldn't have done it without my players," Casey Stengel once said. I say the same for Google and Bill Nack. The Haverford library provided needed information. Friends and colleagues who wrote about these events were invaluable. I thank Al Silverman, Phil Pepe, Angelo Dundee, Dennis D'Agostino, George Vecsey, Steve Cady, Neil Amdur, Bernard Corbett, Paul Simpson, Gerry Eskenazi, Leonard Lewin, Frank Litsky, Ira Berkow, Ray Robinson and Lee Lowenfish. Special thanks to Len Shecter and Larry Merchant. And *Newsday* colleagues Steve Jacobson, Ed Comerford, Bob Waters, Bob Sales, John

Jeansonne and Dotty Antonucci. No acknowledgement would be complete without the kindred spirit, Walter Plinge.